Return on Investment for Healthcare Quality Improvement

Craig A. Solid

Return on Investment for Healthcare Quality Improvement

 Springer

Craig A. Solid
Solid Research Group, LLC
Saint Paul, MN, USA

ISBN 978-3-030-46480-6   ISBN 978-3-030-46478-3   (eBook)
https://doi.org/10.1007/978-3-030-46478-3

This Springer imprint is published by the registered company Springer Nature Switzerland AG
The registered company address is: Gewerbestrasse 11, 6330 Cham, Switzerland

*To my dad, a committed educator
who loved to teach*

Contents

About the Author

Craig A. Solid, Ph.D. is an independent consultant who is the owner and principal of Solid Research Group, LLC. Due to his expertise in the measurement and assessment of healthcare quality and value, and familiarity with federal quality initiatives and the evaluation of health policy and reimbursement, he helps healthcare organizations to navigate the complex world of data and measurement related to healthcare quality and research. His training as a statistician and economist allows him to effectively convey complex analytic and clinical concepts to a variety of audiences. He has given seminars and guest lectures on analytic methods related to continuous quality improvement (control charting, etc.), the process of calculating the return on investment (ROI) for quality improvement, and the steps required to write and format peer-reviewed manuscripts for journal submission. He has co-authored over 60 peer-reviewed manuscripts and has presented work at numerous national and international conferences. Dr. Solid lives in St. Paul, Minnesota with his wife and three children.

Chapter 1
Introduction

1.1 The Current Healthcare Environment

The USA is experiencing rapid change in the healthcare industry and environment in both the public and private sectors. Significant upheaval in the private insurance market has occurred since the adoption of the Affordable Care Act (ACA) of 2010 [1] which yielded changes in the type and amount of insurance coverage offered as well as in the proportion of Americans receiving coverage.

Coupled with the cultural and economic shifts in the overall healthcare landscape, an increased focus has been placed on the "value" of care, both as a concept and as a means to determine the appropriate level of payment or reimbursement for providers and facilities. Public payers, most notably the Centers for Medicare and Medicaid Services (CMS), have begun to move away from the more traditional "fee-for-service" (FFS) payment model in favor of what is frequently referred to as a "value-based" system. Again, the ACA has played a critical role in this transition by specifically allowing for this type of payment design; it was further promoted by the Medicare Access and CHIP Reauthorization Act (MACRA) of 2015, which went a step further.

Specifically, language within MACRA *mandated* the creation of an incentive program for providers where their level of reimbursement would depend, in part, on their performance on a variety of quality measures.[1] Additionally, the CMS Innovation Center was established to test models that may help to improve care by aligning payment policies with proven practices for quality care delivery. As of this writing, the CMS Innovation Center displays more than 90 payment and care delivery models on their site in various stages of development or evaluation. [2] One of these models is the Value-based Insurance Design, or VBID, [3] which is an attempt to explore different

---

[1] More information on programs like the Quality Payment Program (QPP), the Merit-based Incentive Payment System (MIPS), and the Alternative Payment Model (APM) approach can be found at https://qpp.cms.gov/about/qpp-overview.

© Springer Nature Switzerland AG 2020
C. A. Solid, *Return on Investment for Healthcare Quality Improvement*,
https://doi.org/10.1007/978-3-030-46478-3_1

approaches to delivering and paying for health care for those covered under Medicare's risk-based program, Medicare Advantage. The VBID model allows Medicare Advantage organizations to design benefit packages based on beneficiary characteristics, including some related to income. Additionally, these organizations must also develop programs to help beneficiaries plan for future care. Starting in 2021, the VBID will also explore hospice benefits for Medicare Advantage patients as a way to increase access and facilitate care coordination. This is particularly relevant given the significant increase in the proportion of Medicare beneficiaries who are enrolled in Medicare Advantage, from a low of approximately 13% in the early 2000s to a high of 34% (22 million individuals) in 2019 [4].

Given the stated pursuit of aligning payment policies with preferred care practices and the fact that more than one-third of all Medicare beneficiaries are currently enrolled in a risk-based model, clearly the role value plays will continue to gain significance in how health care is delivered and paid for, as will efforts to maximize the financial return of care programs and quality improvement.

Risk-based models, which can often be considered to be value-based, are expanding in the private sector too. Numerous examples exist of private insurers moving to value-based payment mechanisms made possible, in part, because of the explosion in available data on enrollees. A report produced in 2018 by a task force of 41 providers and payers, including the likes of Aetna, Blue Cross Blue Shield, the Cleveland Clinic, Kaiser Permanente, and the American Academy of Family Physicians, indicated that 47% of their members' business was in value-based arrangements by the end of 2017, up from 30% in 2015 and on track to reach 75% by 2020 [5, 6].

In a 2018 survey of 120 payers, nearly $2 out of every $3 paid by those who responded were based on value, which corresponded to significant improvements in measures of quality and reductions in "unnecessary medical costs" [7]. Major payers, including UnitedHealthcare [8] and Cigna [9], have launched value-based initiatives, promoting them as a way to achieve better care at lower costs. All these signs point to a continued push away from FFS and toward value-based models. They signal a need for increasingly sophisticated methods for quantifying and evaluating value.

At the same time of this shift, there is greater awareness of the value tied to the patient experience of care, quality of life, and efficiency in the systems and processes of care delivery. The explosion in the volume and availability of health data allows for more granular information on individual patients as well as the calculation of aggregate metrics to evaluate processes and outcomes. Patients, on the other hand, are demanding more of their care experience and encounters, including the recent push for "price transparency" from providers and facilities. Whether they realize it, they are really pursuing a better understanding of the "value" of the care they are receiving. That is, they want to know not only "What is the cost?" but "How does that cost compare to the quality of the care I received?" which can then be used to determine whether that cost is reasonable or fair.

All these factors underscore the need for greater understanding of how the value of health care is defined, quantified, and compared so that patients, providers, and payers can make informative decisions.

1.1.1 Funding Requirements for Those Looking to Improve Care Quality

In addition to the shift in reimbursement mechanisms from FFS to value-based programs, funding opportunities that focus on improving the quality of care delivery are more commonly asking for some sort of value assessment as part of the application process. Healthcare professionals and organizations that have previously focused on quality metrics now face defining and assessing value metrics, often without much guidance or assistance. Specifically, many are asked to perform return on investment (ROI) analyses for quality improvement activities that they are either proposing or have completed.

This is a natural consequence of raising the profile of the "value" of care in our system. When we associate value with costs and financial commitment, we can expect that requests for the associated "business case" of quality improvement initiatives will only increase. This will happen as funders and key stakeholders are forced to reconcile the fact that the quality of care provided is now directly linked to the bottom line. The difficulty, of course, is that we must balance the fiscal burden with the nonmonetary benefits associated with improved health and a higher quality of life that results.

For example, in some instances improvements in care quality or processes may be expensive but produce significant benefits to patients' experience of care or quality of life. Assuming that the costs are quantifiable (e.g., extra staff, additional steps in the process, more complete follow-up with patients, etc.) but the intangible benefits to patients are not, this improvement could result in a net financial loss if based solely on the measurable fiscal attributes. However, it would be naive to conclude that it therefore produces little to no value, given the obvious benefits patients experience.

As we will see, endeavoring to assess and evaluate these situations requires careful consideration of not only clinical outcomes and the cost to achieve those outcomes, but also the larger concept of value of which ROI is but a part. Even when confined within the framework of ROI, there are aspects regarding the time frame, scope, and perspective of those who incur the costs and receive the benefits that can significantly influence the realized financial return. Certainly, part of a responsible and thorough ROI analysis is to interpret the results for not only financial return but for overall value of the quality improvement activities. But first, we must explore what we truly mean by "value."

1.2 Concepts of Value in Quality Improvement

1.2.1 A Discussion of "Value" in Health Care

A PubMed search of the phrase "value of care" will produce more than 175,000 results, with the number of results per year more than doubling from 2010 (about

Fig. 1.1 Different types of value that quality improvement activities may produce

6500 results) to 2018 (about 13,200 results). While most definitions of value involve some form of effectiveness, safety, and efficiency, no universally shared definition of value exists; instead, the definition is dynamic and often different for different stakeholders [10]. Additionally, concepts of patient satisfaction, quality of life, and social impact also may contribute to the value one assigns to a particular outcome or improvement, but that may also depend on the point of view and the intent of the evaluation.

For providers, improvements in care quality potentially have positive effects on their reputation or "brand." These improvements may carry with them an increase in conceptual value, even if that value is difficult or even impossible to quantify. A nursing home that demonstrates improvements in safety by, for instance, reducing the frequency of resident falls may provide increased peace of mind or reassurance to worried family members. This has value for both the facility and those concerned loved ones (Fig. 1.1).

Clearly, the value produced by the activities intended to reduce falls touches a variety of individuals and organizations, but not all parties experience all of the benefits (i.e., the value), and even those who do may translate those benefits into different forms of value. The outcome of fewer fall-related injuries obviously provides value to patients in the form of better quality of life, better health, and perhaps even extended life. Payers, such as CMS or private insurers, realize a benefit in the form of fewer insurance claims and lower payouts to cover health services for those injured by falls. Family members may experience improved peace of mind knowing that their loved one is housed in a safe environment; staff may experience greater job satisfaction knowing that they are equipped with the tools needed to keep residents safe; and so on. Each of those situations represents value, but in a different way and for a different individual or group. Without specific parameters or a framework for how to consider value, its definition can quickly expand to include intangible and even peripheral benefits that may or may not be of interest to certain players.

Table 1.1 Applying Eq. 1.1 to real situations

Situation	How Eq. 1.1 demonstrates increased value
Maintain quality while reducing costs	The denominator decreases
Increase quality while holding costs constant	The numerator increases

Despite the fact that the concept of value can be varied and multifaceted, some have suggested a very simple equation by which to calculate value:

$$\text{Value} = \text{Quality}/\text{Cost} \tag{1.1}$$

This may be an oversimplification for many cases, but in some instances this definition can be useful to compare the value of two or more time periods or situations (Table 1.1). If one can maintain quality levels while reducing costs, for example, it is reasonable to conclude that value has increased, as reflected in Eq. 1.1, by a decrease in the denominator (cost) which in turn increases value. Similarly, improving quality while holding costs steady also produces an increase in value, this time by increasing the numerator while the denominator remains static. However, the relationship in Eq. 1.1 is not universally applicable and fails to acknowledge much of the nuance and depth involved in understanding and assessing true value. Value is subjective and can change depending on the situation and the perspective.

Some talk about value in terms of "efficiency." In a practical sense, efficiency may reflect a situation where only the appropriate laboratories are ordered and no unnecessary tests are performed. Or it may reflect the correct level of emergency department (ED) staffing to keep wait times short without leaving staff idle. There can be efficiency in administrative processes, the hiring and onboarding of clinical staff, and the coordination of care across departments, specialties, and even settings. In each case, improving efficiency (or equivalently, reducing waste) produces value for one or more interested parties.

However, there is another concept of efficiency, which involves what economists refer to as "moral hazard." Moral hazard refers to how an individual's behavior changes when they have medical insurance. Theoretically, having insurance may make one less averse to potentially risky behavior (referred to as *ex ante* moral hazard because the behavior occurs prior to needing or receiving any healthcare services) or more likely to consume healthcare services (called *ex post* moral hazard because it occurs once services are needed or provided). Reducing the latter is typically the one cited in the name of increasing the value of care in the form of reducing "unnecessary" expenses. Therefore, those who think about health policy are concerned with moral hazard because it informs the structure of health coverage that incentivizes the efficient use of healthcare services and discourages inefficient use (Table 1.2).

Table 1.2 Types of moral hazards

Type	Description	When it is inefficient	When it is efficient
Ex ante	Occurs prior to needing any care and reflects the tendency to participate in more risky activities when one has health insurance	When individuals experience adverse health events from risky behavior	When individuals are incentivized to get preventive care (e.g., vaccinations, checkups)
Ex post	Occurs after an event that results in the need for care and reflects the tendency to use more services than one would if one were paying out of pocket	When individuals receive unnecessary services just because they are covered by insurance (e.g., extra hospital days)	When individuals receive needed care they would have opted out of if paying out of pocket or could not have otherwise afforded

The theoretical basis for the existence of *ex post* moral hazard is that the price of healthcare services (in the eyes of the patient and often in the eyes of the physician) is greatly reduced with insurance coverage, which leads to healthcare services being "overconsumed" at the artificially low price. For example, magnetic resonance imaging (MRI) is a diagnostic tool sometimes used for those with lower back pain. However, some argue that it is used too often and sometimes unnecessarily, and that part of the reason for this is that neither the physician nor the patient incurs the full price of the procedure. This is a classic example of how *ex post* moral hazard is thought to negatively affect the "efficient" use of healthcare dollars.

The price reduction is different than simply a discount or a sale price because theoretically the full price is paid[2]—it is just not paid in full by the consumer. Therefore, the usual balance in supply and demand that is supported by price breaks down because demand is much higher than it "should" be due to the artificially low price. Under this theory of the impact of insurance on prices, you reduce moral hazard and therefore increase the efficiency of healthcare expenditures by raising the price a bit for the individual. This is commonly done by imposing co-pays or deductibles so that the individual receiving the health services pays a larger share of the cost of the service.

Unfortunately, this oversimplifies the situation because in some circumstances arguments for reducing moral hazard break down and can even result in less (economically) efficient use of medical expenditures. For example, often patients lack the knowledge about both the medical necessity and the cost associated with certain services. If your doctor were to suggest that you undergo a certain test or see a certain specialist, you would probably have little to no basis to disagree with her because you are not an expert in that disease area and did not go to medical school.[3] Additionally, often patients are not aware what their insurance covers, and they are trusting that the

---

[2]This is not totally accurate: Most payers have agreements with providers so that the price charged to hospitals or clinics is lower than what would be charged to an individual paying out of pocket, as you have no doubt seen if you have ever examined a medical bill closely.

[3]Not to mention that there may be value to the patient in performing the test simply to rule out certain conditions or maladies, even if the course of treatment would not be altered by the test result.

physician is acting in their best interest, so that the cost or price, or lack thereof, is not a concern, even if it should be (referred to by economists as price insensitivity).

Further, some argue that co-pays or deductibles in the name of lowering moral hazard are pointless for serious and invasive procedures because no one would voluntarily "overconsume" those services. In other words, no rational person would choose to undergo major surgery if it was not medically necessary. There are even situations where the incentives for consuming care services incentivize efficient use of care, like in the case of preventive measures, such as regular checkups, vaccinations, and screenings. In these cases, using these services is higher than it would be if individuals were required to pay for them fully out of pocket; but this type of moral hazard results in reduced utilization because of the preventive nature of the services, and therefore, it ultimately promotes *more* efficient healthcare spending, not less.

It is clear, then, that we cannot present or develop a universally accepted definition of value that will be applicable to all situations and all interested parties. This is key to understand: *Our goal is not to establish one definition of value but to understand how to think about and assess value across the situations we may encounter.* Specifically, we must understand that for each unique case, we will need a framework to operate in where an established scope and perspective will allow us to consistently and reliably identify and quantify the associated costs and benefits. The idea is that once we have established that framework, the subsequent examination of costs and benefits will be inherently transparent and logical so that it is clear what monetary aspects are reasonably included as well as what is excluded.

One of the goals of this book is to encourage you to think about the concept of value and contemplate its meaning in different circumstances. Ideally, you will gain a new appreciation for the complexity of it and will become an advocate for treating it with the same reverence and appreciation that is currently enjoyed by the concept of "quality." We will see that much of what we have learned about defining and measuring quality can be applied to value, and that when we do, the result is a much richer and more textured understanding of the value of the care provided.

1.2.2 The Journey of Understanding Value in Relation to that of Quality

One of the most interesting aspects of the current understanding of value in the healthcare landscape is that much of this terrain has been navigated previously. Over the last twenty or thirty years, the term "quality" has been as ubiquitous as the term "value" is today. Over the decades examining and assessing quality, countless explorations and discussions related to its measurement have shown us that we cannot assume that it means the same thing to everyone or in every situation. Our experiences show us that our ability to affect quality is directly related to our ability to get specific about it. Consider the questions you, as a healthcare professional or quality improvement expert, have learned to ask any time it is necessary to describe, measure, or assess quality. Some of those questions likely include some form of the following:

- How will we define quality in this situation?
- How will we measure quality, and with what data?
- What will those data allow us to do? What won't they allow us to do?
- How will we compare quality fairly (e.g., risk-adjust) and know when there is a meaningful difference or change?
- How will we determine what thresholds reflect "good" quality and/or could serve as a "benchmark"?

Anyone who has worked in quality will understand that as a concept, "quality" is complex and nuanced and that the answers to the questions just asked (and others) will change depending on the situation, the perspective, the objective, and even the available data. Often, the answers are what drive quality. That is, within the sphere of all the possible aspects of care we could potentially improve upon, there is a subset of activities where quality can be measured and therefore where improvement can be demonstrated. So, what is used to define quality is based, in part, on what information is available and measurable.

The same will be true about value. To assess, measure, and eventually affect value, we need to get specific. We need to understand that the same questions we ask of quality need to be asked of value. To design a quality improvement project and measure value, we should ask:

- How will we define value in this situation? Are we interested in only the direct monetary impacts (i.e., costs and revenues), or are we also interested in indirect benefits (e.g., impacts on value-based reimbursements, availability of beds, changes in staff time)?
- How will we measure value? What metrics will we use? What time frame will we look at (during the intervention versus some time into the future, etc.)? If we are interested in less tangible benefits (patient/staff satisfaction, quality of life), how do we plan to measure and quantify them?
- To what will we compare the results? What is a meaningful threshold or benchmark for value, and how will we make comparisons fairly?

Questions like these, and the many others that could be posed, can have a direct impact on how value is calculated and what it represents.

Here and throughout this book, keep in mind that the answers to these questions will evolve as we better understand our systems, our data, and the value that we want to capture. Note that even after all the years of assessing quality, we still have regular conversations and debates about the best way to measure and compare quality to ensure fairness and consistency and reduce uncertainty. It would be naive to not assume that we face a similar journey in the exploration of value (Fig. 1.2).

Decisions Involved in Assessing Value		
Definition	**Measurement**	**Comparison**
- Cost-avoidance	- Metrics	- What is meaningful
- Reimbursement amount	- Data source	- Groups or strata
- Staff retention	- Timeframe	- Appropriate adjustment
- Capacity	- Validity	- Thresholds
- Efficiency	- Reliability	- Benchmarks

Fig. 1.2 Getting clear on how to calculate value and what it represents

1.3 Quality Improvement as an Exercise in Influence

Collectively, as a group trying to improve the quality of care in order to produce better patient outcomes with less expense and less waste, our ability to truly effect change largely depends on our ability to *influence*. For example, consider the physician who has an idea of how to improve care for her patients while also saving time and money, but who cannot get the funding to explore or test her idea on a large enough scale. Assuming she has tried, she has yet to convince anyone, internally or externally, to give her the funds needed to prove that her idea works. Until she does, she will be unable to create the changes she thinks are necessary to improve patient care on a meaningful scale. Her inability to influence potential funders limits her ability to create meaningful change.

Or consider the care solutions that have been proven to be effective but have yet to be fully employed. Multiple randomized clinical trials have demonstrated the benefits of a collaborative dementia care model on patient care and caregiver burden [11, 12]. Unfortunately, barriers associated with how to pay for these new types of models [13] have limited their adoption across the country. As a result, even though evidence shows that the model results in better patient outcomes and less stress and burden for their families, it is unable to reach its full potential in improving care and outcomes for as many patients. That is because policy makers have yet to be convinced of an immediate need for action and a change in policy to support this solution. In this case, even though the care models have been proven to be effective, that alone is not enough to influence providers to employ them, so the affect they can have on the quality of care for dementia patients and their loved ones is limited.

Notably, when ROI analyses are performed, they are typically done so at the two main instances of influence:

1. During the proposal stage of a project, when trying to convince those with money to fund a project
2. After a project has been completed, when those who championed it believe that the results imply that certain actions should, or should not, be taken, and there is a need to convince key people (providers, administrators, policy makers) to

Fig. 1.3 Points of influenceinfluence during the process of quality improvementquality improvement when a ROI analysis may be appropriate

take action or change, or when they are trying to convince those who funded the project that it produced a financial benefit (Fig. 1.3).

In each case, we must bring clinical knowledge, practical experience, and technical expertise related to data and measurement to bear so that the intended audience can see that the project is, or will be, valid, thorough, and statistically rigorous. However, we must *also* convince the audience that the project is important, needed, and impactful. We do that by providing context, citing real-world examples, and storytelling. Just as important as the clinical and technical knowledge are the tools of imagination and creativity, since only through connecting the dots and evoking reactions and emotions to the story can we truly influence others.

Why is this relevant? Because a good ROI analysis is a similar mix of technical and creative inputs and is often used to influence or convince an individual or organization of the feasibility, or even the importance, of a particular activity or endeavor. The intense examination of the steps of ROI in the following chapters will provide a foundation for how to collect and summarize the relevant information; but hopefully it will also allow you to locate and identify the nuance often involved in the process and encourage you to explore, experiment, and even endure to more fully develop and refine your skills in this area. ROI is but one metric within the larger idea of value, which may also encompass things like patient satisfaction, provider reputation, quality of life, peace of mind, etc.

1.4   Return on Investment

1.4.1   How ROI is Used in Other Industries

The notion of ROI is one long associated with manufacturing or banking as a way to justify the purchase of new equipment or facilities or to obtain external funding. Certainly, within the healthcare industry, ROI has played a similar role for administrators for years, but more recently it has gained favor as a way to motivate the funding of quality improvement initiatives. That is, instead of discussing only the decrease in utilization or patient burden that comes from successfully reducing infections, for example, many have started to also ask, "How much money will that ultimately save patients and/or payers?" However, as ROI migrates from boardrooms to the front lines of healthcare delivery and quality improvement, there is a need to understand how to appropriately apply its techniques and accurately perform its calculations.

1.4.2 How We Will Define ROI

ROI does not encompass all of value, nor should it attempt to. Throughout this text, we will talk about ROI and value, but it will be important to remember that ROI is primarily a representation of *monetary returns from a single perspective*, while value can represent a wider spectrum of benefits and utility (to use an economic term) for a variety of individuals and organizations. Said another way, ROI is but one aspect of value, which can be made up of multiple aspects (Fig. 1.4).

However, while ROI is more specific in some sense than the concept of value, no one standard or agreed-upon language or definition for ROI exists. Frankly, this is unfortunate, because while value as a concept can change depending on the perspective or situation, ROI should be an objective measure assigned a fixed definition. We will cover the specifics in a later chapter, including at least one of the alternative definitions that are commonly used; but in general, it is enough to say here that our definition would be recognized by those outside of the healthcare industry.

In addition to being the definition specified by previous experts in the field,[4] our calculation of ROI will be familiar to those in banking or manufacturing, as well as, hopefully, to the general public. That is, a banker's response when asked about the expected return for a particular account or investment will be a percentage, as in, "around 4% or 5%." The formal calculation to arrive at this number involves subtracting the initial investment from what is available for withdrawal after the given time period (typically returns are per year in the financial world) and then dividing by the initial investment. In this way, a 4% return implies the following scenario: Invest $100 today and in a year you will have $104.

Unfortunately, you will see healthcare-related ROI results reported a variety of ways, including as decimals or dollar values. This can only serve to confuse readers

Fig. 1.4 ROI is one aspect of value

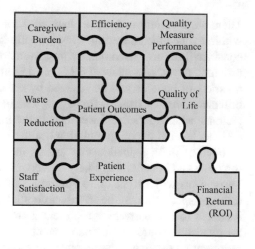

---

[4]Such as in Measuring ROI in Healthcare by Victor Buzachero, Jack Phillips, Patricia Pulliam Phillips, and Zack Phillips. McGraw Hill. 2013.

and audiences and weaken the message. A banker, for example, would never respond to a question about return by quoting values such as "1.04" or "$4"; if they did, those asking would likely be thoroughly confused. The percentage-based definition is more standard and, as it will turn out, more easily understood. This more commonly acceptable form of the ROI used in this book will also allow for a direct interpretation of a negative value. A negative value for ROI will reflect a negative return (i.e., the project's benefits failed to exceed the cost to perform it), contrary to some other metrics that could be used.

At this point, the other key aspect to understand is that ROI is not the only useful metric for evaluating financial return. An appropriate examination of the financial return will typically necessitate quantifying and evaluating return in a variety of ways and calculations. Additionally, the definition of ROI is closely linked to the chosen time frame over which costs and benefits are included, but in healthcare quality improvement, often gains in quality continue to produce financial benefits well into the future. Therefore, any reporting of return without a clear description of the scope and time frame is incomplete, and additional metrics that are invariant to time frames are often merited.

Finally, the goal of some local quality improvement projects is to test their viability so that they may be scaled to larger populations or alternative settings. Therefore, metrics that describe the time until the initial investment is covered by accumulated benefits, as well as metrics that break down benefits on a per-patient basis, will often be useful to provide a full picture of the financial implications of a project.

1.4.3   Unique Challenges for Examining ROI in the Healthcare Setting

There are a variety of unique challenges for examining ROI and value in general within the healthcare setting. **First,** usually several different perspectives could be considered for any given quality improvement initiative, such as those of a patient, provider, payer, or society. That is, during almost any attempt to improve quality, a variety of benefits will be realized by several interested parties. Lower levels of utilization produce benefits for payers, who incur lower reimbursement expenses, for patients, who experience fewer days in the hospital, and for society, which realizes a higher level of overall population health.

Each of these individuals or groups may incur costs and receive benefits, but the costs and benefits will likely be very different and therefore the return of their investments will also be quite different. Complicating things is that in some cases, these perspectives may be in direct conflict regarding the value that is realized— a benefit to one party may represent a cost to another party. For example, fewer hospitalizations are an obvious benefit to patients and insurance payers but may represent a cost (e.g., lost revenue) to a hospital. Depending on the nature of the intervention, it may be necessary to consider multiple perspectives, which can add further complexity to not only the determination of costs and benefits but also to the interpretation and resulting decisions about future activities or health policy.

Second, there is the notion that a good quality improvement intervention not only improves care (or efficiency, or whatever the quality metric is), but that it is also sustainable for the foreseeable future. This has very real implications for selecting an appropriate time frame for evaluating the benefits of the intervention, especially when it comes to forecasting or estimating benefits during the proposal process prior to initiating the improvement activities. Improving the efficiency of the hospital discharge process, for example, should theoretically provide benefits far into the future. That is because saving staff time and streamlining the discharge process should reduce costs and result in fewer patient readmissions for as long as the new process remains effective and employed by the hospital. Therefore, it may be possible to easily inflate the estimated return by simply extending the time frame over which benefits are collected.

What constitutes an appropriate time frame for a given situation or scenario will depend on many things but likely will have practical considerations for both the funding source and those performing the intervention, especially when those are different entities. It will also depend on the level of risk those involved are willing to incur. A small hospital or clinic may be unwilling to wait more than six or nine months to realize a positive return for a particular project, while a large agency whose goal is to improve population health may be willing to endure a negative return for several years if it will result in improvements in care quality and patient outcomes during that period.

Third, intangible and nonmonetary benefits like quality of life and patient experience are often critical measures of success in improving the quality and efficiency of care; but they can be difficult to include in a financial calculation like ROI, for obvious reasons. This is one reason why it is crucial to consider financial metrics of return in concert with quality metrics and to identify how value will be measured at the same time the quality improvement intervention is being planned, not afterward. As we will see, measuring the monetary value of some of the intangible benefits is not impossible but likely will involve some uncertainty and introduce some variability in the results. The best situations show intangible benefits alongside the tangible monetary ones. That way, once a reasonable ROI is established using tangible benefits, the addition of intangible benefits can only improve the value of the initiative in the eyes of the funding source or intended audience.

Fourth, there is a recent push in health care to improve care coordination across settings and between private and community-based organizations. While effective coordination can reduce care utilization and improve patient outcomes, it may be challenging to accurately capture all the costs and benefits across these different organizations so that they may be accurately represented in a ROI analysis. For example, an improvement in the hospital discharge process may involve coordinating after-care with outpatient services or community support programs to ease patient transition back into the community, provide follow-up care and support, and help with medication adherence. However, in reality, a hospital attempting to measure the

Fig. 1.5 Four challenges of
assessing ROI in health care

Challenge #1: Multiple Perspectives May Be Relevant	Challenge #2: Sustainable Change Produces Lasting Benefits
Challenge #3: Intangible Benefits May Be the Most Important	Challenge #4: Care-Coordination Complicates Calculations

value of this new process may have only limited access to information regarding the costs incurred by providers of outpatient services or by the community organizations.

In the best-case scenario, these different organizations would share information and data. However, while this would be valuable for calculating ROI, doing so is likely to be complicated and require extensive measures to protect patient privacy and link data sources, which could drive up program costs. In the worst-case scenario, the hospital will have to estimate or perhaps even ignore the costs incurred by other organizations or ancillary services, thereby reducing the accuracy of the ROI calculation from a payer or societal perspective (Fig. 1.5).

Because of these four main challenges, to establish a consistent and reliable method for assessing ROI in health care, we will need to proceed in a way that acknowledges these challenges and allows us to operate within specific parameters.

In a broad sense, what follows in this book is an attempt to provide a structure and framework that will allow one to make decisions about the value and ROI evaluation such as how to define, identify, and measure costs and benefits and how to determine who they should be attributed to, and over what time frame. Establishing this framework will provide the parameters to work within the constraints and challenges described and allow for transparency in calculations and clarity in the interpretation. Therefore, when specified for those who will ultimately see the results of the analysis, they will be able to interpret the results for what they are, as well as for what they are not.

Once that framework is in place, those performing the ROI analysis will be able to provide a clear sequence that will lead the reader through the steps of identifying costs and benefits in a logical way and that is subject to the assumptions and estimates that are necessary to make regarding recruitment, effectiveness, impact, and the associated monetary implications. This will allow the reader to draw their own conclusions about whether the process is reasonable and credible, which will be essential for any analysis but especially so for prospective analyses performed during the planning or proposal stage when many more assumptions are required. Nothing derails a proposal faster than when a reader cannot follow how the author arrived at a particular conclusion or fails to understand how or why a particular assumption was made.

Throughout the process, we must acknowledge uncertainty and risks, plan for alternatives, and provide context for the values used and the interpretations made. At the end of the day, the costs and benefits in the analysis are just numbers. It will be the job of those performing the analysis to provide an interpretation of the results in a way that instills confidence in the reader that all possible contingencies were considered and that there are transparency and objectiveness that will allow the reader or audience to make their own conclusions.

1.4.4 Differences in Prospective Versus Retrospective Analyses of ROI

A ROI analysis may be prospective or retrospective. Prospective analyses are typically used during a proposal process, to either compare potential interventions or investments one could make or to convince a funding source (internal or external) of the business case of the proposed project. Retrospective analyses are used to summarize past actions to understand the drivers of costs and benefits, determine whether an investment was prudent, or compare a realized experience with what had been anticipated prior to starting the project. Retrospective analyses may also serve to establish the feasibility of scaling interventions to other populations or alternative settings. Throughout this text, we will examine prospective and retrospective ROI analyses in tandem. While most of the key aspects of ROI analyses are the same regardless of whether they are done prospectively or retrospectively, a few differences should be noted.

1.4.4.1 The Use of Assumptions for Prospective Versus Retrospective Analyses

Prospective analyses will typically require many more assumptions and estimates than are required in retrospective analyses, simply because prior to conducting a project there are more unknowns. In a proposal, the ROI analysis will attempt to describe the most likely scenario for how costs and benefits will accumulate and will explore how possible deviations from the assumptions and estimates will affect the resulting return. Prior to beginning quality improvement activities, uncertainties involving the speed and completeness of recruitment or response of the studied entities, the relative effectiveness of the proposed intervention to change the desired measure or outcome, and the associated monetary implications of those changes all require assumptions that are necessary only when performing a prospective analysis. In each case, educated guesses based on prior experience or researched information will be made so that calculations of the realized return can be made.

In contrast, in a retrospective analysis much of the ROI analysis will utilize real data and actual costs and benefits that were observed and collected during the initiative. For example, actual recruitment can be quantified, real reductions in utilization or adverse events can be measured, and the sustainability of the changes can be evaluated. This does not mean that retrospective analyses lack the need for any assumptions or estimates, it just means that they are typically much fewer in number. There still may be assumptions applied to intangible benefits like satisfaction or quality of life, or how reduced utilization or increased efficiency translates into real dollars. Additionally, retrospective analyses may require assumptions when attempting to generalize the results to other settings, situations, or scopes.

1.4.4.2   The Role of Uncertainty in Prospective Versus Retrospective Analyses

Because prospective analyses will be based largely on assumptions and estimates, the role uncertainty plays in the analysis is front and center. Those performing these types of analyses are tasked with identifying and often quantifying uncertainty to assess the likelihood of a "successful" project (however that may be defined), predict potential pitfalls, and develop contingency plans if certain assumptions prove to be incorrect. In a retrospective analysis, uncertainty will play a role when trying to translate intangible benefits into monetary values, extrapolating and generalizing results, or exploring what would have been observed if certain aspects had played out differently. How uncertainty manifests in each case will be unique to the situation and circumstances, but any analysis that fails to explore, let alone acknowledge, the inherent uncertainty in this process should be viewed with significant skepticism and caution.

1.4.4.3   What Information Is Presented for Prospective Versus Retrospective Analyses

For the most part, the information presented when reporting the results of a ROI analysis will be similar for prospective and retrospective analyses. However, prospective analyses will likely be more heavily weighted toward background and supporting information to motivate the need for the project and establish reasonable estimates for key values. Those presenting the information will want to ensure that readers or evaluators understand how certain assumptions or estimates were established. Therefore, they will want to be transparent and thorough when offering supporting evidence for the estimates used while acknowledging the inherent uncertainty that is involved in a prospective analysis.

In retrospective analyses, there will be less need for supportive information regarding assumptions and estimates, since the analysis will involve fewer of both. However, depending on the goal(s) of the analysis, there may be a need to explore what would have been realized under different circumstances, especially if the realized results significantly differed from what was predicted beforehand. In these cases, identifying drivers of the return can help improve future iterations of the intervention or ensure greater success if the activities are to be extrapolated or generalized to other populations and settings. Still another goal may be to compare the realized return to what would have been achieved if the investment had been instead directed toward a different activity, which may require a particular aggregation or stratification of results that allow for direct comparison between (potentially) very different pursuits.

Table 1.3 Differences between prospective and retrospective ROI analyses

	Prospective	Retrospective
Use of assumptions	Typically involves several assumptions and estimates about what is likely to occur	Typically involves fewer assumptions since it evaluates what happened; however, some assumptions or estimates may be used to explore variability and extend results to alternative situations or settings
Uncertainty	Is the result of the use of several assumptions and estimates, each of which may be inaccurate or subject to unforeseen circumstances; exploring uncertainty will be central to a thorough analysis of what is likely to occur	Explored mostly to understand why observed results occurred or to examine what could happen in alternative situations or settings
What is presented	Will often be heavy in background and supporting information to justify the assumptions and estimates used in the analysis	Typically focuses on observed results and realized gains, with less need for background or supporting information

What is presented in a retrospective analysis will be highly dependent on the goals of the analysis (Table 1.3).

1.4.4.4 How Prospective and Retrospective Analyses Are Presented in This Book

Many of the concepts in this book are initially explored in the context of a prospective analysis, for a few reasons. First, it is a natural starting point since a prospective analysis would occur prior to a retrospective one (on the same project). Second, the heavy reliance on assumptions and estimates in the prospective analysis, and therefore the inherent uncertainty, requires careful consideration in light of their potential impact on the resulting analysis, and therefore, there is more to "talk about" for prospective analyses than for retrospective ones. Third, a recurring theme in this book will be the importance of planning for the value analysis in concert with the planning and consideration of other aspects of quality improvement, like identifying quality measures, securing data, and evaluating outcomes. It is impossible to overstate how critical it is that the consideration of the value assessment should not be postponed or delayed until after the quality initiative is planned. Developing them together as part of the same proposal is the single most important activity for increasing the likelihood of a successful ROI analysis.

1.5 Who This Book Is For

This book is written specifically for providers of all types, facility administrators, policy makers, and quality improvement facilitators. It assumes that the reader has little to no analytic training or background (although having some will not invalidate any of the techniques presented; if anything, it may make them more intuitive). The tools and techniques described do not require any sort of statistical testing, modeling, or simulating. Certainly, there are extensions of some of the ideas presented here that lend themselves very nicely to more complex analysis, like forecasting models, time-series analysis, etc. Where appropriate, I have attempted to provide references to additional resources for those who are interested in exploring more analytic possibilities within this arena, and in some instances have explored these in more detail in the chapter on expanded topics.

With that said, this book assumes that the reader has a sufficient understanding of quality improvement concepts and techniques, and ideally has direct experience designing, implementing, monitoring, evaluating, and reporting quality improvement interventions. I will make references to concepts like Plan-Do-Study-Act (PDSA) and Lean, and even to federal or national quality monitoring programs. Additionally, while I will provide a review of some measurement topics like validity and reliability, if previously unexposed to these topics, I encourage readers to consult additional resources to more fully explore basic topics in measurement and evaluation. I provide some references in the text for further reading.

While the chapters appear in a specific sequence to lead readers through a logical progression of the concepts, they are also written so that they may be read out of order and/or used as a reference for those who are more familiar with some of the topics they cover. Therefore, many of the concepts and topics appear throughout the text as they are relevant across stages of the process and the types of interventions, and I have tried to carry several examples through the entire text to provide continuity and highlight common themes.

Additionally, I have included an entire chapter of hypothetical case studies. These attempt to encompass the concepts presented throughout the book and provide examples of how a ROI analysis may look upon completion. In addition to the goal of providing a general blueprint for how to perform ROI analyses, I frequently interject additional thoughts or suggestions for those who may be seeking a more thorough understanding of how to think about and assess value in their work.

Upon completing this book, I hope you will have a better understanding of ROI specifically, but also of "value" generally as it pertains to health care. Several of the concepts discussed under the auspice of ROI can be generalized and applied to other situations and larger conversations of interest to providers, administrators, and policy makers. Also, I sincerely hope that you will gain the understanding required to perform ROI analyses and that you will see quality and value as linked concepts to be considered simultaneously whether you are planning an intervention or evaluating the success of a finished project.

1.6 Summary

The current landscape of health care is pivoting away from FFS models toward more value-based programs. In the public and private sectors, providers, administrators, and payers agree that the future is value-based care. With that shift, however, comes challenges related to measuring and assessing the value of care, especially because of the interest in nonmonetary benefits like patient experience, satisfaction, and quality of life. In fact, any improvement in care quality may be accompanied by several different types of value, many of which may be unmeasurable or nonmonetizable.

Understanding that value is subjective, that it will depend on the perspective, and that it can change over time is key to determining how best to measure, assess, and describe relevant value. Much of the complexity involved in exploring value mirrors what the industry has previously experienced in its quest to define and measure quality, and many of the same questions apply. One component of value is the financial return, or ROI. Throughout this text, we will explore ROI within the larger context of value, acknowledging the unique challenges associated with ROI within the healthcare industry.

1.7 Key Concepts

- No one universally shared definition of value exists; it is dynamic and will depend on the perspective from which it is evaluated. Our goal is not to establish one definition of value, but to understand how to think about and assess value.
- Improvements in care quality may produce several types of value, but only some may be measurable and/or monetizable.
- The quality and value of care are linked; additionally, many of the discussions and examinations of the term "quality" are applicable when exploring the term "value."
- Numerous decisions are involved in assessing value for a particular situation or circumstance, including decisions about how to define it, measure it, and compare it.
- ROI is one component of value and is a representation of monetary returns from a single perspective during a specific time frame.
- ROI is not the only useful metric for evaluating financial return; other metrics can be used in tandem or as alternatives but still leverage financial costs and benefits.
- Four unique challenges for assessing ROI and value in health care exist: the presence of multiple relevant perspectives, the impact of the sustainability of quality improvements, the importance of intangible and nonmonetary aspects of care, and the need for care coordination across settings and organizations.
- We will explore prospective and retrospective ROI analyses; their main differences involve the need for more assumptions and estimates in prospective analyses than in retrospective ones.

References

1. United States Congress (2010) The patient protection and affordable care act. Available at http://www.ncsl.org/documents/health/ppaca-consolidated.pdf
2. CMS Innovation Center (2019) Innovation models. https://innovation.cms.gov/initiatives/# views=models. Accessed 17 Dec 2019
3. CMS Innovation Center (2019) Medicare advantage value-based insurance design model. https://innovation.cms.gov/initiatives/vbid/. Accessed 17 Dec 2019
4. Kaiser Family Foundation (2019) A dozen facts about medicare advantage in 2019. https://www.kff.org/medicare/issue-brief/a-dozen-facts-about-medicare-advantage-in-2019/. Accessed 17 Dec 2019
5. Bresnick J (2018) 47% of payer, provider business tied to value-based care. https:// healthpayerintelligence.com/news/47-of-payer-provider-business-tied-to-value-based-care. Accessed 17 Dec 2019
6. Health Care Transformation Task Force (2017) 2017 transformation progress report. https:// hcttf.org/2017-member-transformation-progress-report/. Accessed 17 Dec 2019
7. Masterson L (2018) Payers moving to value-based care faster than expected. https://www. healthcaredive.com/news/payers-moving-to-value-based-care-faster-than-expected/525900/. Accessed 17 Dec 2019
8. UnitedHealthCare (2019) Welcome to value-based care. https://www.uhc.com/valuebasedcare. Accessed 17 Dec 2019
9. Cigna (2019) Moving from volume to value. https://www.cigna.com/about-us/newsroom/ innovation/moving-from-volume-to-value-based-health-care. Accessed 17 Dec 2019
10. Antonanzas F, Terkola R, Postma M (2016) The value of medicines: a crucial but vague concept. PharmacoEconomics 34(12):1227–1239. https://doi.org/10.1007/s40273-016-0434-8
11. Callahan CM, Boustani MA, Unverzagt FW, Austrom MG, Damush TM, Perkins AJ, Fultz BA, Hui SL, Counsell SR, Hendrie HC (2006) Effectiveness of collaborative care for older adults with alzheimer disease in primary care: a randomized controlled trial. JAMA 295(18):2148–2157. https://doi.org/10.1001/jama.295.18.2148
12. Vickrey BG, Mittman BS, Connor KI, Pearson ML, Della Penna RD, Ganiats TG, Demonte RW Jr, Chodosh J, Cui X, Vassar S, Duan N, Lee M (2006) The effect of a disease management intervention on quality and outcomes of dementia care: a randomized, controlled trial. Ann Intern Med 145(10):713–726. https://doi.org/10.7326/0003-4819-145-10-200611210-00004
13. Boustani M, Alder CA, Solid CA, Reuben D (2019) An alternative payment model to support widespread use of collaborative dementia care models. Health Aff 38(1):54–59. https://doi. org/10.1377/hlthaff.2018.05154

Chapter 2
Planning a ROI Analysis

2.1 The Motivation to Assess Value in Health Care

The need to assess and measure value can be motivated by a variety of factors, experiences, and forces that are both internal and external to the organization. Sometimes, facility or system administrators are considering a capital investment and want to understand the value it will bring to the business of providing care. Other times, a funding agency wants to know whether a proposed method to improve processes or outcomes will yield a financial benefit, or at least not a significant loss, to justify the investment to be made in care quality. Many times, these are fiscal assessments, but by no means does "fiscal" encompass the totality of "valuable." When seeking to understand value in health care, we must first acknowledge that the term "value" can mean different things to different individuals (providers versus patients versus administrators versus payers versus policy makers, etc.), and that there are many different kinds of value. Some value is measurable, some is not; some value can be equated to monetary costs or benefits, some cannot; and some value can be directly attributed to the investment or quality improvement activities, while some cannot.

When confronted with the need to measure and assess value, you must carefully define *what you mean* by value, including answering the question, "Value to whom?" Only then can one begin to determine how value will be measured, which is no small feat. Identifying the appropriate method and metric for measurement will be key to your ability to ultimately assess and interpret value. When considering what to measure in your own work, consider several things you may need to ask yourself or your team, such as:

- Do data exist that can be used to measure value in this situation?
- If not, are there previously developed methods for collecting value data?
- Will our measurement reflect monetary costs and benefits in addition to quality?
- If not, are there additional measurements we can make that will reflect monetary values?

© Springer Nature Switzerland AG 2020
C. A. Solid, *Return on Investment for Healthcare Quality Improvement*,
https://doi.org/10.1007/978-3-030-46478-3_2

Table 2.1 Questions to ask when considering a value assessment

Question	More detail
Do data exist to measure value?	Are there data that will capture the financial or value-based aspects of the improvement in quality? If so, will you be able to obtain and use those data?
Will our measures reflect monetary values?	There is value in improved patient experiences and quality of life, but they may not be sufficient to estimate a financial return of the project. Do the value measures you have available to you reflect monetary gains?
How are measures translated into financial terms?	Is it possible to translate your identified measures into financial amounts? If so, by what method, and how valid is that method?
Can we make inferences from our value metrics?	Will the metrics allow us to make meaningful inferences about the impact the quality improvement activities had on the value for the key stakeholders?

- If so, how does the metric translate into monetary values? Directly (e.g., actual incurred monetary costs) or indirectly (e.g., increased staff satisfaction that is likely to reduce turnover costs)?
- What are the implications for our ability to make valid, reliable inferences from the value metrics? (Table 2.1).

In short, the topic of "measurement" is vast and complex and encompasses issues related to accuracy, validity, reliability, feasibility, and usefulness. The usual challenges associated with developing a good plan for measurement are compounded when assessing value in health care; that is because of the vagueness of the term and the potentially confounding nature of providing health services that stems from the litany of events and encounters that can affect processes of care and patient outcomes.

To identify the most appropriate and useful value measurement requires a thorough examination of the situation, available data, and the intended goal of not only the investment or project but also of the associated analysis.

2.2 The Critical Aspects of Quality Improvement

Although this is a book on value and ROI, it is instructive to examine critical aspects of measuring quality, both because quality is ultimately the driving force behind many measures of value and because quality and value are, and should be, undeniably linked. We can only examine and understand value in concert with an evaluation of quality: Poor care quality has little value, regardless of how cheap it is; exceptional care quality may be extremely valuable, even if supremely expensive. Therefore, your consideration of key aspects of traditional quality improvement will have a simultaneous and corresponding impact on the choices available to you for evaluating value and calculating ROI. Here, we review the considerations related to quality one typically encounters.

2.2.1 Defining Quality

The first step in the development of any quality improvement initiative is to define what quality is for the given situation. The definition of quality will vary depending on perspective and interests; providers, administrators, policy makers, and patients all have their own criteria and motivations for what determines "high-quality care." For example, policy makers believe that one definition of high-quality hospital care is if discharged patients rarely need to be readmitted for the same condition soon after the original hospitalization (defined as within 30 days for many endorsed quality measures).

Providers and hospital administrators, however, would probably argue that a readmission within 30 days is a *result* of care quality. They would also point out that the likelihood of a readmission can be affected by a variety of factors outside of the hospital's control. A patient's ability to understand and follow discharge instructions, their level of medication adherence, willingness to follow up as needed on an outpatient basis, the level of their support at home or in their community, and lifestyle choices regarding diet, exercise, and smoking are all factors that can significantly influence whether their condition, which was improving or resolved upon discharge, deteriorates to the point where they require inpatient care once again. So, who is correct?

Anyone who has studied this issue at length will tell you that *both* are correct in some ways, but they would also probably tell you that it is more complicated than that. Regardless of which one of the players you side with, or even if you side with neither, you can likely see each point of view and understand the reasoning behind each.

You can also probably quickly identify where the lines get blurry so that determining what is true becomes difficult. For example, perhaps one believes that ensuring that patients understand discharge instructions and have the necessary support at home or in the community *could* or *should* be under the hospital's purview. Or perhaps it is reasonable to look at it more holistically and say that it should be *somebody's* responsibility to ensure that patients have the needed information and support once discharged. That is, the system as a whole would be better served if a mechanism existed by which patients were fully prepared and educated about the post-discharge period and were provided with all of the necessary resources to maximize their health and minimize the likelihood that they would need a subsequent inpatient stay.

From this point of view, one might consider that the fact that it is inherently incorporated into the quality metric for hospitals will likely at least pique the interest of the hospital staff and administration; and that once that happens, the staff and administration may then be incentivized to consider how it may be addressed and improved, even if the result is a decision to refer patients to community resources provided by other organizations. Whether this is "fair" to assign to hospital quality is perhaps secondary to the notion that this course of action may result in better system practices by which patients ultimately benefit.

By the same token, it might seem like too much of a leap to assign full responsibility for a patient's readmission to the hospital that previously discharged him or her. Common sense tells us that it is difficult to draw a straight line between hospital care before discharge and the likelihood of readmission a month later; and in the event of a potentially avoidable readmission, it may be more accurate to consider the contributing forces of not only the hospital but of the system as a whole, external forces and events, and yes, even patient behaviors and choices.

This exploration into how theoretical definitions of "quality" manifest in the practical systems and institutions already in place provides a window into the challenges this process can produce. One issue, in particular, is that it can be difficult to establish a link from the proposed definition to what is *measurable* and therefore able to be monitored, evaluated, and demonstrated.

2.2.1.1   What This Has to Do with Value

The challenges and difficulties we encounter when we try to define quality are similar to those we will encounter when defining value. Additionally, as we will explore more deeply in the coming sections, the measurements of quality and value are linked and dependent on each other. Therefore, we need to consider how the definition of one may influence the definition of the other. Defining hospital quality through readmission rates as payers tend to do has implications for the associated value that can be assigned and evaluated for payers, providers, and patients alike. So, reducing the likelihood of a rehospitalization holds different value for hospitals than it does for payers, and it will mean something else for the patient who seeks to avoid another hospitalization, both in definition and in real and relative magnitude.

If instead of using readmissions as the metric hospital quality is defined using some other measure, the result will be different evaluations of value for all parties. This could produce different interpretations for the success or merit of a particular intervention or project. Therefore, the definitions of quality and value ultimately have repercussions both in general and as one gets specific. **Value is linked to both quality and perspective: you cannot ask what the value of something is without asking, value to *whom?***

2.2.2   Measuring Quality

In an ideal situation, we would first define quality and then determine how best to measure it. Unfortunately, that is often not possible. A definition of quality may or

Table 2.2 Examples of how surrogates are used to measure certain concepts

Unmeasurable concept	Possible surrogates
Happiness	Ratings on numerical scales, selection of representative images of feelings
Satisfaction	Likert scale-like responses ("somewhat satisfied," "very satisfied," etc.)
Quality	Readmission rate, number of falls, likelihood of infection
Value	Reduced expenditures and utilization, better patient outcomes

may not include things that are measurable. When assessing quality in health care, quality should be defined in terms of what is measurable, even if it shortens the reach of the definition or dilutes its meaning slightly. To understand this concept, consider how we typically choose to measure "happiness" or "satisfaction." If asked to explain the meaning of these terms, one may describe certain emotions, reactions, and thoughts that one associates with those terms. However, if tasked with defining happiness or satisfaction in a way that could be *measured and tracked*, one would have to adjust the meaning to incorporate measurable aspects into the definition.

Maybe these refined definitions would involve Likert scale-like response categories ("somewhat satisfied," "very satisfied," etc.) to specific survey questions or a numerical scale that ranges from one to ten, where higher numbers reflect higher levels of happiness. These definitions are certainly more measurable than the original definitions, but they also have lost some of their broad applicability and certainly some of the depth of what they may represent. For example, a scale of one to ten provides a series of discrete choices for measuring a concept (happiness) that exists on a continuum. Also recognize that one would likely define them differently depending on the situation and the objectives. When inquiring about satisfaction, for example, the questions may change depending on whether asking about a product, a service, or an experience, and whether the individual being asked is a producer, consumer, or someone else (Table 2.2).

In essence, what is described in the previous paragraph is simply the use and applicability of *surrogates*. The elusiveness of concrete definitions of "happiness" or "satisfaction" forces us to use other measurable concepts as imperfect representations of what we really want to measure. We create definitions in terms of the surrogates (the numerical value for happiness, the Likert scale response for satisfaction), and we feel comfortable doing so when are confident in the link between the surrogate and the unmeasurable concept. The same is true when we examine quality and value—there is no universally accepted definition that applies to every situation and for every perspective. Instead, we are forced to utilize surrogates, and we redefine quality and value in terms of those surrogates, relying on the strength of the link to our imagined concept of either term to establish credibility for the use of that surrogate.

As you can imagine, that link is often the subject of debate: Is it appropriate or not, is it feasible or not, is it measurable or not? In the example of hospital quality presented previously, the rehospitalization rate is the surrogate for hospital quality, and the discussion about whether it is a good representation is really a debate about the strength of the link between that surrogate and the underlying concept of interest. The process of determining what to measure, whether it is to assess quality, value, or something else, is really an exercise in identifying an appropriate surrogate, one that accurately reflects the intended concept and allows us to consistently identify changes or differences.

2.2.2.1 Linking This to Value

The concept of quality measurement is linked to value in two ways. The first is that what is ultimately selected as the metric of quality may very well influence what is used to measure value, and vice versa. When it comes to readmissions, payers may consider it a viable quality metric *because* there is real value for them associated with improving it: Reducing readmissions means reducing encounters and therefore payments in the form of reimbursements. If hospitals were to select a quality metric to reflect care quality, they may select something else, something that not only allows them to more closely examine specific processes or procedures within their facility, but also reflects the value from their perspective.

Examples could be the time it takes to discharge a patient or a survey of discharged patients to get their opinion of their experience and their facility (i.e., the hospital's "image" or "brand" in the eyes of patients). These metrics attempt to measure the same quality that readmission rates attempt to, but they reflect value from a different perspective (Fig. 2.1).

The second way quality measurement is linked to value is through the merits of the surrogate. If the surrogate has limited capability to measure quality, then the associated value of improving that metric will also be a poor representation of the true value to those trying to measure it. Therefore, to identify and use surrogates effectively, we must first understand how to evaluate their appropriateness and ability to perform how we need them to.

Fig. 2.1 Example of how perspective can influence what is a useful metric of quality

Measures of Hospital Quality

From a Hospital's Perspective:
- Time to discharge
- Patient satisfaction
- Staff retention rate

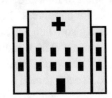

From a Payer's Perspective:
- Readmission rate
- Length of stay
- Utilization

2.2.2.2   Characteristics of a Good Surrogate

A number of aspects of a surrogate inform its applicability and appropriateness for a given situation. The following descriptions are not exhaustive but are intended to provide a general overview of the main concepts one should understand and be cognizant of when selecting and using a surrogate to measure quality or value. In general, two main types of characteristics should be considered: validity and reliability.

Validity

Validity reflects how accurately a measure represents whatever it is trying to capture. Valid measures give us confidence that the chosen surrogate is a true representation of what we seek to understand or evaluate. When we consider the validity of a measure like rehospitalization rate for representing hospital quality, we need to first ask: *What, specifically, do we want it to reflect?* That is, do we want it to capture the quality of the care during the stay, the quality of the discharge process, or both? And then we must ask *how well does it do that?* As in, how robust is it to unmeasurable and uncontrollable factors, like patient attitudes, opinions, lifestyle choices,

Table 2.3 Examples of measure validity

Type of validity	Example
Face validity	A nursing home institutes a new quality measure of medication reconciliation for newly admitted patients; experts from the community review the inclusion and exclusion criteria as well as the rules for when the admitting physician was considered to have completed the reconciliation and found it to be valid
Convergent validity	A home health agency develops a tool to measure how hazardous a home was for those with a fall risk. To assess how valid this new measure was for assessing home safety, the agency compared measure performance with the frequency of falls and home injuries and found that homes that were rated as more hazardous with the new measure correlated with rates of falls and injuries, demonstrating convergent validity of the new measure
Divergent validity	An emergency department hypothesized that having a nurse check-in with those waiting to see a physician at least once per hour would improve patient satisfaction; when measured, administrators found that the more often nurses completed hourly check-ins, the percent of patients who left without being seen was lower, suggesting that the new measure demonstrated divergent validity
Known-groups validity	A new measure that attempts to quantify functional status is given to dementia patients with different disease severity. The new measure revealed poorer functional status for those with more severe dementia, demonstrating known-groups validity for the new measure
Concurrent validity	When a previously validated measure of functional status was applied to the same dementia patients, it produced similar results to the new measure, suggesting concurrent validity of the new measure

or other factors (socioeconomic, access, culture, etc.)? How much is it influenced by circumstances after discharge so that the information it provides is only part of the full picture? There are several ways to assess validity to establish that the values of the measure accurately reflect underlying quality (Table 2.3).

Face Validity

The exception to the notion of quantifying validity is *face validity*. This type of validity involves a subjective assessment, typically by an expert or experts in the topic area for which the measure was developed, as to whether the measure is valid. It is often something that is assessed by someone, or several individuals, who were not involved in selecting or creating the measure but who have expertise in the clinical or topic area it addresses. When assessing this type of validity, one might ensure that the inclusion and exclusion criteria do not introduce bias by unwittingly omitting certain types of patients or situations, or that the data elements proposed are obtainable and are reasonable for what the measure is attempting to reflect.

For example, if a measure attempts to assess how frequently physicians discuss certain information during visits with patients by using only billing codes, one may question the face validity if one believes that those codes are infrequently used, even when the communication occurs. Studies that examine outcomes related to atrial fibrillation often exclude those with valvular disorders because these conditions are thought to not increase the risk of thromboembolism; failure to exclude these patients in studies examining efforts to reduce thromboembolisms due to atrial fibrillation may introduce bias and reduce the validity of the measure for assessing quality related to the intended population. These are aspects of the measure that someone who knows something about the topic could identify, without any data collection or analysis.

Convergent and Divergent Validity

Convergent validity and divergent (also called discriminant) validity involve comparing the correlation or association of different measures that theoretically should reflect similar (in the case of convergent) or opposite (in the case of divergent) concepts. For example, measures of patient quality of life and functional status are measuring similar constructs and therefore could potentially be used to establish the *convergent validity* of each other (since a *higher* level of functioning often equates to *higher* quality of life). Meanwhile, comparing either one of these to a measure reflecting how much daily activities are impeded by chemotherapy side effects could establish *divergent validity*, since one would expect that those who are *more* encumbered by side effects to have *lower* levels of functioning and health-related quality of life.

Known-Groups Validity

Known-groups validity is the extent to which a measure can discriminate between groups known to be clinically different. If one created a measure of functional status and tested it on patients at several stages of a dementia, a valid measure would likely demonstrate differences in functional status by dementia severity, given that we know that patients with more severe dementia are clinically very different than those with only mild dementia.

Concurrent Validity

Similarly, to establish the validity of a new measure, one could compare its performance to a similar measure that has already been established as valid. So, during the process of validation, one would collect data for both the new and the established measure from the same entities (e.g., patients, hospitals, etc.) and then see how well the two measures agree. If the new measure identifies similar differences between groups of patients as does the established measure, then the new measure demonstrates *concurrent validity*.

Threats to Validity

Threats to validity may be conceptual or practical. That is, conceptually there may be reasons why "door-to-balloon" time is or is not a good surrogate for the care quality of patients with acute myocardial infarction; perhaps there are legitimate reasons to delay angioplasty not reflected in the measure, for example. On a practical level, we need to be sure that we accurately and consistently acquire the data used to calculate it. Are the timestamps in the electronic health record accurate? Are certain data fields are always populated?

Those challenging the validity of a measure may do so by demonstrating the impact of slightly altering the measure's definition or inclusion or exclusion criteria, or they may compare the measure to other metrics to try to point out inconsistencies. For example, to challenge the validity of a measure that reflects a process of care (like providing prophylactic antibiotics prior to surgery), one might select a patient outcome thought to result from that process (like post-operative infection) and show the lack of a statistical correlation between the two.

Reliability

Reliability reflects the ability of a measure to correctly discriminate differing levels of quality, or changes in quality, between entities or time periods. That is, if two hospitals or physicians actually differ in their care quality, how likely is it that the measure will detect that difference? The answer tells you about the reliability of the measure (Table 2.4).

Internal Consistency Reliability

This type of reliability reflects whether several items that propose to measure the same general construct produce similar results. The example of patient-reported functional status allows us to imagine a measure that is made up of ten questions asking about different aspects of daily life, where all the questions intend to reflect functional status in some way or another. If this series of ten questions has *internal consistency reliability*, then each of the individual questions should demonstrate "consistency" in the direction and magnitude of the level of functional status, in the sense that those who demonstrate high functioning should do so across all ten questions.

Table 2.4 Examples of measure reliability

Type of reliability	Example
Internal consistency reliability	A composite measure of efficiency of patient discharge is created by combining scores of the speed of discharge following discharge orders, the completion and thoroughness of discharge instructions, and the scheduling of a follow-up appointment; after a period of time, data were analyzed and revealed that scores on the individual components correlated highly with overall scores, suggesting internal consistency reliability
Test–retest reliability	Patients fill out a questionnaire that will be used to create a composite score. Some patients are reassessed by filling out the same questionnaire a week later, and the results are compared. The correlation between the answers individuals gave in their first questionnaire and those in the second questionnaire was high, suggesting good test–retest reliability
Inter-rater reliability	A measure compiled of medical record abstracted data was tested using two different abstractors. They each abstracted the same 50 records, and the results were compared. They each produced the same results, suggesting a high level of test–retest reliability
Responsiveness	After an initiative to improve medication adherence, inpatient utilization remained relatively steady, even among those for whom a significant improvement in adherence was documented. This demonstrated that inpatient utilization was not responsive to improvements in medication adherence
Signal to noise	After collecting measure performance from dozens of individual physicians who each treated multiple patients who qualified for quality measurement, an analyst ran a statistical model to compare the level of variation within individual physicians with the variation between physicians and found that the "signal" (between physician variability) was significantly larger than the "noise" (within physician variability)

Test–Retest Reliability

Test–retest reliability refers to the extent that a measure yields the same results in repeated applications in an unchanged population. Typically, the same measure is collected or administered at least twice from the same group, with the time between the administrations being large enough to ensure that they represent unique measurements but short enough so that no change in condition can be expected. For example, if subjects are required to fill out a questionnaire on their functional status to create a composite measure, to assess the *test–retest reliability*, we would need at least some patients to fill out the questionnaire more than once.

One might wait a week between administrations of the questionnaire, because that might be long enough to prevent the subjects from duplicating their answers simply from memory, but short enough so that one would not expect there to have been much change in the actual functional status. If subjects' responses are relatively consistent between the two time periods, then the measure demonstrates good test–retest reliability.

Inter-rater Reliability

Inter-rater reliability reflects the agreement or concordance among multiple "raters." This can take multiple forms. Let us consider the case of measurements that involve data abstracted from medical charts or obtained from administrative databases. In this case, *inter-rater reliability* reflects how likely different abstractors are to apply the inclusion/exclusion criteria the same way and to produce the same value of the measure. In situations where one is required to estimate or obtain specific values (e.g., the size of a tumor in cm, a manual blood pressure reading), inter-rater reliability reflects how much variation one can expect when the measure is obtained by different individuals. Measures with high inter-rater reliability are robust to who collects or obtains the data used to calculate the measure.

Responsiveness

Responsiveness is important when planning to use the measure to demonstrate improvements over time. The *responsiveness* of a measure reflects its ability to detect clinically important changes, even if the changes are small. Typically, this involves demonstrating two attributes: that the measure does not change much when care quality stays relatively stable, and that the measure changes, and in the appropriate direction, when quality changes. Establishing responsiveness requires that one is able to detect change using some other method (e.g., a previously validated measure, other data, etc.), so that the performance of the measure of interest can be compared to what the other method indicates is true (i.e., has there been a change).

Signal to Noise

This measure of reliability is perhaps the most straightforward. It attempts to quantify the variability in measure performance seen across the entities that are being compared. Reliable measures are ones where the signal is larger than the noise, so that observed differences between entities (hospitals, physicians, etc.) can be trusted to represent true differences in quality. As stated by Adams, Mehrotra, and McGlynn: [1].

> The signal in this case is the proportion of the variability in measured performance that can be explained by real differences in performance. A reliability of zero implies that all the variability in a measure is attributable to measurement error. A reliability of one implies that all the variability is attributable to real differences in performance.

A variety of methods can be used to estimate signal-to-noise ratios.

Threats to Reliability

Challenges to reliability occur when too much of the variation in measurement performance happens for reasons other than differences in the underlying quality of care delivery. Small sample sizes, unintended biases, and uncontrolled factors may make it difficult to reliably and consistently differentiate entities that truly differ in the quality of care they deliver.

Strategies exist that attempt to mitigate threats to reliability. Risk adjustment, for one, attempts to normalize differences that may be due to uncontrollable factors known to affect the measure. In our rehospitalization rate example, we immediately recognize that the readmission rate of a small rural general hospital is likely to differ from that of a large urban trauma center because of case mix, geography, resources, volume, and a host of other things. Therefore, to reliably compare their readmission rates, we can risk-adjust the results to try to account for those aspects so that any remaining difference can be assumed to be due to differences in care quality.

Those who challenge the reliability of a measure may also challenge the effectiveness of these strategies. In the case of risk adjustment, a common dispute is the adequacy of the method to address underlying differences, so that comparisons remain unfair because they reflect more than just quality. Whether the issue is with the particulars of how the risk adjustment was performed, or whether one simply does not believe adequate risk adjustment is possible for that measure, it is a dispute about the ability of the measure to reliably detect true differences or changes in quality.

2.2.3 Assessing and Evaluating Quality

Once we understand the concepts of quality measurement and have established that our intended measures are valid and reliable, we must also consider the implementation and the assessment of the observed results. The implementation of a quality improvement initiative involves a series of efforts that occur over a period of time. Whether activities involve training and education, changes to the physical environment, the institution of new care protocols, or developing and activating electronic health record alarms or clinical decision support systems, part of planning the intervention involves determining the appropriate length and intensity of the activities. When planning an intervention, we not only identify the measures to use and the data from which they will be calculated but also how that data will be collected, at what time period(s), by whom, and so on. PDSA cycles and other similar methodologies involve iterative sprints and intermediate measurement and assessment. Additionally, there is often a need for pre-determined criteria for when to terminate an unsuccessful, or unintentionally harmful, intervention.

We must also consider the type of comparison that will be made. The attributes of the comparison group(s) inform the ability to isolate the effects of the intervention and thereby attribute observed benefits (and monetary gains) to that intervention. For example, if attempting to demonstrate change over time (a pre-post design), we must consider any changes in other aspects of care, facilities, staff, health policy, or outside factors that may have also changed between periods. Then, we must determine how, if at all, they could have affected the results. If the comparison involves two or more groups simultaneously (treatment versus control, facility A versus facility B, etc.), it may be difficult to mitigate potential spill-over effects that can dilute the observed

Table 2.5 Considerations needed to assess quality

Consideration	Description
Measures used	Need to identify valid and reliable surrogates that can be measured
Data needed	Need to ensure that the necessary data are available (or can be collected) and that they will provide the information required to calculate the chosen measures
Study type or comparison	Whether it is a pre-post, treatment versus control, or some other design, the timing and makeup of the groups and data collected need to be established
Intended audience	The frequency and vehicle for presentation and dissemination can inform how the data are collected or what measures are used

benefits for the treatment group. Whatever the case, we must consider advantages and disadvantages and think about the potential implications for the resulting ROI analysis (Table 2.5).

We should also consider how the results will be summarized and presented, and to whom. This often involves considering the audience(s) targeted, the necessary context and level of complexity, as well as the venue or vehicle (e.g., a summary report, a peer-reviewed paper, a conference proceeding, etc.). Remember that the ultimate goal of the ROI assessment, and likely the document or presentation in which it resides, is to convince or influence an individual or group of the merits of the quality improvement activities, either to secure funding or inspire change in practice or policy.

2.2.3.1 Translating This to Value

The specifics of the intervention, including its length and intensity, will impact value through how quickly costs are incurred and over what time period benefits are realized. The complications regarding the implementation process, terminating an unsuccessful intervention, and collecting the necessary data to assess quality can all complicate or influence the components of value and how it is measured and evaluated. All of these aspects can complicate the assessment of value and certainly the estimation of realized costs and benefits prior to implementation. But, one must recognize that they are a necessary and real consequence of undertaking activities where human lives are affected.

2.3 Measuring Value

Throughout the remainder of this book, we will explore details of how to define, measure, and assess costs and benefits of quality improvement initiatives to determine the return on investment of these activities. But, there are some general concepts that follow from our understanding of quality improvement and quality measurement that we need to first consider. These are applicable to more than just ROI analyses, but hopefully they will encourage you to think about value as you have been no doubt thinking about quality in your work up to this point.

2.3.1 Considering What Can Be Improved, Measured, and Monetized

When determining what to pursue for a quality improvement initiative, we fully understand the practical constraint that not all things that can be improved can also be measured. For example, we may strive to improve the culture of a facility or department, but we may struggle to specifically define what that means in a way that can be quantified and compared in order to demonstrate definitive improvement. Similarly, within the realm of improvable and measurable aspects of quality, only a subset of aspects can be linked to direct and specific associated monetary value.

Extending the previous example, while culture may not be directly measurable, perhaps several aspects of employee experience may be measurable, such as general satisfaction, turnover, or the frequency of complaints. However, among those measurable aspects, perhaps only turnover has any chance of having an associated monetary value assigned to it, and even then, it might take effort or require one to employ some assumptions to do so (Fig. 2.2).

In general, measurable aspects of quality that allow for an exploration of an associated monetary value are those linked to care utilization (treatments, procedures, diagnostics, and facility use like room charges), staffing (salaries, overtime, turnover), efficiency (resource use, capacity, reduced waste), and potentially changes in penalties or bonuses from federal programs or risk pools. By far the most common monetary benefit explored in quality improvement is cost avoidance associated with lower levels of utilization. In part, this is a natural result of the goal of most types of quality improvement initiatives: to reduce incidence or prevalence of disease, avoid adverse events, improve patient outcomes, or reduce waste or errors. Achieving those

Fig. 2.2 An example of selecting measures that can be measured and monetized

Table 2.6 Targets of quality improvement

Most common targets of quality improvement
Reduce incidence or prevalence
Avoid adverse events
Improve patient outcomes
Reduce waste or errors

Table 2.7 Monetary benefits

Most common monetary benefits
Cost avoidance of lower utilization
Reduced staff effort
Process efficiency (capacity, reduced waste)
Reduced penalties

goals ultimately reduces the need for care, producing a benefit of avoiding the cost of providing that care (Tables 2.6 and 2.7).

As we will discuss in more detail later, the representations of value most relevant to ROI analyses will be those that are measurable, monetizable, and attributable (MMA) to the intervention in whole or in part (Fig. 2.3).

This does not imply that other sources of benefits or other measures of value that may be of interest do not exist; they do indeed exist. But, commonly, quality improvement initiatives will have at least one of the just mentioned sources of value as the primary metric. There are ways to apply monetary values to quality of life, satisfaction, patient and caregiver burden, and other intangibles, but they can be difficult, costly, and imprecise.

Fig. 2.3 Venn diagram of measurable, monetizable, and attributable to the intervention, with improved safety as an example aim

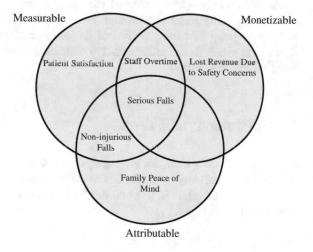

2.3.2 Planning the Value Assessment in Tandem with the Quality Assessment

Given the need to consider which quality measures can be associated with a direct monetary cost or benefit (i.e., "monetized"), it should be no surprise that planning the evaluation of the value of an initiative should be done in tandem with the planning of the initiative itself. As discussed earlier, quality and value are linked so that the decisions of how to measure one can and will influence how to measure and assess the other.

Unfortunately, it is all too common to explore the value analysis only after the initiative has been fully developed and scoped. This will most likely lead to an inadequate, or at least incomplete, value analysis or a revision of the original plan of what to measure. In some cases, it will be possible to select quality measures that are appropriate for both the assessment of quality and the analysis of associated value; but in other cases, there may be a need to supplement the measurable, but nonmonetizable, quality indicator with one or more additional metrics that can be translated into monetary values. Those who begin to explore value determination and ROI soon discover that the level of validity and reliability of quality metrics can also impact the ability to accurately capture associated costs and benefits.

Other considerations when planning the value assessment of a quality improvement initiative may involve the nature and timing of the activities. For example, it may be prudent to explore questions such as the following: How will implementation affect how value is measured and quantified? Will there be a delay between the intervention and benefits? Will it be possible to attribute the selected benefits to the intervention? What else is going on? Does the plan for summary and presentation allow for how to easily and smoothly incorporate the results of the value? If not, why not? And so on.

At this point, we have explored the general ideas driving quality and value in healthcare quality improvement and have started to describe how they are linked. Before we jump into the specifics of designing and carrying out a ROI analysis, we need to establish the definitions and metrics that we will employ throughout the remainder of the book.

2.4 Definitions and Terms

As we will discuss later, for any analysis of value you perform and present, it is standard and necessary to clearly define the metrics you will use. Below are the main metrics we will explore in this text and their associated definitions, which you will see several more times.

2.4.1 ROI

We will use a definition of ROI that reflects realized net benefits relative to costs as a percent. This will allow us to present ROI in the same way that monetary returns are presented elsewhere. For example, a ROI of 10% will represent a situation where the individual who made the initial investment has recouped their costs and received an additional 10%:

$$ROI = (Benefits - Costs)/Costs \times 100\% \qquad (2.1)$$

Therefore, if quality improvement activities cost \$25,000 to implement and produce \$35,000 in benefits (we will get into how to quantify this later), then the calculated ROI is:

$$(\$35,000 - \$25,000)/\$25,000 \times 100\% = 40\%$$

Again, this definition allows for a straightforward interpretation: Positive returns (those greater than 0%) reflect situations where benefits exceed costs, while negative returns reflect the opposite. A ROI of 0% is the break-even point: The realized benefits exactly equal the costs of the intervention, so one is no better off (fiscally) having done the project than if it had not been attempted in the first place. This interpretation is strictly related to the monetary aspect at this point. That is, if the quality of care targeted by the intervention significantly improved without resulting in a negative return (even if that return is 0%), the project is likely to be considered a success by some criteria. This highlights the added complexity ROI enjoys in the healthcare setting. That is because there may be situations where a negative ROI would be acceptable if it corresponded to a significant improvement in the quality of care provided. We will return to this and other discussions of what constitutes a "good" or "acceptable" level of ROI later.

A disadvantage of the ROI metric is that can be highly dependent on the chosen time frame. The benefits and costs included in the calculation are those that occur during the specified time frame, and shortening or extending the time frame will likely produce different results. This can be troublesome when most of the cost occurs at the beginning of the intervention while the benefits continue to accrue as long as the change is sustained. A negative or insufficient ROI in such a scenario may simply be because not enough time has elapsed to allow benefits to sufficiently accumulate. Other metrics are more robust to the chosen time frame.

2.4.2 Benefit-to-Cost Ratio (Benefits per Dollar Spent)

In addition to the ROI definition above, the most common alternative definition of ROI is what is more appropriately referred to as the benefit-to-cost ratio, or BCR.

[2] Its formula is simply:

$$BCR = Benefits/Costs \tag{2.2}$$

The lure of this metric is rooted in its simplicity and its often-relatable interpretation of the "benefit per dollar spent." In the previous example of the $25,000 initiative that produced $35,000 in benefits, the BCR is simply the ratio of those two values, or 1.4, which allows one to say, "For every $1 spent there was a benefit of $1.40."

However, the interpretation can get confusing when using the BCR to describe negative returns. Because the BCR is a ratio, it will always be greater than zero,[1] and the financial break-even point is at 1. Values between 0 and 1 reflect situations where the benefit is less than the cost (a negative ROI), while a BCR greater than 1 indicates that benefits exceeded costs (a positive ROI). Unfortunately, some will define their ROI using Eq. 2.2, but then suggest an interpretation that is inconsistent with that definition. For example, I have seen the following written:

> ROI is defined as benefits/costs [which is actually BCR], and a ROI < 1 reflects a *negative* return.

That can be confusing because it is not intuitive to consider a value greater than zero as reflecting a negative value. However, as calculated, a value of 0.8 reflects a situation where costs exceeded benefits, so that if ROI was calculated as we have defined in Eq. 1.1, it would be negative; specifically, it would be equal to -20%.

Further confusing the issue, some authors will use the term "net benefits" even though it is clear from their context that they are not considering benefits "net" of anything. To clarify: "net benefits" implies that costs have already been subtracted from the benefits, as in "benefits, net of costs."[2] Be careful when reading *and when writing or presenting* findings so that the meaning is clear to all who may encounter it. While we could use the term "net benefits" in Eq. 2.1 in place of "(Benefits − Costs)," it is presented as is to allow for consistency with what "benefits" represents in the BCR calculation (Eq. 2.2) and the metrics that follow.

As with the ROI calculation, the BCR can be highly dependent on the time frame, which can be misleading if not presented appropriately.

2.4.3 Savings per Patient

The metric of savings per patient reflects a value for the realized net benefit of the intervention that is scaled to the size of the affected population. Specifically, it is:

$$Savings\, per\, Patient = (Benefits - Costs)/Number\, of\, Patients \tag{2.3}$$

---

[1]Unless the intervention makes care *worse*, which almost never happens.

[2]When you report your "net income" to the IRS at tax time, it represents the value that is obtained after subtracting appropriate expenses and deductions from your gross income; that is, gross income net deductions.

Again, using the previous example but now assuming that the project involved a total of 34 patients, the attributable savings would equal ($35,000 − $25,000)/34 = $294.12 per patient. This metric can be helpful to put projects that are large in scope or numbers of participants into a more relatable perspective: When benefits and costs reach into the tens of millions of dollars, it can be difficult to know what is "good" or "acceptable" while savings per patient may allow for a more direct comparison with known values.

For example, if it is known that a payer spends an average of $300 per patient per year for a particular medication, calculating the benefits of a medication adherence initiative on a per-patient basis allows for the comparison of the project value in relation to the overall per patient spending for that drug. If an intervention is found to produce a savings of $30 per patient per year, the interpretation of the significance of that result can be viewed in light of its relative magnitude: It represents 10% of the average annual medication costs per patient.

Savings per patient can also help compare value between interventions of different-sized populations or over multiple time periods. For example, imagine a scenario where recruitment of participants is slower during the initial stages of an intervention than later during the intervention. If calculating benefits in the aggregate to compare to the fixed cost to launch the project, subsequent time periods when recruitment is larger may produce higher benefits and appear to produce a better return. In this case, considering results only in the aggregate may cause one to misinterpret a greater benefit in the subsequent time periods as reflecting the effectiveness of the intervention as opposed to being a function of the size of the participating cohort. Comparing the net benefits on a per-patient basis can help level the playing field and allow for a more meaningful comparison. The example in Table 2.8 reflects a situation where the aggregate net benefits are higher in the second six months ($63,000) than they were in the first six months ($48,000), but when scaled to savings per patient, it is clear that value was greater in the first six months ($240 vs. $180 per patient).

A disadvantage of savings per patient is that it may imply to some readers that each patient receives equal benefit, which may not be true. And, while it can add perspective to projects with a large scope, it can also mask the aggregate costs and benefits associated with the initiative.

Table 2.8 An example of how savings per patient can scale results by population

Time period	Recruitment	Total benefits-fixed costs	Savings per patient
First six months	200 patients	$48,000	$240
Next six months	350 patients	$63,000	$180

If comparing aggregate net benefits, one would consider the second time period as providing more value, but if comparing savings per patient, the opposite conclusion would be made

2.4.4 Payback Period

The payback period [2] reflects the amount of time, usually in months or years, until the accumulated benefits from a project will negate the total cost up to that point. It is calculated by determining or estimating the per-period benefit and dividing that into the total investment:

$$\text{Payback Period} = (\text{Total Costs})/(\text{Monthly Benefits}) \qquad (2.4)$$

While Eq. 2.4 uses months as the time period, it would be equally appropriate to use weeks or quarters or even years, depending on the situation. To see how it is used in practice, consider again our $25,000 quality improvement initiative described previously. If we could expect it to produce $4500 in benefits per month, the payback period would be $25,000/$4500 = 5.5 months. That is, assuming we do not incur additional expenses, our $25,000 investment would be recouped in just under six months.

This interpretation can be appealing when the initial ROI in the short term is negative. If in the previous example we performed a retrospective ROI analysis three months after the initiation, we would produce a negative ROI: (3 months × $4500 per month) = $13,500, which is less than our initial investment of $25,000 and reflects a ROI at month three of −46% (i.e., a negative return). If framed appropriately by also providing the payback period of 5.5 months, one can conclude the following: "To this point our ROI is negative, but we anticipate recouping our full investment in another 2.5 months." When considered together with the associated improvement in patient care or experience that one may expect, this metric can help establish the cost of an intervention as truly an investment in quality that will eventually recoup the investment and produce additional monetary dividends in the future.

However, this metric can get complicated if ongoing maintenance costs or costs to shut down an intervention exist, or if the intervention will produce varying levels of benefits over time and/or cease to produce benefits after a certain amount of time. Additionally, payback periods over twelve months should consider whether it is appropriate to discount the future value of benefits, which can further complicate calculations.[3]

2.4.5 Other Metrics

The four metrics just defined are not the only ones available, but together often provide the necessary information for most ROI analyses (Table 2.9). If other metrics are used and reported, they should be clearly defined and interpreted for the intended audience. The four just defined, or variations, will encompass the ones used in this text.

---

[3]We will cover discounting in a later chapter.

Table 2.9 Commonly used metrics to describe financial return

Metric	Pros	Cons
ROI	Most are familiar with this concept in general	Highly dependent on the time frame used for analysis
BCR	Allows for an intuitive interpretation of "$X in benefits for every $1 spent"	Highly dependent on the time frame used for analysis
Cost savings per patient	Can provide a tangible savings or benefit in analyses with a large number of patients	May be interpreted that each patient receives equal benefit, which may not be true; costs and benefits are likely accrued in the aggregate
Payback period	Effective when ROI is negative and when a sustainable intervention will provide benefits for an extended period	Often assumes that benefits will continue to aggregate in a consistent way, which may not be realistic

2.5 Basic ROI Design

A complete ROI analysis will typically involve several key components. The importance of providing context, scope, and perspective prior to identifying and aggregating costs and benefits cannot be overstated. While this step often receives little to no attention, it is crucial to allow the reader or audience to follow the examinations and calculations that follow. Before you can describe and evaluate the value of a project, you must first explain what you mean by the concept: value from *what*, value to *whom*, and value over *what time period?* Each section we will now describe will be explored in more detail throughout this text (Fig. 2.4).

2.5.1 *Scope and Perspective*

As mentioned previously, defining the scope and perspective of the analysis provides a framework and establishes some parameters regarding what will be considered to be costs and benefits. We have already explored some of the challenges associated with performing ROI analyses in the healthcare setting, including the potential for

Fig. 2.4 Four basic steps of ROI analysis

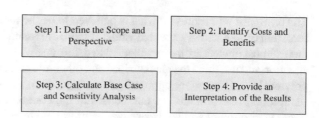

Step 1: Define the Scope and Perspective	Step 2: Identify Costs and Benefits
Step 3: Calculate Base Case and Sensitivity Analysis	Step 4: Provide an Interpretation of the Results

several interested parties (patients, providers, facilities, payers, policy makers, etc.) who may each incur costs and receive benefits of different types and magnitudes from the same activities. Therefore, before we begin to accumulate and aggregate costs and benefits, we need to specifically define things like who incurs the costs and who receives the benefits.

It will be necessary to explain why we are focusing on this particular perspective when multiple parties may be affected. For example, if we are applying to an external agency to solicit funds to perform a quality improvement initiative, we will likely perform the analysis from that agency's perspective (i.e., the costs and benefits that agency can expect), even though others, like patients, may also experience costs or benefits from the initiative.

2.5.2 Costs and Benefits

This section is really the bulk of the ROI process and represents what most people probably think of when they think of ROI analysis. Here, we will identify and quantify the specific monetary costs and benefits, including how they are or will be measured, quantified, and monetized. We will explore sources for each and how any assumptions or estimates we make may impact the accuracy or variability of these quantities. During this process, we may have to frequently make a case for certain assumptions or estimates and will return to these aspects in the sensitivity analysis to examine how they may influence our resulting value assessment.

The activities involved in this section will vary significantly from project to project. In some circumstances, costs or benefits will be limited to only a handful of sources and may be very easily quantified, resulting in a relatively brief description of how they were accumulated. Other times, however, this section will involve extensive explorations of published literature and the consideration of multiple sources and circumstances which could, or did, arise. Transparency and thoroughness will be important attributes of this section, so that those evaluating the analysis and the intervention it reflects can adequately determine of its merits based on the information that is presented, without wondering what was omitted or glossed over.

2.5.3 Base Case and Sensitivity Analyses

The base case will represent what is believed to be the most likely or credible representation of realized or expected value. If there are assumptions or estimates (which there almost always are), one will need to determine which are most applicable to the situation and use them to calculate ROI and other relevant metrics that were described previously. To the extent appropriate (as opposed to doing so in the Interpretation section), an interpretation of the metrics in the context of the intervention and the larger environment and landscape can be presented here.

Performing sensitivity analyses is not only instructive to help us identify the crucial pieces of our intervention, but it is essential to establishing credibility in the eyes of the reader or audience who will appreciate a full understanding of what could, or did, go right or wrong and the resulting effects of those scenarios. What happens if recruitment does not go as planned or if our intervention is not as successful as we had hoped? Does a positive ROI depend on everything going as planned? Or have we built in appropriate alternatives to deal with the inevitable snags that will occur along the way? Answers to these and other questions as well as an exploration into intangible or nonmonetizable benefits will allow for a full and complete examination of the costs and benefits associated with the quality improvement activities.

2.5.4 Interpretation

Here is where we will explore what our analysis says about the financial feasibility and viability of our project or intervention. What are/were the key aspects that drive ROI? What does this imply moving forward either in the current project or for future endeavors either locally or more generally? Is the return "reasonable," "acceptable," "good," or something else in light of the corresponding improvements to care quality or efficiency?

Striking a balance between providing an informative summary and remaining objective regarding the assumptions and estimates can be a delicate process. The audience often benefits from some guidance regarding how to view the results in light of the larger context or circumstances, but they must also consider the path by which the results were obtained to be credible and reasonable.

2.6 Hypothetical Case Studies

To assist in illustrating the key points throughout the text, we will consider four specific examples that highlight different aspects and nuances of each step of the ROI process. They will provide concrete, although fictitious, examples that we can refer to throughout the text. By defining them here, we can also ensure some consistency across the chapters so that it becomes clear how everything fits together. Chapter 7 contains fully developed examples of these case studies.

2.6.1 Example 1: Nursing Home Falls

Let us imagine that a facility, university, or quality improvement organization is applying for external funding to initiate a program to reduce the number of serious falls in a local nursing home. To allow this example to be generalized to other types of externally funded quality improvement projects, let us assume that the perspective for the ROI is CMS.[4] This type of example is emblematic of projects that attempt to reduce any number of common adverse events, like infections, hospital-acquired conditions, medication errors, etc. For a prospective analysis, the goal is to produce a ROI calculation that can be included in the proposal to demonstrate the economic benefits to the funding source associated with this project. If done retrospectively, the goal would be to summarize the reduction in falls produced significant cost savings to the funding agency.

2.6.2 Example 2: Improved Hospital Discharge Process

While this, too, is often a topic of interest in federal quality monitoring programs, let us assume the following in this case: This opportunity is initiated by hospital administrators who see it as a way to provide better care, improve coordination with community partners, and, hopefully, improve their bottom line by reducing 30-days rates of readmission and mortality that can impact reimbursement. In this case, hospital administrators need to be convinced that activities to improve the discharge process are worth pursuing instead of using available time and resources in other areas (the purchase of equipment, spending on facility improvements, additional staff, or quality improvement in other specific areas). Therefore, the perspective will be that of the hospital and its administration.

This example would be applicable in: (1) the case where an administrative body is trying to determine its own best course of action, or (2) where an outside organization is looking to recruit the facility to participate in activities that have already been funded. This example, too, can serve as representative of all sorts of process-improvement examples (increasing vaccination rates, improving handoff procedures for shift changes in a psychiatric facility, reducing door-to-needle time, etc.).

2.6.3 Example 3: Introducing a Collaborative Care Model

Significant evidence demonstrates that collaborative care effectively manages multiple chronic conditions in a way that coordinates care and provides the needed education and support to patients and their caregivers. If a physician or department wanted to implement care that incorporated the key aspects of these collaborative models, she would likely need to convince multiple parties, such as institution administrators or potential donors, of its feasibility and financial viability. Therefore, in proposing such a project, she would need to consider costs and benefits from a variety

---

[4]We will dive more deeply into the appropriate perspective in the next chapter. For now, just know that for this example the ROI will be calculated by considering the costs and benefits to CMS, who may be funding the program and ultimately evaluating its financial merits.

of perspectives, including those of patients and their caregivers. Ultimately, however, the goal of the ROI may be to convince staff that the program is financially feasible to continue for future years. This example will serve as a model for interventions intended to change the standard of care and/or a series of processes associated with patient care, well-being, and experience.

2.6.4 Example 4: Investing in Facility Improvements

While facility improvements may technically fall outside of some definitions of quality improvement, certainly investments in examination rooms, equipment, or other facility aspects could directly improve care efficiency and quality. In this example, we will explore the impact of a renovation to an ED in an attempt to reduce waiting time and thereby the percent of patients who leave without being seen by a physician.

This example could be representative of any investment in internal facilities that facility administrators would like to determine the financial return on. It could also be representative of staff training or development in a similar scenario. Other similar types of investments could be purchases of equipment such as an MRI machine, increasing staff levels, switching to a new EHR vendor, or even spending on activities intended to combat physician burnout (Table 2.10).

Table 2.10 Hypothetical examples explored throughout the text

Example	Other scenarios this example is emblematic of
Example 1: Reducing falls in a nursing home	Reducing adverse events like: Infections Hospital-acquired conditions Medication errors
Example 2: Improved hospital discharge process	Improving care delivery processes, like: Increasing vaccination rates Improving handoff procedures for shift changes Reducing door-to-needle time
Example 3: A collaborative care model	Changing the standard of care, like: Creating a clinical pathway Improving the patient experience Extending care across settings or to include others (e.g., family members)
Example 4: Renovating the ED	Making investments in facilities or equipment, like: Purchasing an MRI machine Increasing staffing levels Switching to a new EHR vendor

2.7   Summary

There may be a variety of motivations for assessing value and specifically ROI, and one can ask several key questions to assist in this venture. As noted previously, a strong link exists between quality and value, and the critical aspects of quality improvement (namely, defining and measuring quality) must be addressed before value can be ascertained. Because "quality" cannot typically be measured directly, we employ surrogates that we want to accurately reflect the underlying concept (validity) and allow us to detect true changes (reliability).

Defining and determining how to measure value should be done in tandem with defining and determining how to measure quality. However, additional considerations when assessing value include whether a particular measurable aspect can be monetized for inclusion as part of the financial calculation. Of all the possible results of quality improvement activities, only a subset will be measurable, monetizable, and directly attributable to the intervention. Once the measurements and metrics have been defined, there are several components that are common to most ROI analyses: identifying the scope and perspective, identifying and quantifying costs and benefits, calculating base case and sensitivity analyses, and providing interpretation.

2.8   Key Concepts

- The motivation to assess value can stem from a variety of sources, both internal and external to the organization.
- Defining value is necessary for each situation and may depend on aspects such as the availability of certain data, the perspective, and the scope.
- Given that quality and value are linked, it is first necessary to ensure that quality can be assessed, which means developing a specific definition of quality given the circumstances and identifying the appropriate measures.
- Defining value and determining metrics should be done in tandem with defining and identifying measures of quality.
- When considering potential definitions and measures of value, one needs to be aware of what value is measurable, monetizable, and attributable to the quality improvement activities.
- We will explore several key metrics in this text: ROI, the benefit-to-cost ratio, savings per patient, and the payback period.
- Most ROI analyses involve these major sections: defining the scope and perspective, identifying and quantifying costs and benefits, calculating base case and sensitivity analyses, and providing interpretation.

References

1. Adams JL, Mehrotra A, McGlynn EA (2010) Estimating reliability and misclassification in physician profiling. RAND Corporation, Santa Monica, CA
2. Buzachero VV, Phillips J, Phillips PP, Phillips ZL (2013) Measuring ROI in healthcare. McGraw Hill, New York

Chapter 3
Initial Steps

3.1 Define Scope and Perspective

The chapters that follow will dive into the details surrounding identifying costs and benefits, calculating the base case estimates, performing sensitivity analyses, and the interpretation and presentation of results. However, before any of that can occur, we must first consider the scope and perspective of the resulting ROI analysis to clarify what will be included in the costs and benefit calculations. We must also do this to ensure, when planning a project, that the proposed activities and measurements will allow for the necessary computations (Fig. 3.1).

3.1.1 Perspective

There may be multiple stakeholders in the quality improvement initiative, but for any specific ROI examination, one must be specific in terms of the perspective, even if multiple perspectives are considered simultaneously or side by side. The easiest way to specify the perspective is to answer this question: Who incurs the costs and receives the benefits? Typically, the answer will be patients, providers, facility administrators, payers, society, or an outside funding agency. If the answer to that question is "several," then you can either determine to focus this particular analysis on only one, or you can perform multiple analyses from multiple perspectives.

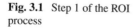 **Fig. 3.1** Step 1 of the ROI process

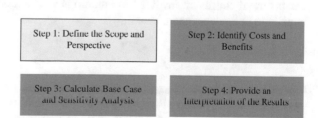

© Springer Nature Switzerland AG 2020
C. A. Solid, *Return on Investment for Healthcare Quality Improvement*,
https://doi.org/10.1007/978-3-030-46478-3_3

A common perspective is that of a payer, like CMS. In this case, from their perspective the costs incurred include the funding amount, if any, plus any additional reimbursement directly attributable to conducting the intervention, and benefits are typically reductions in Medicare and/or Medicaid reimbursement associated with lower utilization. Costs incurred or benefits realized by others impacted by the intervention, like those of facilities, providers, and patients, are not expressly included in the ROI to CMS. That is because they are costs and benefits incurred and realized from others' perspectives. That does not imply that those costs and benefits are unimportant, only that they do not represent a cost or a benefit for the entity for which the analysis is being conducted.

In truth, CMS, or other payers or funding agencies, are likely to be interested in the type and magnitude of those costs and benefits, and a thorough examination of the intervention would include and interpret them in some way, shape, or form. But in regard to the ROI analysis, when you specify a perspective you are setting parameters for which costs and benefits will be included in the ROI calculation; and if the chosen perspective is CMS, then those amounts are limited to those incurred and realized by CMS.[1]

Alternatively, the relevant costs and benefits for a locally funded initiative would be very different. If an individual facility or organization is funding a quality improvement initiative, then from their perspective the costs to quantify are those related to staff time, materials, training, and/or any facility or operational investments (structural, electronic, new equipment, etc.) that the facility or organization incurs. Realized benefits may result from changes in costs, revenue, or efficiency (e.g., required FTEs and/or overtime). Some benefits may be easy to identify and quantify, while others, such as changes in payments from insurance risk pools or quality reporting programs, or the impact of increased bed capacity, may be more nuanced. Additionally, the facility or healthcare system in which the activities occur may experience nonmonetary benefits such as improved staff and/or patient satisfaction, which may not be monetizable at all.

We will dive into the details of how to quantify these types of costs later, but these examples illustrate how the relevance of costs and benefits is directly tied to the perspective of the ROI analysis (Table 3.1).

Finally, note that a benefit to one party may be a cost to another. Reimbursement amounts or risk pool bonuses can reflect a cost to a payer but a benefit to a facility. Therefore, we must establish a perspective up front so that there is clarity regarding what constitutes a cost versus a benefit. This is also why the consideration of multiple perspectives requires separate analyses, even if they are presented together, to avoid the potential confusion involved in situations where a change can simultaneously constitute both a cost and a benefit.

---

[1]Note that this has real implications in value-based and bundled payment systems, as efficiencies and improvements funded by a payer may produce benefit at the provider or facility level that is not directly realized by the payer. We will dive into this concept more deeply in a later chapter.

Table 3.1 Examples of how relevant costs and benefits of the same intervention can change based on perspective

	Payer perspective	Provider perspective	Patient perspective
Relevant costs	Funding of initiative	Staff time Materials IT support	Time away from work Transportation
Relevant benefits	Reduced utilization	Increased efficiency Staff satisfaction Reduced turnover	Better outcomes Quality of life Lower caregiver burden

3.1.2 Scope

Together with specifying the perspective, early in the process it will be necessary to define the scope. Like perspective, the scope can be viewed as an answer to a question; specifically, who is involved and over what time frame? However, also like the process of specifying the perspective, determining the scope is not as straightforward as it may initially seem.

While it is true that part of determining the scope is identifying the number of patients, providers, or facilities involved in the quality improvement activities, it is typically necessary to define the scope in more detail to more accurately frame and guide future steps. For example, perhaps only a subset of patients is the true target of the intervention, or maybe the available resources dictate the setting or length of the intervention or data collection periods.

Additionally, the scope should consider when costs and benefits will be incurred and realized and ensure that the selected time frame is defined to fully capture those values. For example, if a hospital implements a new discharge process requiring more staff time, then the additional staff-related costs associated with that intervention will continue for as long as that facility maintains the new process. In this example, the cost is directly proportional to the length of time (i.e., the scope) involved in the ROI calculation. Alternatively, investing in a new piece of equipment is typically a one-time purchase regardless of the time frame considered for the ROI analysis, and therefore, its cost remains the same regardless of the time period chosen to examine ROI. Whatever the case, the scope of the project has major implications for how you will determine which costs and benefits to include as well as how to measure them (Table 3.2).

Table 3.2 Aspects of project scope to consider

Potential aspects of scope
The patients to include
The facilities, departments, or areas to include
The time frame
The processes or outcomes to measure

Additionally, the scope may have implications for the generalizability of the results and whether it is possible to scale or apply the ROI estimates to other patient populations or care settings. Interventions that are possible on smaller scales may not be feasible in large systems or across multiple facilities so that the value realized through a short but intense intervention locally is not applicable on a grander scale where the same level of intensity is not possible.

The intentions or goals regarding generalizability need to be considered in case certain adjustments are necessary to increase the likelihood that results can be generalized. For example, one could potentially add certain types of patients or consider potential variations that may be required in different settings or facilities. As another example, if trying to avoid adverse events like hospital-acquired infections, one may need to consider whether it is reasonable to assume that a successful intervention would reduce events across all of the settings and patients included in the intervention. Or, one may need to consider whether it is more likely to succeed only in a specific setting and/or among a subset of patients. The answer directly impacts the costs and benefits that should be included in the ROI calculation. And, if there is uncertainty about how widespread the impact may be, it would be prudent to explore various scenarios in the sensitivity analysis of a prospective analysis.

As a side note, it is entirely possible that a successful intervention could reduce revenue for a facility, at least in the short term, because of shorter stays and reduced utilization. Whether this is a benefit or a cost is directly related to the scope and perspective: A payer would consider it a benefit (reduced cost), while the facility itself would consider it a cost (reduced revenue).

As for the time frame, realized returns may vary significantly by time period. Some interventions may have an inherent delay in realized returns. Particularly for interventions that target patient outcomes such as 30-day readmission or 90-day mortality, a determination of changes in quality, and therefore the associated value, will be delayed until the appropriate amount of time has elapsed. In some cases, the real benefits of an intervention may not be realized until long after the implementation is complete. Additionally, if targeting a reduction in events that are already somewhat rare, significant follow-up time may be necessary to observe enough instances to confidently establish changes in rates and to assess differences from what they were prior to the intervention.

Alternatively, some circumstances and certain types of interventions benefits may be realized almost immediately, but then diminish over time. For example, perhaps a training session has an immediate impact on workflow efficiency that produces significant value initially, but over months or even years its effects fade as staff forgets the training and turns over. Even though a large portion of the benefits may be realized over a short time period, to accurately estimate the amount of ongoing benefit that could be expected, one would need a long enough time frame so that the rate of decline either levels off or becomes predictable in its path. In each case, the period of time during which associated costs and benefits are measured can have significant implications for the resulting ROI calculation(s) (Fig. 3.2).

Selecting the appropriate time period is a function of several things, and varying the time frame as part of the sensitivity analysis can be an effective method

Fig. 3.2 How scope can affect costs and benefits

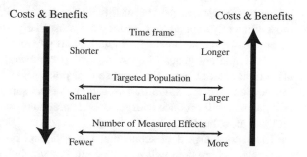

for illustrating its importance. Further complicating the selection of an appropriate time frame is the notion that successful interventions produce sustainable change, even after the intervention has been completed. Theoretically, therefore, the benefits associated with such an intervention could continue for months or even years after implementation, if not indefinitely. Even if future values are appropriately discounted, the ongoing benefits of a successful intervention will eventually surpass the initial investment, and the analysis will become less about establishing a reasonable return and more about establishing an acceptable payback period (the length of time until costs are recouped by ongoing benefits).

3.1.3   Practical Examples of Defining the Scope and Perspective

At this point, it is prudent to leverage the hypothetical case studies introduced in the previous chapter to illustrate how the definition of scope and perspective provide a framework for subsequent ROI activities.

3.1.3.1   Example 1: Nursing Home Falls (A Prospective Analysis)

Given that a facility, university, or quality improvement organization is applying for external funding to perform activities to reduce falls, the appropriate perspective for this prospective analysis would be the funding agency (CMS). In this scenario, the group applying for the funding is attempting to demonstrate not only the need and merit of the quality improvement initiative but also the value that a successful project would provide for the funding agency. Namely, that cost avoidance from reductions in care utilization stemming from fewer fall-related injuries will exceed the cost to perform the intervention.

As for scope, the applicant will need to determine multiple things. First, whether the intervention will target all residents of the nursing home or only those who exhibit specific risk factors for falls. The argument for targeting only those with risk factors is that they represent the "biggest bang for your buck," specifically that funds are most efficiently applied to those who are most likely to benefit from fall prevention. Alternatively, the argument for including all patients in the nursing home is that it may have a larger general impact regarding the overall safety of the facility. There is no right answer, but what is chosen for purposes of quality assessment will have implications for the value that is captured. The same relative reduction in high-risk patients will produce a larger overall monetary return per patient than one that includes all patients.

The second aspect of scope that the applicant needs to determine is the time frame over which data will be collected. Presumably, efforts taken to improve the physical space, heighten awareness, and increase residents' physical activity will be permanent changes in the process and culture of care. Therefore, any associated reductions in falls would sustain for an extended period of time. The applicants will need to select a prudent time frame to calculate return, but they may also find that a metric like payback period will be useful in demonstrating the financial feasibility of the project.

3.1.3.2 Example 2: Improved Hospital Discharge Process (Prospective)

The way that this scenario is presented, the intent of the analysis is to allow hospital administrators to determine how best to proceed. Therefore, the ROI analysis should be performed from the facility's perspective. Regarding scope, those performing the analysis will need to determine whether the intervention will target all patients discharged to all locations (home, another care setting, etc.), or whether it will be focused on a subset. Also necessary will be to establish a reasonable time frame over which to assess change and accumulate both ongoing costs of any new systems or procedures (i.e., staff time, any equipment investment), as well as benefits realized through performance-based reimbursement. In this scenario, however, those assessing ROI will most likely need to address the issue of how much of the realized benefits can be directly attributed to the stated intervention.

As discussed previously, much can influence the likelihood of readmission. Therefore, attributing changes to readmission entirely to the new discharge process will likely overstate the value in the case of significant decreases in readmission and understate value if readmissions stay stagnant or increase. In either case, the value associated with readmissions may not be a good representation of the value of the project. Here, the facility and its administrators may want to consider whether there are other metrics of value that they wish to collect and leverage to assess their progress. If so, they need to be considered in terms of the costs and benefits associated with them and of how the scope may need to be adjusted to include them.

3.1.3.3 Example 3: Introducing a Collaborative Care Model (Retrospective)

In this retrospective analysis, the goal is to ascertain what the ongoing benefits of the program will be so that the healthcare system can determine whether to continue the program. Therefore, the perspective will be that of the healthcare system that pays the salaries of staff who perform the main duties of the program. The scope chosen for this scenario will need to be one that accurately portrays what has been realized up until the point of the analysis but in a way that allows for the results to be used to make decisions about the future. Additionally, because the healthcare system is not looking to scale this intervention or demonstrate its viability to other populations or settings, the appropriate costs are those that are internal to the organization, as opposed to more general estimates that may reflect national or regional averages.

3.1.3.4 Example 4: Investing in Facility Improvements (Retrospective)

For this example, too, the appropriate perspective is that of the administration that funded the facility improvement. The goal will be to determine whether the combined costs of renovation plus lower capacity during construction will be recouped by the improved ability to care for patients going forward, and if so, when. The scope will also be limited to this particular facility and to the period of time preceding when the analysis is being performed. This will allow administrators to assess the return of the project to the current point and make decisions about the future.

3.1.4 Major Assumptions and Their Implications

For a prospective analysis in a proposal, when you define the scope and perspective you inherently make assumptions about the size, intensity, and length of your intervention and the associated costs and benefits. For some interventions, there will be solid evidence or data to support the assumptions being made, for others there may be significant variation in how things could play out. You should clearly identify and explore these assumptions, including what could happen to the value produced if the assumptions are incorrect, as well as what contingency plans are, or should be, in place. This exercise will allow those designing the intervention to quickly see where the key assumptions lie, not only those related to quality but also those that influence value. As a result of this process, those designing the quality improvement activities may decide to reconsider certain aspects of the proposal to either mitigate the risk associated with their uncertainty or to avoid them altogether.

Let us consider another example. If you are preparing a proposal for how to reduce hypertension-related strokes, you may describe the potential impact in terms of the reduction in the number and rate of strokes one could expect from the proposed intervention. There may be data available from previous experience or a pilot project that could be used as direct evidence of the potential impact. Another option would be to pull information from published studies that have performed similar interventions in similar populations.

In addition to these values and estimates, other quantities are necessary to include when estimating the potential value associated with this improvement, such as the number of patients included and affected (i.e., recruitment, volume, etc.), the proportion of the observed improvement attributable to the intervention (how much of the reduction is due to improved blood pressure control versus other potential changes made by patients), and the expected decrease in utilization stemming from fewer strokes. These values, too, will require that there exists either sound data to draw from or reasonable assumptions that can be applied (Table 3.3).

When specifying the exact scope and perspective, in this example a reasonable strategy would be to calculate the number of strokes one would expect both with and without (or before and after) the intervention. Depending on the size of the target population, the baseline stroke rate, and the length of the observation period, the observed effect (i.e., reduction) may only equate to a handful of strokes. It might be so small, in fact, that if actual recruitment is less than expected or the intervention is less effective than anticipated, the observed benefit may quickly evaporate. Reducing a stroke rate per 100 patient-years by 15–20% represents an improvement in quality; but if it translates into only two or three fewer strokes during a three- or four-month observation period, then it may be difficult to demonstrate an acceptable financial return. That is to say, there may be too high of a risk of realizing an inadequate return.

In reaction to this risk, one may decide that it will be necessary to enlarge the target population or extend the observation period in order to capture more of the realized value. Unless this type of exploration is performed prior to undertaking the project, one may proceed assuming that any improvement in quality will translate into an adequate financial return. However, only by examining in detail the potential variability prior to starting the initiative is one likely to identify this type of situation and have the opportunity to either alter the plan or pursue other opportunities.

For a retrospective analysis as part of a summary report, this exercise involves either (a) evaluating the accuracy of the pre-intervention assumptions and the effect

Table 3.3 Examples of assumptions commonly required	Potential assumptions needed
	Number affected (recruitment, participation, etc.)
	Baseline or pre-intervention quality (rate of events, likelihood, etc.)
	Effectiveness of intervention
	The implications of improved quality (how much less utilization, etc.)
	How much of the change is attributable to intervention versus other factors

they had or (b) exploring the key drivers of value for the intervention to better understand where future opportunities may exist to focus efforts to realize the greatest benefit. For example, if the recruitment of patients or facilities was less than anticipated, it may be reasonable to explore what level of value *would* have been realized if recruitment had reached anticipated levels. If it turns out that achieving the targeted level of recruitment was tantamount to an acceptable return for the project, this can inform how many resources to allocate next time to ensure a minimum level of participation.

3.2 Determine What to Measure

It is clear, then, that the selected scope and perspective inform and even dictate what value is captured and how. In some cases, it may need to be adjusted due to the nature of what is being targeted as part of the quality improvement intervention. At the end of the day, however, the realized ROI of a project is a function of two primary outcomes:

1. The effectiveness of the intervention
2. The (relative) magnitude of the associated costs and benefits (Fig. 3.3).

The first result is intuitive since it is simply saying that the realized value is in part a reflection of the amount of quality improvement that was achieved. That is, the more efficient the workflow becomes, the more adverse events that are avoided, the more the infection rate can be reduced, the larger the resulting value. This illustrates, again, how quality and value are linked and why they should be considered together.

The second result, however, is a little more nuanced and can be a function of a number of things, such as the following: how rare the disease or event to be reduced or avoided is to begin with (basically, how much improvement is possible), how much the intervention costs per unit of quality improvement, and how much cost savings will be realized by avoiding or reducing the disease or event. Put more plainly, cheaply solving common and expensive quality problems produces a large ROI. For example, hip fractures are expensive to treat, so interventions that successfully reduce their occurrence will produce significant monetary benefits. Whether that results in a large ROI depends on how common they were to begin with and how expensive the quality improvement activities are to implement.

Fig. 3.3 Two primary outcomes that drive ROI

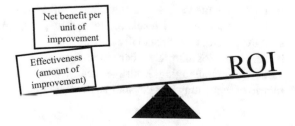

	Full-time personal aides	Reminders + adjusting environment
Effectiveness	High	Moderate
Cost	High	Low to moderate

Table 3.4 Comparing effectiveness and costs of efforts to reduce hip fractures

Even though full-time personal aides would likely be more effective and therefore produce more benefit than only reminders and adjusting the environment, it is not clear which would produce a higher ROI. That is because the more effective intervention is also the more costly one

More specifically, reducing hip fractures within a high-risk population that has several risk factors (e.g., frailty, risk of falling, cognitive impairment, lack of assistance in the home, etc.) will likely produce a higher ROI. That is simply because there is more opportunity for improvement and more value available to go after than there would be in a population with a lower baseline risk of fracture. By the same token, while reducing emergency department wait times to reduce the proportion who leave without being seen by a physician may not produce much benefit per individual, the value may be massive for large EDs that serve upward of 30,000 patients a year, even if the improvement is relatively small.

Often, the effectiveness and cost of an intervention are correlated so that increased effectiveness is accompanied by higher costs. In the example of reducing hip fractures, hiring a full-time one-on-one aide for each at-risk individual is likely to be extremely effective, but it is also likely to be cost prohibitive and may even produce a negative return. Alternatively, an intervention that involves only simple reminders and minor adjustments to the environment (e.g., moving furniture, etc.) will be relatively inexpensive but is likely to be less effective in reducing the fracture rate (Table 3.4).

The subsequent difference in the two types of efforts on ROI is unknown because financial return of a solution is driven by the amount of the benefits *relative* to the cost required to implement it. A less effective activity may produce a higher ROI than a more effective activity, even though the absolute benefits are smaller than they would be from the more effective, and more expensive, alternative (Fig. 3.4).

Similarly, a novel community-based care model that provides customized in-home care for individuals in an attempt to reduce repeated ED visits may be wildly successful in reducing acute care utilization and produce a sizeable monetary savings for payers and providers alike; but the overall ROI may be small given that it is likely very expensive to administer. By all accounts, the intervention may result in immense value and result in significantly improved patient quality of life and care experiences but financially may produce only marginal savings on a per-patient basis. Scenarios like these can make the interpretation of ROI, and ultimately of value, very challenging. Multiple factors should be considered, and more than one metric of value may be relevant to assess the intervention. As mentioned previously,

Fig. 3.4 Interventions that
produce the most benefit may
not produce the highest ROI

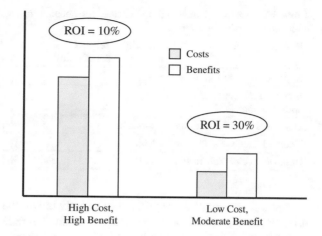

understanding that ROI is but one consideration is key to making informed, prudent
decisions regarding the merits of an opportunity.

Another important concept is that the demonstrated effectiveness of the intervention is in part a function of what is measured and how it is measured. And, because
this has a direct impact on the realized value of the project, we need to ensure that
what is measured not only allows for the assessment of quality, but also of value. In
each situation, multiple measurements could be used to demonstrate improvements
in quality, but it is unlikely that all would allow for a value assessment.

For example, demonstrating the effectiveness of a staff training program on
infection prevention could be measured by:

- Improved performance of staff on a quiz regarding key concepts
- Increased frequency of use of an infection-prevention bundle
- Decreased rate of infections
- Reduced lengths of stay or resources during the stay (antibiotics, ICU, consults,
  etc.)
- Improved patient satisfaction regarding their care.

Clearly, while all of those measurable results reflect some aspect of quality, only
some could feasibly be used to estimate the associated monetary benefit or cost-
avoidance of the intervention to reduce infections. Unfortunately, sometimes measuring quantities that allow for value assessments may reduce the ability to meet the
originally stated quality goals.

In the example just given, the most immediate and tangible reflections of staff
knowledge and behavior (and therefore those possibly considered to be the most
reflective of quality) are the first two measurements: improved performance on a quiz
and more frequent use of an infection-prevention bundle. Unfortunately, these are also
the two that are least amenable in that list to ascertaining an associated monetary
benefit. Fewer infection events and shorter lengths of stay (the third and fourth
measures on that list) have direct monetary implications. From a quality standpoint,

Table 3.5 Example of trade-offs to consider for potential measures of the effectiveness of an infection prevention intervention

Possible measurements	Ability to reflect of effectiveness of training	Ability to ascribe a monetary value
Improved quiz performance	High	Low
Increased frequency of anti-infection bundle	High	Low
Decreased rate of infections	Moderate	High
Reduced length of stay	Low	High
Improved patient satisfaction	Low	Moderate

however, they may be more difficult to directly link to the training exercise than the direct measurements of staff knowledge and behavior reflected in quiz scores and the use of the infection-prevention bundle. Therefore, in a sense, *if not willing to measure more than one thing, ensuring that value can be reliably measured and quantified will sometimes make it more difficult to measure quality, and vice versa.* These are some of the considerations one makes when defining the scope and perspective: what to measure, how to measure it, on whom, and over what time period (Table 3.5).

Although anyone familiar with quality improvement certainly understands many of the common decisions required when determining what to measure, it is worth reviewing some of them to explore how they influence the ability to measure value.

3.2.1 Process Versus Outcome Measures

The first distinction is one made by the previous example: The frequency of the use of an infection-prevention bundle is a process measure, while the rate of infections is an outcome measure. By their very nature, these measures are different and can be influenced by different things. *Process measures*, while related to patient care, really evaluate actions and decisions made by providers. They answer questions of quality like, did the provider perform a certain task or administer a particular treatment? These types of measures typically reflect actions that occur at the time and setting of the care provided and are therefore direct feedback regarding that care. Additionally, they may also be relatively robust to uncontrollable factors if they are correctly defined and measured.

Outcome measures, on the other hand, are truly patient focused (e.g., death, remission, hospitalization, progression-free survival, etc.). These types of measures will reflect care that is received but will also be influenced by uncontrollable, and sometimes unmeasurable patient characteristics like age, comorbidity burden, race, gender, socioeconomic status, and patient behaviors, like adherence/persistence to therapy, diet, smoking, etc. Additionally, they may occur days, weeks, or even months after the care that is provided, resulting in measurements, and therefore value assessments, that occur after the care event.

In terms of assessing value, outcome measures are often more attractive because they typically reflect events or utilization, which can be directly attributed to monetary value to demonstrate ROI. However, it may also be difficult to attribute the outcome directly to care (e.g., the portion of the reduction in infection events or rehospitalizations are attributable to the intervention). This may complicate the resulting value assessment because it is no longer simple subtraction of what "would have been" without the intervention from what was observed in light of the intervention. Also, as mentioned previously, an outcome measure may be rare or commonly occur outside of our scope's designated time frame, so that data on its occurrence does not accurately reflect a change in quality of care delivered.

3.2.2 Individual Versus Composite Measures

Individual measures are those where there is a single numerator and denominator calculation or a single reading or measurement that is made (e.g., the number of days until referral, the percent of patients receiving antibiotic prophylaxis, etc.). *Composite measures* are a combination of two or more individual measures in some way. There may be multiple ways to develop a composite measure, as shown in Table 3.6.

Often, additional challenges are associated with determining value associated with composite measures. The first stems from the difficulty of creating a valid and reliable composite measure in the first place. Issues related to whether patients appear multiple times in a composite numerator and denominator, or whether correlation between individual measures introduces bias into the composite, are common concerns.

Additionally, the statistical variability inherent within individual measures is compounded when measures are added together or combined, heightening the level of uncertainty and variability for the composite measure. In other cases, however, composite measures are combined specifically to address or avoid confounding that can exist. For example, when using hospitalization or rehospitalization as an outcome,

Table 3.6 Examples of composite measures

Example of composite measure	Description
Percent achievement	Identify a threshold for several individual measures (door-to-needle time less than 30 min, discharged on aspirin, etc.); instead of reporting results for each measure for each patient, summarize results by providing one value: percent of measure thresholds achieved
Aggregated percent	Sum the numerators and denominators of several measures to calculate an aggregated percent
Overall or mean performance	Take the average of the performance on several measures

some argue that mortality is a "competing event" and can skew or confound what the measure tries to represent. Therefore, a composite measure of *either* death or hospitalization may be examined as a way to better understand the patterns of patient outcomes. This combined event, however, may be more difficult to ascertain value, since avoiding one outcome may be associated with significant cost savings while the other may not.

3.2.3   One Versus Many Measures

In addition to combining measures into a composite measure, one may also choose to examine multiple measures individually, and there may be instances when it is appropriate to do so. Some may more accurately capture quality while others more easily reflect value. Or, there may be multiple aspects of quality affected by the intervention, each of which has its own value that one can reasonably sum to obtain an overall return. In the example described previously regarding the staff training in infection prevention, several of the potential measures listed may be useful.

- The "increased frequency of use of an infection-prevention bundle" may help demonstrate improvements in the processes of caring for at-risk patients and reflect a true improvement in the quality of care provided, but it may have little to no direct monetary benefits one could identify.
- The "decreased rate of infections" certainly has implications for both quality and value, especially from a payer's perspective, since the reduction in the adverse event translates into lower levels of utilization.
- Similarly, "Reduced lengths of stay or resources during the stay (antibiotics, ICU, consults, etc.)" can reflect both quality and value, perhaps from the perspective of either patients who endure shorter stays or the facility and providers who are spending less time and fewer facility resources on these patients. A more value-centric version might be something like "Reduced laboratory orders for blood cultures"; this may not always easily be equated to improved quality, but it certainly has implications for value in the form of efficiency and reduced resource use.
- Finally, "Improved patient satisfaction in case" likely holds value for patients, but it also hold value for providers and facilities if it translates into an improved reputation or "brand" (that it may be unmeasurable is a different issue). And it may also hold value if it translates into increased reimbursement from a federal program that incorporates patient experiences, through the Hospital Consumer Assessment of Healthcare Providers and Systems (HCAHPS) or some other method.

Using some combination of these measures may more readily allow for an assessment of the quality and value.

3.2.4 The Impact of Project Characteristics on Measures

As with many analytic endeavors, considering aspects of the general framework, like scope and perspective, can greatly add to the usefulness and robustness of the results. Assessments of the value associated with quality improvement activities often involve several assumptions and estimates. So being intentional and specific about *who* incurs costs and benefits and over *what* time frame provides the necessary guidance for identifying and quantifying those values. When considering this, there are implications regarding what are chosen as relevant measurements and the applicability of certain data. As mentioned previously, developing these aspects in concert with relevant aspects of the assessment of quality will produce the most thorough and relevant analysis possible. Additionally, understanding the importance of this process allows one to make informed decisions about how to select which quality improvement opportunities to pursue.

3.3 How to Select Quality Improvement Opportunities for Value

Value and quality go hand in hand, but as mentioned previously, improvements in quality are not always accompanied by monetary returns, at least in the short term. Therefore, when selecting and vetting quality improvement opportunities for their potential value or ROI, you should consider not only the potential improvement in quality, but also the fiscal impact in relation to the costs needed to achieve it.

Obviously, holding the level of quality improvement equal, interventions that target "big ticket" conditions (i.e., those that make up a significant portion of spending and resource use in many populations) will typically produce a larger ROI over shorter periods or per event avoided. This does not mean that lower revenue or rarer events or conditions should be ignored due to their limited capacity to produce large returns; on the contrary, these situations require the most skill in framing the issue appropriately in order to accurately capture associated costs and benefits. Teams can ask several questions as they are identifying and vetting potential quality improvement opportunities to pursue.

3.3.1 Questions to Ask

3.3.1.1 Question 1: Does an Opportunity to Improve Quality Exist?

In many cases, an outside agency or funding source will provide the target of quality improvement, and the role of those charged with bringing about change need only to focus on *how* to do it, not whether to do it. However, it is common for those

Table 3.7 Different types of quality improvement opportunities

Type of opportunity	Description
Adverse outcomes	Infections, falls, readmissions, etc.
A breakdown in process	Inadequate clinical pathways, misdiagnoses, etc.
Waste or inefficiency	Delays in time until treatment, the need for retesting, etc.
Oversight or prevention	Inspections, regulations, insurance, etc.
Penalties (or lack of bonuses)	From federal monitoring programs or insurance risk pools, can also include legal costs, settlements, etc.

who work on the front lines of care to identify and recognize where opportunity for improvement exists. When determining the extent of the opportunity, it can be helpful to think about it in terms of what type of detriment the current situation or process poses to care delivery or patient outcomes (Table 3.7).

Considering opportunities in this way can allow one to better assess how much of an opportunity exists and what would be necessary to address it. That is, each potential opportunity will likely have associated with it:

- A cost of it remaining unaddressed (i.e., continued waste, unacceptably high error rate, etc.).
- A cost to address it (i.e., the cost of quality improvement).
- Benefits of improving it.

The last one is often a mirror image of the first one, but not always. In some situations, improving the issue provides some benefits but does not completely alleviate the cost burden. Depending on the opportunity, even if there is significant cost associated with it remaining unaddressed, the costs to try to improve it could be prohibitive. While the last two in the bulleted list reflect the costs and benefits included in ROI, the first one reflects the cost of maintaining the status quo, which may involve some level of investment just to ensure it does not get any worse. An example might be that while the current physical environment is dated and incurs high costs to run (electricity, heat, etc.), rebuilding the entire facility might be prohibitively expensive but smaller investments in the form of upgrades in the heating or electrical systems may suffice for the time being.

3.3.1.2   Question 2: What Is the Demand for the Opportunity Among Key Stakeholders and How Does the Potential Return Affect that Demand?

At times, the demand for an opportunity is strong and based largely on the potential for improved patient care and outcomes. When this occurs, it may not be that ROI is unimportant, but it may be that ROI is not a driving force and one only needs to demonstrate that the return is not prohibitively poor. It may even be the case that a negative ROI could be acceptable, depending on the improvement in quality. In that case, the ability to measure value and return may not greatly influence the decision of whether to pursue the opportunity. On the other hand, if stakeholders have made it clear that a certain return is expected or even required to move forward, then ensuring adequate data and measurement is paramount, as is ensuring that the measurements can be translated into monetary value to demonstrate the level of return. The questions that follow are relevant to this latter situation.

3.3.1.3 Question 3: What Will the Length and Intensity of the Intervention Be Versus the Timing of the Benefit (If Not Immediate)?

Interventions can be brief, and improvements in quality can level off or reach a particular goal, but the potential benefits associated with changes in quality may extend for some time. For example, a successful intervention may reduce the infection rate to specified goals within three months and then simply sustain this improvement for the rest of the year. However, the financial benefits associated with the lower infection rate occur over the entire time period, not just the first three months.[2] Along these lines, when considering what to measure, consider whether there is a different tolerance for the size and timing of the financial benefit than for meaningful clinical improvements in quality. For instance, what if you expect to achieve an improvement in quality after a month but do not anticipate recouping the initial costs for another year? Is that okay? Will you have a full year to allow for the benefits to accumulate so that you can demonstrate the needed return?

As a side note, what this issue really addresses is whether there is sustainability. One might argue that a key characteristic of a successful intervention is one that is sustainable long after the intervention is over—improvements in quality that are only temporary are not really an improvement. If that is true, then there is value in sustainability so that it is often reasonable to consider the financial gains associated with the sustaining of an improved quality metric.

3.3.1.4 Question 4: Are the Necessary Data Available and/or Easily Obtained?

Often when designing a quality improvement intervention, we only consider the data needed to quantify and track changes in quality, not value. Remember that there may be processes or outcomes that are measurable but not monetizable. Therefore, when considering what data are available or obtainable, we should consider needs for both quality and value. Where quality data are available while value data are not (e.g., the measures of quality will not be monetizable), we should ask whether it is

---

[2]One of the benefits of evaluating projects based on their associated value is that it can emphasize the importance of sustainability: Simply maintaining an achieved level of quality can continue to produce monetary benefits indefinitely.

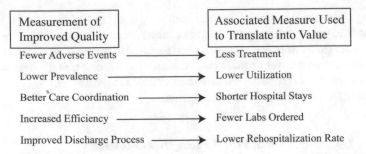

Fig. 3.5 Translating quality improvement into measures that can be assigned value

possible to identify and/or collect additional data that can inform the impact on the value of the intervention. When quality metrics need to be translated into dollars by using prior experience or published information on the associated reduction in care utilization or cost avoidance, a relevant question within this topic is: Will you be able to identify relevant information for calculating the value associated with improvements in quality?

Basically, this question is asking whether there is information available that demonstrates how an improvement in quality (e.g., reduced infections, lower prevalence, faster discharge time, more frequent referrals, etc.) translates into cost savings or changes in utilization (e.g., less treatment, shorter hospital stays, fewer readmissions, etc.). If the answer is not immediately apparent, it may require a preliminary search to see what type of information is available. You will not want to pursue an idea and then later discover that there is a paucity of data regarding how your chosen metric translates into monetary value (Fig. 3.5).

As an example, consider an intervention that attempts to improve blood glucose control for diabetics, where hemoglobin A1c values are used to define the "success" of the project. How these measures are framed and used could potentially have implications for what is monetizable. One way to establish success would be to aim for an absolute reduction in the mean A1c value. An alternative would be to try to increase the percent of the target population whose A1c is <7%, a common target for diabetes interventions. (This situation is often encountered when laboratory values are used, whether it is glucose, triglycerides, blood pressure, or some other metric; in addition to the raw laboratory value, there are often thresholds that represent clinical goals to be in "control" or in the "normal" range.)

From strictly a quality standpoint, there may be reasons to select one type of metric over the other. However, when selecting the appropriate measure of value, one should consider the available data. Published studies will often classify patients on their level of control (i.e., the percent whose A1c is <7% or some other threshold) instead of their absolute glucose value. Therefore, information regarding the risk reduction of adverse events associated with achieving that threshold may be more plentiful than information quantifying the benefits of an absolute improvement. Obviously, other important considerations will arise when determining the best way to frame quality-related measurements, but this type of exploration can help us recognize how best to identify and leverage available data.

3.3.1.5 Question 5: What Assumptions Will Be Made that May Affect the Value Assessment?

In any prospective analysis, assumptions will be made regarding recruitment, feasibility, achievable impact, and its translation into monetary returns, among other things. At times, these assumptions and estimates are based on highly reliable and relevant data or information. Other times, it is clear that there is more uncertainty. Consider how the potential variability of your assumptions and estimates may influence the ability to identify benefits, translate them into monetary benefits, and attribute them directly to the intervention. This can help strengthen the plan and allow for additional contingencies.

If the primary assumptions carry with them a significant amount of uncertainty so that the likelihood of a positive return is highly dependent on their accuracy, one may want to reconsider whether the opportunity is appropriate or explore whether there are contingencies that could be put into place to mitigate that risk. Again, this may frequently be done in regard to improvements in quality, but it tends to be a rare endeavor as it relates to value.

3.3.1.6 Determining the Necessary Sample Size

Inevitably, before you begin an intervention there will always be questions like, "How many patients should we include?" and "How long should we follow them?" and others which are basically, "How much data do we need?" Most of the time, the answer will largely be driven by the need to be able to detect change, which is not specific to value or ROI but instead an issue related to detecting improvements in quality. As mentioned previously, a positive ROI is driven in part by the effectiveness of the intervention. More accurately stated, what is required is that one can achieve an improvement and empirically detect and demonstrate that it occurred and is attributable to the intervention. In addition to the attributes of measured quantities described previously (validity, reliability, etc.), this is also driven by the amount of data available (i.e., the sample size).[3]

A common question regarding sample size is how does the determination of the necessary sample size change when considering value in addition to quality? The answer: often it does not. The necessary sample size will largely be driven by the quality metric that has been chosen, and specifically:

---

[3]The need or desire to demonstrate statistical significance in the demonstrated value is uncommon, and such demonstrations are usually limited to changes in measures of quality. A thorough sensitivity analysis of the value calculation is usually sufficient to address uncertainty.

1. The amount of a change you want to be able to detect (what is meaningful).
2. The level of variability you will observe (the level of precision).
3. How certain you want to be that you're right (the power).

As with any sample size calculation, you may or may not have prior knowledge regarding meaningful differences or expected level of precision, so these can become estimates as well.

Good sources for helping you determine the appropriate sample size can be found through simple online searches. However, always keep in mind the additional stumbling blocks when considering the amount of data necessary, like:

- Not everyone will return a survey; consider likely response rate in the sample size calculation.
- Often, available data will have missing or invalid data, which can either reduce the sample size or require a procedure for imputing missing values.
- If an under-represented group is of interest, it may be necessary to oversample individuals from that group or simply increase the overall sample size.

From a statistical standpoint, there may be no need to separately consider representations of value (i.e., money) when determining sample size, with a few exceptions:

- Representations of value can sometimes help determine what amount of change is meaningful; perhaps improvements in efficiency are only considered effective if one can achieve a certain savings per event or patient.
- If comparing monetary values using statistical methods (hypothesis tests, confidence intervals), recall that the ability to do so validly often requires an underlying assumption of the distribution of the variable of interest (e.g., normally distributed), which are frequently violated when examining monetary values due to the common skewness introduced by a few large values. However, this can be addressed by:

  - Ensuring an adequate sample size of monetary values so that *mean values* are normally distributed.
  - Using techniques related to distribution transformations in analysis.
  - Comparing differences, which are normally distributed even when individual values are not.

Details of these concepts are beyond the scope of this book. However, hopefully the ideas above will help you identify potential pitfalls or areas of concern for your project. Consulting a statistician prior to collecting any data or progressing too far with an analytic plan is always a good idea.

3.4 How to Estimate the Expected Effectiveness and Associated Value

When considering the questions given in Table 3.8, it can be difficult to know how to answer them. Often, it is necessary to rely on prior experience, either our own or the experiences of others detailed in published articles or other mediums. Sometimes, these experiences provide specific information that can be used, while other times we must translate the experiences of others' improvements in quality into value. However, there are things to consider in either case.

3.4.1 Pulling from Your Own Experience

Whether your experience is from a hospital, clinic, healthcare system, nursing facility, quality improvement organization, or something else, and whether you are a provider, administrator, facilitator, analyst, or policy maker, you may be able to speak to a number of aspects of the project.

General day-to-day experiences are likely to inform aspects related to feasibility and sustainability. Specifically, you may have experience attempting to incorporate a new workflow, improving emergency efficiency, recruiting patients or providers for a study, etc. These experiences are likely to highlight potential barriers, challenges, and general feasibility of the intervention and timeline being proposed. These are key insights and should be leveraged to more accurately predict aspects like the size of the target population and effectiveness of the intervention. They will also serve as a reality check for the proposed time frame and intensity of an intervention, which are frequently estimated too aggressively. These types of insights often stem not from formal projects or studies but from the real-world experiences of the day-to-day business of caring for patients and keeping the facility up and running.

Experience with more formal endeavors, like pilot projects, are more likely to inform more specific aspects of the study like necessary sample size, generalizability,

Table 3.8 Questions to ask when selecting quality improvement opportunities

Demand	What is the demand for the opportunity among key stakeholders and how does the potential return affect that demand?
Scope	What will the length and intensity of the intervention be versus the timing of the benefit (if not immediate)?
Data	Are the necessary data available and/or easily obtained?
Availability of information	Will you be able to identify relevant information for calculating the value associated with improvements in quality?
Necessary assumptions	What assumptions will be made that may affect the value assessment?

and realistic expectations regarding costs and benefits. Here, too, there will likely be important knowledge regarding sustainability.

3.4.2 Pulling from Published Literature

When using published literature to inform key assumptions about a proposed quality improvement intervention, you should engage in some primary activities.

The first will be searching and identifying studies that are applicable to your proposal. It can be helpful to break down all the different aspects of previous studies that may be applicable to your situation or proposed intervention. In each case, a previous study may be similar to your situation in its:

1. Affected population. This could be the demographic or clinical characteristics of patients (e.g., the same age group or those with the same clinical history, such as those receiving a certain type of medication) or in the case of a process improvement within a facility or organization, it could be the characteristics of the facility (e.g., urban hospitals, healthcare systems with at least 500 providers, etc.).
2. Targeted condition or issue. This should be self-explanatory. If your intervention targets heart failure patients, studies on care of heart failure patients may be relevant, if only to provide baseline or pre-intervention estimates of utilization and outcomes.
3. Care setting. This, too, should be self-explanatory. If you are planning an intervention in an ambulatory surgery center (ASC), studies of quality of ASCs can provide needed context and baseline estimates.
4. Intervention or quality improvement activities. There may be one or several aspects of the previous study's intervention that matches up with yours, such as the materials or tools used, the time frame, or what's being measured (falls, infections, length of stay, etc.).

Obviously, the more of these that match up with your study, the more applicable and useful the study is likely to be for you. A study with the same, or similar, intervention in the same care setting targeting the same condition within the same population can provide ample information and strong support for assumptions you make in your own proposal.

At the same time, a study does not need to have more than one aspect in common with your project to be of use. Any study of your targeted condition may provide relevant estimates of baseline incidence, prevalence, event rates, costs, quality of life, care utilization, etc., even if the study differs from your project in its care setting or intervention. But, for those aspects that do not match up with your proposed project, you need to think critically about how those differences may affect your estimates. A common occurrence is to find published incidence or prevalence estimates that apply to more general populations or conditions than what you are targeting. For example, there may be a published estimate of the prevalence of "any cognitive impairment" as opposed to the specific type of dementia you seek to affect; or there may be published hospitalization rates for all ages but not specifically for those aged 70 and older, as in your target population.

Regardless of the type of difference, when using estimates from published studies that differ from your proposed project, consider how the resulting estimate likely differs from what would be applicable to you, and in what direction (i.e., is it more conservative or less conservative than what you hope will be true for your project?). Ideally, you will find several articles that will provide multiple estimates that together will provide a range that you feel covers the likely scenarios you may encounter in your project. Even so, you should be able to defend why your chosen assumptions differ from other published results based on differences between your project and the published studies.

You will also want to pay special attention to any measures of costs or benefits (and any measures that could be translated into costs or benefits, like utilization, changes in incidence, prevalence, or event rates, etc.). Notice the source of the costs/benefits, how they are quantified and monetized (if at all), and who they are a cost and/or benefit to (patients, providers, payers, facilities, etc.). Consider the data that are used and how they compare to what you plan to use. They can either provide inspiration for how to measure certain aspects or validate your plan by providing an example of what has been done previously.

It is also possible to estimate costs and benefits for studies that did not explicitly attempt to do so. Often, there is enough information in the study to estimate:

- Costs associated with staff effort or facility investments.
- Ongoing costs associated with maintaining the efforts.
- Realized improvements in quality and how they translate into benefits.

Doing this can provide guidance on what type of costs and/or benefits you may be able to expect in your project and reveal insights about what aspects may drive return in your situation.

Let us look at an example to further illustrate how previous published literature can be leveraged.

3.4.2.1 Hypothetical Example of Estimating Costs and Benefits from a Published Study

Article Title: Improved Care Coordination Through the Use of a Care Management System

Introduction: At a small hospital (120 beds) in a rural community, providers and administrators were concerned about the large amount of acute care utilization focused within a small group of high-frequency utilizers. This article describes a quality improvement intervention involving the implementation of a care management system that successfully reduced repeat and unnecessary utilization by matching patients' acuity with more appropriate levels of care, connecting them with community resources, and improving self-management of medication adherence.

Methods: In June 2018, we assigned two RNs to serve as care managers by allocating a total of 0.5 FTEs between the two of them. Their roles were to maintain communication with patients identified as high-frequency utilizers and liaise with providers and ancillary care services to meet the specific needs regarding non-acute, non-serious health needs. As part of the biweekly communication with patients, the care managers provided information on available community resources and educational material regarding self-management of medication adherence. When necessary, care managers coordinated appointments with both the appropriate department and specialists and had informal interactions with family caregivers to suggest resources they could access for information and support.

Results: Prior to the implementation of the care management program (January–May 2018), the 26 high-utilizers accounted for 47 ED visits and 34 hospitalization events. By comparison, during the same months in 2019 (January–May), which was six months after the June 2018 initiation of the care management program, the 23 patients who were still alive and treated by our hospital had 32 ED visits and 14 hospitalizations. These represent a 32% and 59% decrease in ED and hospital visits, respectively.

Discussion: The care management program resulted in a significant reduction in acute care utilizations among patients previously identified as high utilizers. We credit this improvement to several sources: first, patients were directed toward the correct level of care based on their needs, whereas previously these patients would have likely gone to the ED or hospital for every need. Second, patients utilized community-based support services to help with care in their own home, due to the information provided to both the patients and their informal caregivers. Third, it is likely that medication adherence improved thereby increasing the level of disease control.

This is obviously an oversimplification of a full manuscript, but the key aspects are there: a description of the setting and patients, details of the intervention and the resources used to implement it, and tangible results using several quality measures. Using this information, it may be possible to estimate the individual, or at least a range of reasonable estimates, of costs and benefits this hospital experienced.

Estimating Costs of the Published Study

It appears as though the main cost of the program was the RN staff time. While few details are offered, it is likely that salaries and benefits could be reasonably estimated using general knowledge or experience, to arrive at an estimated cost for 0.5 of a full-time equivalent (FTE) of RN time per month. If one can assume that an annual RN salary is roughly $80,000, then 0.5 FTE would be roughly $3300 per month.

During the five months between January and May 2019, that equals approximately $16,500 in costs.

In reality, there may also have been costs related to:

- IT or software necessary to track patients and interactions.
- Training for the RNs or other staff regarding the program and its materials.
- Developing and printing educational materials for distribution.

If prudent, it would be reasonable to estimate some of these costs based on the size and scope of the intervention and the number of patients involved. For the current example, we will assume that these costs (which are likely incurred only once as opposed to monthly) are minimal compared to the staff costs and therefore will not appreciably affect ROI.

Estimating Benefits of the Published Study

On the surface, the benefits presented by the study reflect the reduced utilization of the targeted population. Depending on the perspective, however, this may or may not be a benefit of interest. For example, if these are reimbursed events, the hospital may not see this reduced utilization as a monetary benefit. However, for the purposes of this example, we will assume that those estimating the ROI are doing so to gain understanding of what kind of benefit would be realized by a payer (like CMS) if they were to fund this sort of intervention.[4]

To estimate the monetary benefits, we need to establish the relative improvement in rates of utilization and apply a monetary value for cost avoidance. As presented, the counts of ED and hospital visits and percent improvement are in real values as opposed to rates per time at risk (more on this in a later chapter). However, because we are assessing costs and benefits over the same time period, we can simply total each over the window of comparison to arrive at net benefit and ultimately ROI. Using the raw counts, there were 15 fewer ED visits and 20 fewer hospitalizations. Assigning a value of $\$X$ to each ED visit and $\$Y$ to each hospitalization, the total realized benefit in cost avoidance would be calculated as:

$$(15 \times \$X) + (20 \times \$Y) = \text{Total 5-Month Benefit} \qquad (3.1)$$

Various values for $\$X$ and $\$Y$ could be explored depending on available information and various assumptions regarding type and length of visit.

Estimating ROI of the Published Study

Although the program started in June 2018, the window of comparison is January through May 2019. Ideally, we would try to establish the total costs and total benefits starting in June 2018, but without additional information it may be inappropriate

---

[4]That is not to say that there may not be hospital benefits: These high utilizers have likely resulted in elevated readmission rates for this hospital which could have imposed monetary penalties. Reductions in their utilization may translate into cost savings for the hospital through reduced readmission-related penalties. To estimate that, however, we would need more information regarding previous financial penalties.

Table 3.9 Summary of estimated ROI from published study

Estimated costs	0.5 FTE for $3300 per month	$16,500
Estimated benefits	15 fewer ED visits and 20 fewer hospitalizations	15 × value of each ED visit avoided + 20 × value of each hospitalization avoided
Estimated ROI		(Row 2 − Row 1)/Row 1 × 100%

to assume that the reduction in utilization demonstrated in early 2019 was realized during the latter half of 2018 as well. Our willingness to apply assumptions and make estimates about that period will dictate whether we are comfortable estimating ROI including that time period, or whether we prefer to limit it to the period where there are real data reported.

For this example, we will limit the ROI to the window of comparison provided by the paper; we could also estimate a net benefit per month and then perhaps use that to forecast forward or backward, if desired.

The realized ROI *during the five months* between January and May 2019 is calculated as:

$$[\text{Total 5-Month Benefit; (Eq. 3.1)} - \$16,500]/\$16,500 \times 100\% \qquad (3.2)$$

As one can see, this value is subject to several of the assumptions made throughout the process, and adjustments to those assumptions will produce a different ROI. Additional explorations could be made by incorporating other costs, additional time frames, or attempting to estimate per-month benefits to understand the financial viability of the program going forward. However, at this point, the example sufficiently illustrates the general procedures involved in estimating the financial return for a previously published study (Table 3.9).

This type of exploration may provide multiple insights. First, it may provide a benchmark for what one could expect as a financial return for a similar intervention or at least provide the starting point from which one could estimate it. Adjustments could be made to account for differences in the setting, the scope, or other characteristics of the proposed project. Second, it may reveal components not previously identified or potential barriers that may need to be addressed. These barriers may be technical in nature, such as potential issues with the chosen measurements or available data to provide the necessary values. Or, the barriers may be conceptual and highlight limitations of the intervention so that adjustments are necessary for the project being proposed. In either case, the exercise provides valuable information for anyone planning quality improvement activities where value will be assessed.

3.5 Secure Buy-In and Recruit Partners

Often, to implement an intervention you will need to convince others to participate and either buy-into the process or allocate time and resources toward the implementation and maintenance of the project. In addition to convincing them that the intervention is worthwhile and feasible, you may need to demonstrate either a positive return or that a slightly negative return is accompanied by a significant improvement in care and/or efficiency in a way they care about.

For internal audiences, the goal is to secure demand and convince key players that their participation, and that of their staff, is worthwhile. Influential individuals within an organization understand that unless a project is financially feasible it will be unsustainable, even if it is highly effective in improving quality.

Sometimes, there is a specific need for an organization that is developing and designing an intervention to recruit outside entities and individuals to participate in their project. This happens frequently in larger interventions that span wider geographic areas and/or involve multiple settings of care or the coordination between private healthcare delivery systems and community resources or state-funded organizations. In these scenarios, there is a need to identify and approach organizations to gauge their interest in participating. Often, these outside organizations will have altruistic motivations and will willing to participate simply if they believe that it will improve care quality and patient outcomes. However, there may be times when it is necessary to demonstrate that it will result in an acceptable ROI for their organization.

Many of the same considerations needed when presenting ROI in an application to secure funding are also needed when asking outside organizations to participate in quality improvement activities. However, the key difference will be in the perspectives that are explored. That is, while potential partners may be interested in knowing the funding agency's potential ROI in order to evaluate the likelihood that you will secure the funding, to secure their commitment to participate it may be helpful to present the ROI that they, as partners, could expect. They may not require a significantly positive ROI. They may simply want to know that they will not incur significant losses. However, they will probably need to be confident that you have identified the key assumptions and have developed contingency plans to handle unforeseen circumstances. In essence, this is about quantifying and minimizing or mitigating the *risk* to this outside organization. If they feel that their overall level of risk is low, they will be more likely to agree to participate.

For example, assume that an independent quality improvement organization has developed a project aimed at reducing infections at ambulatory surgical centers and needs to recruit centers to participate. To convince those centers to invest the staff time, resources, and effort to the cause, they will be interested not only in the improvement in quality experienced by their patients, but they likely will also seek to understand what the financial implications are for their organization.

Clearly demonstrating the costs incurred by a participating ambulatory surgical center as well as the expected benefits related to fewer infections likely involves a collaborative effort with clinical and administrative members of that center. How fewer infections could increase capacity (from shorter stays), reduce penalties from post-operative transfers to acute care, or other efficiency or outcome-related benefits may be easily identified and quantified by those internal to that organization.

There may be several ways to frame this information, depending on the situation. For instance, some centers may have previously identified infections as a primary focus and simply had not been able to find the time or resources to devote to it. In this situation, it may be prudent to highlight not only the costs and benefits that would be accrued but also any savings in costs or time that the center may experience by participating in this larger project compared with tackling it on their own.

If your intervention does not quite mirror an opportunity they had thought of pursuing independently, you may alter or add to your intervention to include an aspect this organization would like to have measured and evaluated so that they feel they are getting something from their participation.

When communicating the estimated costs and benefits, describe what they will be in totality across the entire project as well as what this individual organization can expect. The outside organization may be more willing to participate if they understand their place in the larger scheme even if their individual ROI is minimal. Also be specific about whether their commitment involves a one-time investment or will require ongoing costs. Finally, indicate whether their organization will realize a benefit only in the short term or whether they can expect that the project will continue to produce benefits over the long term.

However it is presented, a clear and transparent demonstration of relevant costs and benefits as well as subsequent calculations of estimated ROI or payback period will help facilitate the necessary conversations regarding their potential participation.

3.6   Summary

The initial steps of embarking on a ROI analysis involve several crucial decisions. Establishing the scope and perspective provide the framework that help to define everything else that follows. The selected scope and perspective affect what constitutes costs and benefits and how they are monetized and summarized. Further, they inform how the chosen measures can and will be translated into monetary values and represent relevant aspects of the quality improvement initiative. During the initial steps, examining the necessary assumptions and their implications is necessary to ensure that the analysis will accomplish its stated goals and provide the required information for those assessing the project. Along these lines, understanding this process and the elements included can help identify quality improvement opportunities that are likely to produce measurable value. Once in place, the initial decisions will allow us to proceed to identify and quantify the relevant costs and benefits.

3.7 Key Concepts

- The first step in a ROI analysis is to define the scope and perspective, which outline for whom the costs and benefits are being attributed and over what time period.
- Scope can include things such as patients or providers to include, geographic or organizational areas that will be involved, the time frame over which costs and benefits are accumulated, and measures or outcomes that are assessed.
- The quantified costs and benefits can vary significantly by perspective; those perspectives, other than the one chosen are not insignificant but must be addressed separately.
- Several aspects of the scope (e.g., length of the time frame, the target population, the number of measured effects) can impact the quantity of costs and benefits identified.
- In any analysis, but especially in a prospective one, several estimates or assumptions are needed; these should be carefully considered and clearly communicated to the audience or reader.
- The ratio of costs and benefits will produce the ROI but does not reveal the absolute magnitude of either costs or benefits; large benefits may be accompanied by a small ROI, and vice versa.
- Several things should be considered when selecting quality improvement opportunities to pursue, such as the potential for improvement, the demand for improvement among stakeholders, and the availability of the necessary data.
- Estimating the value in a prospective analysis can be achieved by leveraging one's own experiences or looking to outside resources (such as published literature); these can provide values for use in the analysis as well as potential benchmarks for overall return.
- When it is necessary to recruit partners or participants for quality improvement activities, demonstrating the value from their perspective can be an effective way to secure their involvement and buy-in.

Chapter 4
Costs and Benefits

4.1 The Impact of Scope and Perspective on Costs and Benefits

As described in the previous chapter, the scope and perspective of the ROI analysis relate, in general, to who incurs the costs and receive the benefits, in what setting, and over what time period. Therefore, as we explore in more detail how to identify and quantify costs and benefits throughout this chapter, we must do so within a specifically defined scope and perspective. In each case, the perspective (and scope, as we will discuss in a moment) will inform the kinds of costs or benefits that will be included and even how they are quantified.

From a payer's perspective, costs may simply involve the awarded amount, while benefits will likely take the form of cost avoidance stemming from reduced utilization, lower incidence and prevalence of disease, fewer adverse events, or shorter treatment time. Internally funded projects will often face costs related to staff time and facility resources, while benefits may follow from improvements in efficiency, changes in reimbursement amounts, changes in performance-based rewards or penalties, or some other source.

The scope, including the time frame, will also play a role in how costs and benefits are quantified and applied. The identified breadth of the intervention regarding the setting, specific departments, patients, and staff involved will obviously dictate which costs and benefits will be included. Knowing, or assuming, that certain interventions may have spillover effects across other populations or areas within or around the facility or organization may inform the decision about the appropriate scope. Regarding the time frame, the existence of ongoing costs associated with maintaining a new hospital discharge process means that a longer time frame for the analysis will produce higher costs. In contrast, a one-time purchase of new medical equipment will produce the same cost, regardless of the length of the time frame.

© Springer Nature Switzerland AG 2020
C. A. Solid, *Return on Investment for Healthcare Quality Improvement*,
https://doi.org/10.1007/978-3-030-46478-3_4

4.2 Costs

Several steps are involved in identifying and summarizing the appropriate costs for a ROI analysis, regardless of whether it is a prospective or retrospective analysis. In the coming pages, we will discuss sources of costs, how to estimate and monetize costs, and finally how best to aggregate costs so that they can be easily understood, clearly demonstrated, and thoroughly examined through sensitivity analysis (Fig. 4.1).

4.2.1 Identifying Cost Sources

The appropriate cost sources will vary depending on specific attributes of the intervention and setting, as well as the funding source and the chosen scope and perspective. For some interventions, identifying cost sources will be relatively straightforward; for others, it may require more time and effort. Some interventions will have many cost sources. Others will have only one.

For projects funded by external sources with a chosen perspective of that external source, there may be a single cost source and a single cost amount: the dollar amount provided by the funding agency. This does not mean that no other individuals or organizations incur costs, but from the perspective of the funding source, the amount of the award represents their entire investment and therefore will serve as their total cost for the ROI analysis.

At the other extreme, if the intervention is funded entirely internally and the analysis is undertaken to determine what the internal return would be (or was), there may be several cost sources: staff, travel, materials, facility operations, consultants, equipment, software, training, data collection, analysis, and other sources. Within these categories, there may be several subcategories and multiple individual line-level cost sources, and accurately capturing them all can require substantial time and effort (a cost in and of itself).

Additional scenarios are possible; the point is that the number and type of cost sources will vary depending on several aspects of the intervention, setting, and funding source. Also remember that costs of development and implementation may be only part of the overall cost of improving quality. There may be costs associated with identifying the opportunity (i.e., what needs improvement), maintaining the solution

Fig. 4.1 Step 2 of the ROI process

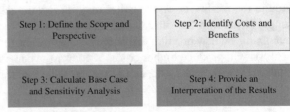

after the intervention ends, and reporting results to key stakeholders. Depending on the selected scope and perspective, these costs may or may not be prudent to include.

In general, the chosen scope and perspective should provide much of the guidance for identifying cost sources and determining what is or is not appropriate to include. This is why we must define these aspects of the analysis up front.

4.2.1.1 Examples

Example 1: Reducing Nursing Home Falls

As it is presented, this example reflects the situation where the ROI analysis is taking the perspective of the funding agency (CMS) and the amount awarded represents the entire investment, or cost, for that analysis. Notice that developing the necessary materials for the intervention, holding calls and meetings to recruit facilities and plan, training staff, collecting data, tracking results, performing the necessary analysis, and developing summary reports are all activities that incur costs to individuals and/or organizations. However, from the perspective of CMS and to evaluate the financial return they receive for their initial investment, the only costs that must be considered are those incurred by CMS to fund the quality improvement activities. Presumably, the costs of the individual activities will be covered by the funding amount.

Example 2: Improving the Discharge Process

This example is quite different from the previous one. In this situation, the facility is trying to decide whether to use its own money to fund the activities necessary to improve the discharge process; it also wants to assess what kind of financial return it can expect as a result of the change. Therefore, administrators may want to consider costs stemming from several sources and for specific types of activities, including:

- Developing the intervention, which may involve assessing the current process, identifying specific ways to improve the process, developing protocols or materials, designing the implementation process, including sprint cycles or necessary feedback loops
- Training of staff, which will require staff time, trainer time, room/facility time, and training materials
- Changes to staff makeup or duties, since the new process may call for additional staff or for certain staff members to devote more time to the new process, which leaves less time for some of the things they currently work on
- Technology, equipment, and facility costs, which could include health IT systems, EHR interfaces, or changes to the physical environment of the facility
- Data collection and analysis, including determining what to measure and how to measure it, staff time to collect and manage data, time and resources for analysis, and the time necessary to develop reports or presentations for key stakeholders.

Depending on the nature of the intervention, there may also be ancillary costs associated with communication and/or coordination with community partners or external organizations. There will be costs related to the planning (before the intervention), implementation (during), and maintenance (after) of the activities, so it is likely there will be ongoing costs in addition to the original investment.

Example 3: Introducing a Collaborative Care Model

Cost sources for this example will depend on the specifics of the individual program and intervention planned. However, these types of programs frequently involve care coordinators, regular communication (e.g., phone calls), and internal meetings and administrative activities to coordinate and manage the multiple conditions and, often, multiple care providers. Therefore, much of the costs are likely to be related to staffing. This could take the form of new positions that are created specifically for the program (often a new administrative role or perhaps a nurse coordinator), but it may also simply involve a reallocation of staff efforts in the form of percent time or FTEs. In addition to these staff costs, other cost sources that may be incurred, depending on the specifics of the program, could include:

- Transportation services for patients
- Materials and/or facility resources to train staff
- Capital investments in technology or the physical environment necessary to provide the care and house administrative staff
- Other sources relevant to the chosen care model.

From the specific perspective of the facility or administration, costs incurred to patients and caregivers would not be explicitly included in the ROI to the administration but would likely be considered to determine if they would impose undue burden on those the care model aims to serve. For example, if the care model requires frequent face-to-face visits by patients, there would be costs to the patients and caregivers for travel and lost work time, at a minimum. Presumably, if the selected care model has previously been established as effective, those types of potential barriers would already have been mitigated or addressed so that the costs to patients and caregivers would be minimal or at least not prohibitive. Note that like the previous example, this intervention is likely to have ongoing costs to continue providing the collaborative care model.

Example 4: Investing in Facility Improvements

Often, capital investments in the facility are considered to be one-time investments, even if they occur over a period of time. That is, construction of a new wing or a renovation may last several months or even years, but eventually the costs associated with it will end, or will transition from construction costs to maintenance costs, which are typically a fraction of the initial investment. Therefore, one might consider there to be only one cost source: the capital investment. However, that one cost source will be made up of several sources, some of which will vary and be the main drivers for any overages that may be experienced.

Whether performing a prospective or retrospective ROI analysis, in some situations it may make sense to identify cost sources separately to allow for a sensitivity analysis; this can also help one understand where variation can influence total costs

Table 4.1 Examples of possible cost sources

Hypothetical example	Potential cost sources
Reducing nursing home falls (perspective = external [CMS])	The cost to CMS to fund the project
Improving discharge process (perspective = internal)	Developing the intervention, training staff, changes to staffing, investments in technology, equipment, or facility, data collection, analysis, and presentation
Collaborative care model (perspective = internal)	Staffing needs, training, transportation, materials, investments in technology or the facility, specific needs of the chosen care model
Facility improvements (perspective = internal)	Renovation costs

and ultimately the return that is realized. In some cases where the capital investment limits the ability to provide care for some period of time, costs for this intervention could also include lost revenue due to these limitations. In our example, that would include any reduction in ED capacity or availability that may be due to unavailable space or services during the renovation (Table 4.1).

4.2.2 Estimating and Monetizing Costs

For a retrospective ROI analysis, often specific costs are known because they have already been incurred. However, some aspects of care may qualify as costs but are not straightforward to monetize. In the example involving the renovation of an ED, the loss in capacity during renovation may be measurable and known after the renovation is complete, but there still may be estimation involved in translating that to a monetary value. That is because one must determine how much capacity was reduced and essentially estimate what the volume would have been if there was no loss of capacity.

In a prospective analysis, in addition to having to estimate the monetary value for some types of costs, there is also uncertainty regarding how much of any one type of cost may be incurred. For example, if we prospectively evaluated the impact of an ED renovation, we would want to estimate the amount of capacity that would be lost and for how long. We may also have to make additional assumptions in order to translate that cost into a monetary value. This is an example where prior to beginning the project, some costs may be known with some degree of certainty (e.g., the actual construction costs to renovate the ED), while others may require estimating values and the inherent uncertainty that involves (e.g., lost revenue from the temporary reduction in capacity).

Table 4.2 Costs that may require estimating or monetizing for a proposal

Cost source	Requirements to monetize cost
Staff time	Estimates of hours (including overtime) or FTEs
Changes in productivity or efficiency during implementation	Estimates of impact on patients served, monetizing that value
Data collection	Estimates of frequency and intensity necessary (i.e., response rate to a survey, patients' willingness to participate) to obtain an adequate sample size

Other examples of costs that may be known with a high degree of certainty prospectively include the cost of new equipment, the salary and benefits of a new hire, or specific services like training or education. But for many of the costs in a prospective analysis, multiple estimates will be needed to arrive at an overall estimate of the cost. Table 4.2 contains examples of costs that may require either estimating or monetizing in a prospective analysis.

When it is necessary to estimate values and translate them into monetary terms, multiple methods can be used.

4.2.2.1 Using Knowledgeable Opinion (Including from Previous Experience) to Estimate Costs

It is likely that those involved in the planning and development of the intervention are familiar with the setting, the situation, and the potential issues and challenges that may be encountered. Therefore, they may be well positioned to provide accurate and precise estimates for what should be expected in terms of the time and resources necessary to prepare for and implement the selection intervention. Those asked to provide these estimates may do so in terms they are most familiar with, which would then need to be converted into the units of measurement chosen for the analysis. For example, a shift manager may be able to estimate the hours necessary for each staff to fulfill certain roles, but these would need to be converted into estimated hours or FTEs for the prospective analysis, so that they can be monetized and used to calculate the return.

Knowledgeable opinion can also be obtained externally. Experts in the field, individuals from other organizations who have participated in similar activities, or those from partnering organizations all may be able to provide reasonable estimates for certain–uncertain costs. Information from these knowledgeable individuals may come in the form of estimates regarding both the estimated quantity and monetary value of the costs. Or these individuals may simply provide information for the first step in the estimation process (e.g., the number of hours likely required by each staff) which would then need to be converted into monetary values (e.g., salary and benefits) by staff internal to the organization performing the prospective analysis.

Previous experiences by both internal and external individuals can not only inform knowledgeable opinions used to estimate costs, but these experiences can also provide tangible data that can be leveraged to estimate costs. Data from a pilot study or a previous quality improvement intervention may provide ample information regarding the required time, resources, and efforts needed to prepare for and implement a future intervention. At a minimum, they can establish a starting point from which adjustments can be made (e.g., "We are planning on recruiting 20% more patients than we did for the previous intervention, so our costs are likely to be about 20% higher…").

4.2.2.2 Using Published Literature or Trusted Sources to Estimate Costs

In cases where experience is lacking and knowledgeable opinion is difficult to come by, previously published studies can provide guidance when making estimates for certain types of costs. In some ways, this information is used in the same manner as that of the information provided through knowledgeable opinion: There may be information on quantities as well as monetary values, or only on one or the other. Often, however, by leveraging multiple studies one can arrive at reasonable estimates for the quantities and monetary value of all the necessary costs.

Later in the chapter, when discussing benefits, we will dive into more detail regarding how to abstract information from published literature, but in general, studies that more closely reflect your specific population, setting, and intervention will be the most useful and provide the most robust estimates with which to work. Ideally, one would hope to find a number of relevant articles to provide a range of possible values that will be useful not only for pinpointing the base case estimates but also for the sensitivity analysis.

There may also be trusted sources for obtaining certain estimates or values. National organizations or federal agencies may provide values based on information they have gathered or obtained from other sources. In some cases, there may be industry standards (e.g., federal fee schedules, etc.) that can be leveraged to establish credible estimates. The level to which these values are applicable to the local or specific situation may vary depending on many factors. As with information from any other source, the values or estimates obtained from these sources should be vetted for their relevance for the project being proposed and either altered or used for guidance to establish more appropriate values.

4.2.3 Aggregating Costs

Sometimes, it is prudent to aggregate costs into specific categories or time frames. That is, there may be reasons to aggregate costs by different characteristics of the intervention, such as:

- Calendar-based time periods (per month, per year)
- Intervention time (pre-intervention, during, post-intervention, shutdown)
- Duration of costs (one-time versus ongoing)
- Activity type (planning, training, implementation, maintenance, monitoring)
- Cost or budget source
- Department or facility.

It can be difficult to know the best criteria by which to aggregate costs; certain considerations can help identify the most appropriate and useful arrangement. First, consider which costs to explore in the sensitivity analysis. For example, if staffing costs are a source of uncertainty, it may make sense to report costs by their sources so that you can freely vary staffing costs during the sensitivity analysis while holding other costs constant. If instead the uncertainty lies in the amount of the ongoing maintenance costs, perhaps it would be prudent to present costs by the intervention

Table 4.3 Alternative methods to aggregate costs (hypothetical data)

Method 1: by month

	January	February	March	April	May	June
Staff time	$8500	$5500	$5500	$5500	$5500	$5500
Materials	$1500	$0	$0	$0	$0	$0
IT support	$800	$400	$400	$400	$400	$400
Data collection	$0	$0	$0	$550	$550	$550
Analysis	$0	$0	$0	$0	$0	$2400
Total	**$10,800**	**$5900**	**$5900**	**$6450**	**$6450**	**$8850**

Method 2: by time period

	Pre-intervention	Post-intervention
Staff time	$3500	$32,500
Materials	$1200	$300
IT support	$600	$2200
Data collection	$0	$1650
Analysis	$0	$2400
Total	**$5300**	**$39,050**

Method 3: by frequency

	One-time	Recurring
Staff time	$3000	$33,000
Materials	$1500	$0
IT support	$400	$2400
Data collection	$0	$1650
Analysis	$2400	$0
Total	**$7300**	**$37,050**

In each situation, the total costs equate to $44,350

time period to allow the intended audience to view the variability in the ongoing costs separately from the costs incurred during the planning and intervention stages.

Another approach is to consider how benefits will be accrued. If it is anticipated that benefits will need to accumulate over some time before the initial costs are recouped, then presenting costs on a monthly or yearly timeline may allow for an easy representation of the payback period.

As shown in Table 4.3, the same costs aggregated differently provide different information for those evaluating the project. There may be instances when you should examine costs in a variety of ways.

4.3 Benefits

When accruing benefits, the activities can be thought of as split between two types of benefits: those that are measurable, monetizable, and directly attributable to the intervention, and those that are not. The former provides the most tangible financial return for the investment, but many key components of care quality and value come in the latter form. Here, we will explore both.

4.3.1 Measurable, Monetizable, and Directly Attributable Benefits

In an earlier chapter, we explored the similar challenges faced when attempting to affect quality and value. As we have seen so far, many changes or improvements could be "valuable" or a "benefit," but they may not all be measurable, monetizable, or directly attributable to the intervention. We must identify and distinguish between these types of benefits in both prospective and retrospective analyses. In the proposal stage, this type of exploration can assist in defining the intervention, deciding what to measure, and determining the criteria used to deem it to be a success.

4.3.1.1 Measurable Versus Unmeasurable Benefits

In this context, when we say that something is measurable, we are simply saying that we can define and specify it, and there exist (or will exist, after we collect them) usable data. Whether this measurement and these data are adequate to serve our purposes (i.e., are valid and reliable) is a separate issue. At this point, we are simply interested in identifying whether it is something we can, at a minimum, *attempt* to measure. In all likelihood, there will be benefits that are within the scope of the intervention and that are important but may simply lack a working definition or data to assess them. An example might be the improvement to a facility's "brand" that results from a remodel of their facility or waiting room. Outside of performing a complex market analysis that employs a firm with experience in assessing and quantifying "brands," this type of benefit will likely fall outside of the set of benefits that we can consider to be measurable. Perhaps instead it would be sufficient to assess changes in patient perception and satisfaction through surveys, but that likely will not fully encompass the facility's brand. Other examples of potentially unmeasurable benefits[1] include things like engagement, innovation, reputation, and culture.

Another type of unmeasurable benefit might be one that is simply outside of the scope of the current analysis or beyond current capabilities to measure. For example, even though a good intervention is one that is sustainable, we may not be able to adequately estimate effects more than a few months or years into the future. Successfully implementing a collaborative care program that takes hold and changes the future of care for chronic conditions will likely have significant benefits many years into the future. However, it is likely outside of the scope to analyze its effect on reduced utilization five, ten, or twenty years into the future. Too many other factors could influence it, and there may be too many unknowns. Or, there may be behaviors of patients or others where changes could be measured if the correct data were collected, but it is beyond the project's capability to do so (for reasons related to the budget, available technology, etc.).

There may also be quantities that are measurable in theory but are not measured in your project or with the available data. In the example of reducing falls in nursing homes, significant reductions may reduce the anxiety of patients of high fall risk, improve their comfort level with continued exercise, or ease the worry of family members who have entrusted their loved ones to the facility. These are important benefits to mention and consider, but they may not be directly measurable for the project as designed.

Similarly, some quantities may be measurable but are not estimable prior to conducting the project. In that same nursing home example, the facility could choose to track all falls and delineate which ones require medical attention ("serious falls") and which ones do not ("minor falls"). These are measurable quantities and will be collected during the intervention; but perhaps during the proposal stage when a prospective ROI may be performed, these individual quantities are not available (i.e., they were not previously collected separately) and are therefore unavailable in this form for the prospective analysis. This type of situation is typically rare because one can usually rely on either published literature or knowledgeable opinion to arrive at an estimate of some degree of accuracy.

Sometimes, there are ways around data deficiencies that are appropriate in a prospective analysis. For instance, the following example nicely illustrates how one can creatively use the information available to estimate necessary quantities. In an economic evaluation of reducing hospital falls, Spetz et al. [1] identified several

---

[1]These are sometimes referred to as "intangibles," but I believe it is more useful to classify them based on whether they are measurable, monetizable, and attributable to the intervention as a way to better understand why they can or cannot be quantified or included in the ROI calculation.

Table 4.4 Examples of potentially unmeasurable benefits

Hypothetical case study	Unmeasurable benefits
Reducing nursing home falls	Lower levels of patient fear, increased peace of mind of family members, facility reputation
Improving the discharge process	Improved connection and rapport between staff and patients
Implementing collaborative care	Reduced utilization 20 years later, increased likelihood that caregivers will be proactive about their own future care given their confidence in the program
Renovating the ED	Improved patient perception, better workflow, improved "brand" of the facility

The benefits listed as unmeasurable may be so due to inherent difficulties in identifying reasonable surrogates, quantifying them, or simply because they are outside of the scope of the project

studies that measured "all falls" and several that measured "injurious falls." They collected the reported rates of each and used them to estimate the rate of *noninjurious* falls by subtracting the average injurious fall rate from the average of the overall fall rate.

Average noninjurious fall rate = Average rate of all falls – Average rate of injurious falls

While perhaps not the most statistically rigorous method (this was not a meta-analysis estimate or aggregated rate, but simply the average of the reported rates across studies that differed in their populations and sample sizes), it provided at least a ballpark estimate of what the authors needed. It is also a good example of the kind of thing that can be done to create estimates needed for analysis. Whether this type of back-of-the-envelope calculation is appropriate will be entirely situation dependent. Often, there are simply unmeasurable quantities where little to no recourse exists for those who would like to measure them.

Table 4.4 displays several types of important benefits that may not be measurable in certain circumstances or for certain interventions.

4.3.1.2 Monetizable Versus Nonmonetizable Benefits

The issues raised regarding what is measurable are true for assessments of quality as well as value. In a nursing home, for example, many things could be improved, but to demonstrate an improvement in quality you need to be able to measure it. Falls are a common choice, in part because they are easily measurable. However, to demonstrate a fiscal benefit, what the quality improvement activities affect also must be monetizable so that their value can be quantified in dollars. Perhaps within the nursing home setting, any and all falls are measurable, but only "serious" falls are monetizable (Fig. 4.2).

The most common examples of monetizable benefits include things like changes in utilization, resource use, time, and adverse events (which lead to utilization). Benefits that are often more difficult or impossible to monetize include ones such

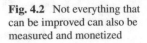

Fig. 4.2 Not everything that
can be improved can also be
measured and monetized

as satisfaction, individual effort and buy-in, quality of life, and changes in capacity or efficiency. These are often measurable by some standard or with some tool (e.g., a survey to assess satisfaction or quality of life), but equating them to monetary values can be challenging or may be more closely scrutinized by those evaluating the analysis (Table 4.5).

A note about ambiguity: None of the lines drawn by these distinctions are definitive. Attempts can be made to estimate benefits that may not be immediately monetizable. When confronted by these types of situations, use your own judgment and weigh the need for these types of estimates with the decreased certainty or "credibility" of your process.

Table 4.5 Benefits that are
usually measurable

Benefits
Changes in utilization
Reduced resource use or waste
Reduced time to treatment
Avoidance of adverse events

Table 4.6 Reasons why benefits may not be directly attributable to the intervention

Reason	Example
Confounding variables	Multiple interventions, or interventions occurring during changes in policies or practice guidelines
Inherent bias	The observed patients in the study self-selected into a particular group
Preexisting trends	Even though rates of infections declined during the intervention period, they were already declining prior to the initiation
Too many steps	Reducing physician burnout improves patient–provider interactions which increases patient satisfaction as demonstrated by higher HCAHPS scores and ultimately increases reimbursement

4.3.1.3 Benefits Directly Attributable to the Intervention

Just because a benefit is measurable and monetizable does not necessarily mean that it is appropriate to use in the calculation of ROI. To be included, it should be directly attributable to the intervention, either in whole or in part. If it is attributable only in part, it is also necessary to estimate the proportion of it that is directly attributable.[2] There may be multiple reasons why a benefit may not be directly attributable to the intervention. A common reason is when there is confounding with other interventions or changes in health policy and practice guidelines. For example, if multiple interventions are occurring within the same facility at the same time, it can be difficult to determine how much improvement is due to each specific intervention and how much is due to the cumulative effect of multiple interventions. Or there can be inherent bias in the groups studied, since often quality improvement is performed using convenience samples or as fully observational studies (Table 4.6).

Attribution can also be a challenge in light of existing trends in whatever is being measured. Detractors of the effectiveness of national programs to reduce mortality in Medicare patients, for example, have pointed out that mortality rates were already declining prior to the program's initiations. They suggest that it is difficult to know how much of the observed decline was directly due to the program and how much would have been observed simply as a continuation of the already existing trend.

Similarly, simply declaring one's intention to measure an event or process can impact its rate. Some studies reporting on the effectiveness of interventions to reduce patient falls have observed an initial *increase* in events immediately after initiation. There can be several reasons for this, including an increase in awareness and "looking for" the event of interest, an increase in documentation of events that sometimes would not be documented, or even a subconscious desire by staff to inflate the rate of

---

[2]Many resources on ROI will classify benefits as either "direct" or "indirect." I have avoided this language here because I think it can be confusing. Typically, "direct benefits" refer to those that are measurable and monetizable, and "indirect benefits" are really intangible benefits. But, I think considering whether benefits are measurable, monetizable, and directly attributable provides more specific guidance about whether or not to include them in the analysis, and how to do so.

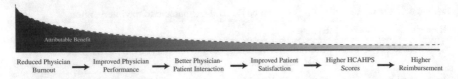

Fig. 4.3 Amount of the benefit that is attributable to the intervention decreases the further away the measured quantity is from the improvement activity

occurrence early in the study to increase the likelihood of observing an improvement over time. Regardless, these phenomena can reduce our ability to determine how much of a change is directly due to the intervention or activities.

Here is another situation where it can be difficult to attribute a benefit to the intervention: when numerous intermediate steps exist between the activities involved in the intervention and those that are both measurable and monetizable. For example, an intervention that reduces physician burnout can improve the well-being of physicians, which can improve physician–patient interactions and thus patient satisfaction, which in turn can improve HCAHPS scores that are tied to reimbursement. However, it may be difficult to ascertain how much of the improvement in HCAHPS scores is directly due to the steps taken to reduce physician burnout because at each intermediate step other reasons or factors may be affecting each result along the way (Fig. 4.3). Similarly, there may be benefits that are observed after an intervention, but there is no observable link (or there is a tenuous link) between the intervention and the benefit. For example, after improving the hospital discharge process, if the facility also observes increased efficiency in their ED, it may not be clear how that benefit could be a result of the original intervention.[3]

Also note that while we have previously suggested that sustainable interventions may provide benefits well into the future, the further one gets from the original intervention, the more difficult it may be to attribute the observed improvement to those activities.

Combinations of these situations may be especially difficult to reconcile. For example, attributing a readmission to the discharge hospital's quality is difficult because there may be several steps between the quality of care delivery and the outcome and because of confounding variables that also contribute to the likelihood of readmission, such as availability of community resources, the presence of a family caregiver, medication adherence, and lifestyle choices.

Ensuring Benefits Are Directly Attributable to the Intervention

As with the issue of what is monetizable, the lines dividing benefits that are and are not directly attributable are blurry and may warrant discussion among those planning or evaluating the intervention as well as exploration during the sensitivity analysis.

---

[3]That does not mean that it is necessarily *not* a result of the intervention, but to include the benefit of increased ED efficiency in the ROI calculation, one would have to demonstrate how they are linked.

Some of the issues just described will be unavoidable, but for others one can take actions to mitigate their effect. What follows are some strategies for how to ensure that benefits can be attributed to quality improvement activities.

Control as Much as Possible

When feasible, isolate the intervention by limiting other quality improvement activities that may also affect your targeted result. Understand that even seemingly unrelated interventions in different areas or departments can unknowingly impact your results. When viewed as the complex systems that they are, the different parts of a healthcare system are not silos, and the interdependence of its members means that anything will impact the system as a whole [2].

Use Randomization and Matching

Include random assignment if feasible and reasonable. Clearly, this is only applicable to certain types of comparisons and is not common in many quality improvement efforts. That is the case because of the situations and opportunities available. But, even if it is impossible to randomize participants to specific groups, it may be possible to randomize other factors that could influence the outcome, thereby mitigating some of the confounding that may occur naturally. For example, if multiple trainers will be used to train staff for the new discharge process, instead of sending staff to training sessions by department, randomize who gets sent to which session. Otherwise, if one trainer is better than the other, it could muddy observed differences seen in the discharge process by department or even clinical specialty. At a minimum, just being aware of the potential biases or confounding related to personnel, physical environment, patient selection, etc., can sometimes help identify how to address them.

When random assignment is difficult, sometimes it is possible to match units of measurement between the comparison groups (either treatment versus control group or pre-post). Examining differences within patients of similar ages and disease burden may help more accurately identify true changes in the rates of falls, especially if the demographic makeup of the facility changes over time.

Be Strategic About Data

When using preexisting data sources, select an appropriate "pre-intervention" time frame to draw from that eliminates the possibility of bias associated with ideation of the project. Consider whether there are preexisting trends or seasonal effects that should be accounted for (e.g., perhaps rates of an event or utilization should be compared to the same month in the previous year, as opposed to simply the prior month) or plan to incorporate statistical methods that can adjust for complex time trends. Determine whether it would be helpful to use data that are not subject to potential biases related to data collection (e.g., administrative or claims data).

When collecting data, try to do so "quietly" and seamlessly with existing workflows and duties. Identify unique events that may unintentionally influence observed data and plan accordingly (e.g., a new hire, a new policy or guideline, changes in the organization's budget, holidays, etc.).

Consider Alternatives

In the case of multiple interventions occurring simultaneously, consider whether it is possible to combine the interventions into one analysis by aggregating the costs and benefits. If it is not possible to separate the impact of each individual intervention, together they may demonstrate a positive return. From that point, you can either argue for their merits individually or simply laud the joint activities as a success without attempting to attribute specific gains to either intervention.

Another alternative would be to consider whether other measurements are also available that would be more readily attributed to the intervention. For example, if it is difficult to attribute reductions in 30-day readmissions to the new discharge process, perhaps there is a corresponding reduction in the staff time necessary to discharge patients or the time it takes from orders to release for patients. These quantities may be measurable and monetizable and may be more clearly directly attributable to improvements in the discharge process. Similarly, instead of trying to associate reductions in physician burnout with increases in HCAHPS-related reimbursements, perhaps a more immediate measure would be the rate of physician turnover. This measure would also be measurable and monetizable.

4.3.1.4   MMA Benefits as a Fraction of the Whole

Among all the potential benefits of a quality improvement intervention, only a fraction will likely be measurable, monetizable, and directly attributable. As an example, Table 4.7 includes a list of common benefits one might expect to achieve from improving care delivery or processes, but when the desired attributes are applied, fewer and fewer make the cut.

Table 4.7 Identifying benefits that are measurable, monetizable, and attributable

All potential benefits	Measurable…	…and monetizable…	…and directly attributable
Efficiency	Efficiency	Efficiency	Efficiency
Informed patients	Informed patients	Readmission rate	
Patient satisfaction	Patient satisfaction		
Caregiver satisfaction	Readmission rate		
Lower caregiver stress	Medication adherence		
Medication adherence			
Improved provider–patient communication			
Readmission rate			

Constructing a similar table for a proposed intervention can help identify benefits that may be considered for estimating the value of the activities. While the categories are often not cut and dried, the exercise may provide insights or may identify potential pitfalls before they are encountered during the intervention or data collection process. This type of table can serve as a point of discussion as individuals or groups identify opportunities and develop interventions, including which data to collect.

4.3.2 Estimating MMA Benefits

So far, we have focused on benefits that are measurable, monetizable, and attributable (MMA) to the intervention. While other benefits should not be discounted or assumed to be unimportant, MMA benefits are often the only ones included in the base case of the ROI analysis. Therefore, we will begin our exploration into the estimation of benefits by continuing to focus on these types of benefits. Often, it is reasonable and responsible to explore benefits that are not MMA in the sensitivity analysis either in concept or by making some attempt to estimate the monetary value associated with them. Later, we will discuss some ways one might estimate and monetize benefits that are not MMA, and you will see how that is a more fluid and creative process.

4.3.2.1 Benefit Sources

Sources of benefits associated with patients include those related to improved outcomes as a result of higher care quality: reduced utilization, lower incidence and prevalence, improved safety, a better patient experience, more satisfaction, and so on. Benefits experienced directly by a facility or care provider include increased efficiency (less staff time/overtime), better workflow/patient flow, increased capacity, expanding life of facilities or equipment, and less waste (fewer unnecessary laboratory tests).

Note that some of the benefits in the previous list may not be MMA in many situations; other times they will be. For independent organizations looking to partner with healthcare delivery systems (hospitals, clinics, etc.), these types of benefits may be vitally important to help with securing partners and support, but may be difficult to come by. As we discussed in an earlier chapter, part of the recruitment of partners will need to involve these types of conversations where facilities can provide these data or where facilities can at least be prompted to examine them internally to more fully address their needs and establish demand for the proposed solution.

Examples

In reducing nursing home falls, MMA benefits are achieved through a reduction in care utilization and cost associated with treatment for injuries that result from a serious fall. Therefore, the benefits will be a function of how much each type of injury is avoided and how much cost savings is associated with avoiding the need for treatment of that type of injury.

The benefits associated with the introduction of the collaborative care program are similar: namely the cost savings associated with the reduced utilization due to better management of patients' multiple chronic conditions.

In the example of improving the hospital discharge process, the chosen measure of benefits from the facility's perspective is the increase in bonuses (or decrease in penalties) associated with improved 30-day readmission rates. While directly measurable and monetizable, this example involves benefits that we have mentioned may be difficult to directly attribute to the intervention.

In renovating their ED, the facility in this example is hoping to realize benefits by reducing the revenue losses associated with patients leaving the ED prior to being seen by a physician. They estimated that the renovated space would reduce wait times enough (a driving factor for leaving the ED for low-acuity patients) to reduce the percent of patients who leave without being seen.

4.3.2.2   Estimating Benefits

For each of the examples just discussed, as well as other situations, estimating the magnitude of the intervention on the benefits can be accomplished through leveraging relevant prior experience, preliminary data, national estimates, published literature, or knowledgeable and expert opinion. Data related to patient-associated benefits such as care utilization or event rates may be equally likely to come from a number of resources, including internal systems and external examples or published literature. Benefits to facilities and providers, however, may be more likely to come from internal data and/or personal and institutional experience. Fortunately, often the motivation for those types of interventions stems from an examination of internal data and experiences so that they are readily available. Plus, details regarding potential impact on staff time, efficiency, workflow, and the like may be specific to the unique situation, staff, and patient population of the specific facility.

Using Prior Experience and Preliminary Data to Estimate Benefits

This is a common resource simply because it is often through personal or institutional experience that one identifies opportunities to improve care quality that may also provide a fiscal benefit. This may certainly be true for hospitals and other healthcare delivery systems: As they seek to improve care either from internal motivations or through encouragement of national programs or policies, they can typically rely on data they have available to provide a clear picture of the current (pre-intervention) situation. Independent organizations that seek to obtain funding to improve care in other settings (e.g., quality improvement organizations what want to improve care in hospitals, clinics, EDs, nursing homes, etc.) may obtain these data from prior collaborations with care providers or from partners they are engaged with.

Using Knowledgeable or Expert Opinion to Estimate Benefits

Either an external expert or anyone with legitimate knowledge of the situation, facility, patient population, or opportunity may be in a position to contribute to the understanding of the current situation and even the potential for improvement. Often, this person works on the front lines of care and has anecdotal knowledge as well as a general feel for the current level of quality. Their opinion(s) can often be used in tandem with the preliminary or local data that is available.

For example, current records may reveal that the current fall rate is around 2.5 per week at a nursing home, but the head nurse may suggest that those data only reflect a certain type of event (e.g., unaccompanied falls, not counting those where they only drop to one knee, or some other description). Using information from a combination of resources can be instrumental in providing the most accurate and precise estimates of key measurements. The potential disadvantage of both this resource and preliminary data is that there may be limited information that can be generalized to a different setting or population.

Using Published Literature or Trusted Sources to Estimate Benefits

Another common resource for obtaining estimates of pre-intervention rates, levels of improvement, or potential thresholds for quality improvement can come from national estimates or published literature. These resources are not better or worse than sources we have mentioned previously; however, if the goal is to generalize the project's findings to larger populations or other care settings, these types of data may be more appropriate because they may reflect a more heterogeneous population or account for geographic variations. The danger with this resource is that in some ways these estimates are open to more critiques or criticisms: Readers may disagree with the sources cited or the method used to combine information from multiple articles into a single estimate.

To accurately and effectively identify and apply estimates from national sources and published literature, a few things can help ensure that your resulting estimates are seen as applicable and reasonable.

Abstracting Information from Published Literature

When identifying relevant information, examine the details of the source or study to determine how closely they match the situation to which you wish to apply them. That is, consider the study type (pre-post, treatment versus control, randomized versus observational, matched versus unmatched, etc.), population (demographics, disease burden, access to care, social determinants, etc.), situation and setting (type of facility, geographic location, how participants are selected and recruited and included, etc.), and intervention (type, length, intensity, scope, etc.) (Table 4.8).

Also be aware of what kinds of estimates are needed. Common estimates obtained from the literature include rates of incidence, prevalence, events, utilization, etc. Sometimes, these values are provided in a form that is easily transferable to other situations, like "rate per time at risk." Other times, they are presented simply as

Table 4.8 Key components to abstract from published literature

Component
Study type (pre-post, treatment versus control, randomized versus observational, etc.)
Population (demographics, disease burden, access to care, social determinants, etc.)
Situation and setting (facility type, geography, patient selection, etc.)
Intervention (activity type, length, intensity, scope, etc.)
Estimates (incidence/prevalence, utilization, event rates, changes or improvements, etc.)
Monetary conversions (from events avoided, efficiencies, waste reduction, etc.)

Fig. 4.4 Process to collect relevant information from published literature

A Quick Read-through

Highlight relevant information and gain a general understanding of the paper.

Abstract Specific Information

Reported counts and rates, definitions, limitations, and results

Compare Values Across Studies

Select the appropriate values for the base-case and sensitivity analysis counts or percentages, and there may or may not be enough detail provided in the study to convert them to a form that could be applied to your situation.[4]

To collect and use relevant information from multiple studies, I suggest the following process (Fig. 4.4):

First, do a read-through and highlight relevant information such as the study population, reported measures (counts, percentages, rates), definitions, and limitations. Do not skip the limitation section, because the items contained in that section can include key information that can help determine whether the estimates included are applicable and usable for your application. Repeat this process for several studies before diving deeper into any one in particular. Also, identifying reviews, literature summaries, and meta-analyses can be especially useful, in part because they will have done much of this work already.

After completing an initial read-through of several articles, you should abstract the relevant information into each article into a central location. In addition to documenting information about the study population, intervention, and relevant estimates, you will want to include space to insert notes regarding the study or the estimates.[5]

Once you have abstracted several articles, you can more easily compare the studies and determine which estimates are the most applicable to your situation and why, and which may be more useful in sensitivity analyses. The studies can also provide insight regarding what adverse events or outcomes may be affected by your intervention. This can be especially helpful when considering any unintended consequences or spillover from your intervention that you want to be sure to capture.

Depending on the specifics of the project and ROI analysis, a common type of estimate obtained from published literature is rates of utilization. The other is event rates that will be used to estimate pre-intervention and post-intervention counts and costs to ascertain the attributable benefit due to cost reduction or cost avoidance. In most cases, the ideal form of these estimates is as a rate per time at risk. There may be situations where flat percentages are fine (e.g., "$X\%$ of those who arrive at the ED with a suspected stroke receive thrombolytics within 30 min"), but most often the preferred form of these values is as rates per population or per time at risk (e.g., "falls per patient-week," "strokes [or other event] per 1000 patient-years," etc.). This allows you to apply these rates to whatever time period is appropriate for your intervention by simply applying the rate by your population's estimated time at risk.

Unfortunately, often the available information is presented in percentages and includes nonspecific or extended time periods, as in "12% of those aged 65+ with BP over 160 SBP will develop heart failure in their lifetime." This poses several problems for anyone who needs to establish an estimated rate of heart failure incidence for a prospective analysis.

First, percentages by themselves do not account for time at risk, so unless your proposed intervention will span the same length of time that is represented by the study that reported the percentage, it will not be an accurate reflection of what you

---

[4] A discussion regarding why rates per time at risk are more universally useful than counts and percentages follows shortly.

[5] A template for abstracting this type of information is provided in a later chapter.

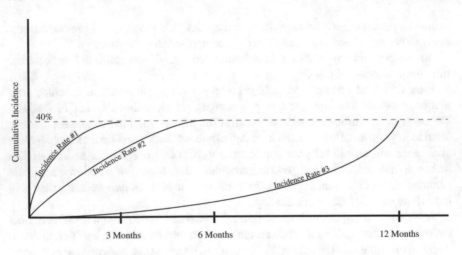

Fig. 4.5 Three incidence rates producing the same cumulative incidence

can expect in your population. Second, the indefinite time period limits the ability to convert the reported percentage into a rate per time at risk. This, in part, is because it is unclear how much total time at risk is involved and, in part, because doing so assumes that the rate of incidence is equally spread across that time frame, which is often unreasonable to assume. Figure 4.5 illustrates that without knowing the time at risk, a reported incidence of 40% may reflect several different incidence rates and so by itself is not very useful.

Sometimes, reported percentages or counts can be converted to estimates of time at risk. Consider the following examples:

Example: "The cohort of 34 patients was followed for 6 months and incurred a total of 13 infections."

The information is there to calculate a rate per time at risk by dividing the total number of events (13) by the total time at risk (34×0.5 years $= 17$) to produce a rate of 0.76 infections per patient-year. This ignores, of course, that when a patient has an infection, he or she is not at risk to develop one, so that our time at risk is likely a little overestimated and therefore our rate is slightly underestimated. But, for the purposes of an estimate it would be adequate.

Example: "During the 12-month follow-up, mortality was 17.5%."

In this scenario, we may not have the necessary information to calculate a rate per time at risk. Assuming we know the original sample size, we could calculate the total number of events, but without knowing *when* during that time frame patients died, we cannot accurately estimate the time at risk.

For example, if most of those who died did so near the start of the follow-up period, there will be less time at risk and a higher rate; if the opposite were true, the rate would be lower. As a solution, depending on the situation, one option would be to assume an "average" time at risk for those who died. If in this example there were 40 patients at the start of follow-up, 17.5% mortality would equate to seven patients. That means that for the other 33 patients, the time at risk was a full year, and if we assume that the average time until death for the seven who died was X months, then the total time at risk is 33 years + ($7 \times X$). Whatever we choose for X (six months, for example), we can calculate the total time at risk and use it to calculate the rate = 7 deaths/[33 years + (7×0.5 years)] = 7/36.5 = 0.192 deaths per patient-year, or 19.2 deaths per 100 patient-years.

Depending on the quality of the study and information as well as the situation we are hoping to apply it to, these types of numerical manipulations may or may not be prudent. There is a fine line between cleverly leveraging available information to produce usable estimates and hand-waving. If possible, collect information from multiple sources and through multiple methods to give you, and ultimately your intended audience, a thorough examination of the evidence available.

Concepts to Consider for a Prospective Analysis

Estimating Effectiveness: Post-intervention Rates or a Relative Improvement?

When determining the necessary estimates, in addition to the baseline or pre-intervention rates of utilization or events, you will need to estimate the effectiveness of the intervention. One option is to seek out estimates of relative improvement (e.g., "a 5% relative reduction," "60% less likely," "two times more efficient," etc.); this estimate, combined with your estimates for how things were before the intervention, will allow you to calculate things like: events avoided, time saved, etc.

An alternative is to identify studies that involve a population that has already experienced what your intervention is striving to achieve, and use the rates observed within that population as the post-intervention rate. For example, if the goal is to improve medication adherence to blood pressure medications to reduce hypertension-related adverse events, then literature that reports rates of acute myocardial infarctions or strokes among persons with medication-controlled hypertension may provide reasonable estimates of the post-intervention rates you could expect for those patients whose hypertension becomes controlled. These types of studies are likely more common than those directly reporting the relative reduction in adverse events observed within hypertensive patients achieving blood pressure control after previously being above acceptable thresholds. However, you would still need to estimate what percentage of your target population would achieve this ideal. This, too, is a function of the effectiveness of your population, and you would likely need some way of estimating what is reasonable to expect. Maybe a previous study or your previous experience will tell you that this type of intervention can be successful in producing control in 40% of hypertensive patients targeted, for example.

Difficulty of Rare Events and/or a Short Time Period

Here is one of the common barriers experienced by those attempting to perform a prospective ROI analysis: They are limited by relatively small sample sizes and/or limited follow-up. For example, individuals with hypertension are more likely to have a stroke. But, if this population is expected to experience 20 strokes per 1000 patient-years and a project is proposing to follow 300 patients for six months (or the equivalent of 150 patient-years), one would only expect to see only 3 total strokes, on average, prior to any attempts to improve care. That does not provide much opportunity for achieving improvement and therefore for realizing the monetary benefits associated with improvement. This is yet another reason to explore the achievable value of a project during the initial and early planning stages of the intervention. Identifying potential issues like this early will allow one to explore alternative measures or adjustments to the proposed time frame to ensure the opportunity to demonstrate sufficient value.

Exploration of a Hazard Ratio Versus Rate Ratio or Relative Risk

For a number of reasons, one of the most common types of analyses in healthcare research is that of time-to-event analysis and Cox proportional hazards modeling. This semi-parametric method attempts to compare the "hazard" rate of two populations or treatments by considering the number of events during a specified time frame, while assuming that the ratio of these rates will be proportional over the time frame observed. While we will forgo an exploration into when this is reasonable to assume, it is necessary to discuss the nature of the resulting hazard ratio estimates and what they provide and what they do not. The hazard is the "instantaneous risk" of an event. Specifically, it is the likelihood that the event of interest will occur in the next very short time period *given* that it has not yet occurred. To make this concept more tangible, consider a hospital where every day an individual patient has a 5% chance of getting an infection. At the end of each day that they do not contract an infection, they wake up the next day and their risk for that day is again 5%. That is a hazard rate—it does not matter how many days previously they have gone without the infection, each new day brings with it the same risk of an infection that day.

Hazard rates and ratios, while common in health studies, should be used with caution, if at all, when trying to estimate the rate or relative rate of an event over a period of time of any significant length. That is because hazard rates give you the likelihood of an event in the immediate future, or over a very short period of time. In general, the hazard ratio will always overestimate the risk reduction—and the more so the longer the time period. For very short time periods, the hazard ratio may be a reasonable approximation, but for any reasonable length of time the actual reduction in the risk of the outcome or event will be much less severe than what the hazard ratio expresses [3].

To illustrate, let us examine a short example, which is strongly motivated by the examples given by Sashegyi and Ferry in their excellent article cited in the previous paragraph. Assume that a study claims to have reduced the weekly hazard rate of some adverse event (it could be a fall, an infection, etc.) per week from 5 to 3.5%, which is a 30% reduction in the hazard (likely reported as a "hazard ratio of 0.70"). To arrive at that value, they likely modeled the "time to incidence" using a common distribution for survival analysis, such as the exponential distribution.[6]

---

[6]The details of this are not crucial here: You could just as easily perform this exercise by assuming a weekly incidence of 5% versus 3.5% instead of assuming an exponential distribution.

If we apply those hazard rates to two populations using the exponential distribution, we would find that after one week the cumulative incidence would be 4.88% (for a hazard of 5%) and 3.44% (for 3.5%), respectively. That equates to a relative reduction in the incidence risk of 29.5%, which is very close to the relative reduction in hazard of 30%. However, after 10 weeks, those weekly hazards would result in cumulative incidences of 39.4% and 29.5%, respectively, which is a relative reduction of about 25%. And after 20 weeks, the relative reduction is 20%—significantly lower than the 30% relative reduction reflected in the hazard ratio. Some of the calculated values are shown in Table 4.9, and a comparison of relative reductions in hazards and risks is shown in Fig. 4.6.

This illustrates why a hazard ratio will always overestimate the achievable effect of the intervention over any significant period of time. Additionally, a hazard ratio alone, without the individual hazard rates that produced it, does not provide enough information to extrapolate to a risk reduction over time. That is because larger or smaller hazards that produce the same hazard ratio will produce different cumulative incidences that will drive the risk reduction. If we had used hazards of 15 and 10.5% in the above example, even though their ratio is still 0.70, the relative risk reduction is much less: After 10 and 20 weeks, the lower hazard will reflect a relative risk reduction of 16% and 7%, respectively.

If individual hazard rates are provided, it may be possible to use them to estimate a relative risk reduction over a desired time frame, as in the example just supplied.

Concepts to Consider for a Retrospective Analysis

Obviously, much of what is covered in the previous sections does not apply when performing ROI retrospectively on an intervention that has already occurred. You will no longer need to estimate baseline and post-intervention rates of events or utilization because you will have actual observed data. However, while more straightforward in

Table 4.9 Example of how a hazard ratio translates into relative risk over different periods

Week	Weekly incidence*		Cumulative incidence*		Relative risk reduction**
	Hazard = 5%	Hazard = 3.5%	Hazard = 5%	Hazard = 3.5%	
1	4.88%	3.44%	4.88%	3.44%	29.48%
2	4.88%	3.44%	9.52%	6.76%	28.96%
3	4.88%	3.44%	13.93%	9.97%	28.44%
4	4.88%	3.44%	18.13%	13.06%	27.93%
5	4.88%	3.44%	22.12%	16.05%	27.42%
10	4.88%	3.44%	39.35%	29.53%	24.95%
20	4.88%	3.44%	63.21%	50.34%	20.36%

After one week, the relative risk reduction is similar to that of the reduction in hazard; but over 10 or 20 weeks, the hazard reduction provides a poor estimate of the true risk reduction
*Calculated assuming an exponential distribution; weekly incidence is $1 - \exp(-\text{hazard})$, and cumulative incidence at week "t" is calculated as $1 - \exp(-\text{hazard} * t)$
**Calculated as 1 − the ratio of cumulative incidences

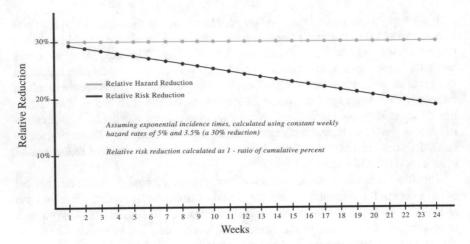

Fig. 4.6 Comparison of relative hazard reduction and relative risk reduction

many ways, this type of analysis also requires some of the deeper explorations that appear in proposals.

Often of primary interest when performing a retrospective ROI analysis is whether the intervention proceeded as expected and whether its effect was as anticipated. Specifically, how many participants were recruited compared with what was proposed? Was the intervention completed within the expected time frame and with the expected intensity? Did the observed effect or change reflect what was expected? While the answers to these questions may not impact the calculations performed for the actual ROI analysis, they are crucial for providing context when interpreting results and preparing for future projects and interventions. That is, if the anticipated level of return was not achieved, these questions will likely uncover the key reasons why.

Whether it is lower recruitment, less effective intervention than anticipated, or some other reason, answers to the questions just pose will help you identify which unexpected circumstances most contributed to either the higher costs or lower benefits (or both), and then infer which assumptions were unreasonable versus those that were reasonable but were subject to unforeseen circumstances. This will not only provide crucial information for future iterations of interventions of this type or in this setting or situation, but it may also allow for the results to be viewed in a perspective that is wider than that provided by the ROI analysis alone. Further, in addition to the actual calculated ROI, it may be reasonable and relevant to explore what the ROI *would have been* if certain assumptions had turned out to be correct.

Therefore, it is still important to obtain information related to what similar interventions for similar populations or in similar situations experienced, if for no other reason than to frame your results within a larger context.

Keep in mind that improving care quality may actually produce a negative benefit to a facility in the form of reduced revenue. Multiple examples of this exist, and while it is likely not to be the goal of the intervention, it may be a very real possibility. Whether it appears here as a "negative benefit" or in the cost section is a matter of preference; it may depend on where it comes naturally for the reader to encounter. For example, perhaps there will be impacts to multiple types of services or utilization and it will be clearer to list all of them in the same section, as opposed to separating them and putting some as costs and others as benefits.

4.3.2.3 Monetizing Benefits

Once the necessary estimates have been obtained to quantify the effect of the intervention through changes in events, incidence, prevalence, efficiency, or other metrics, the next step is to monetize that effect for inclusion as a benefit in the ROI analysis. As mentioned previously, benefits often take the form of cost savings or cost avoidance associated with lower utilization, fewer rates, and overall improved health and outcomes. Therefore, monetizing benefits frequently involves equating different types or aspects of utilization (inpatient stays, number of days in the hospital, procedures, etc.) to their financial equivalent from the perspective of the entity of interest. In doing so, you should consider several aspects.

Locally Versus Nationally Sourced Monetary Values

Often, multiple data sources are available to obtain the monetary value of different types of utilization. When determining the most appropriate data source for a situation, one required decision is whether to use "local" information and values versus more general estimates. Local data are those that are available at the setting or site of the intervention, such as the hospital's internal administrative database regarding the cost of care. More general estimates are those available from regulatory bodies or from large nationwide studies of clinical areas and care utilization.

Using local data is likely to produce estimates of value that are accurate and relevant to the individual site or setting because they reflect the experiences specific to that setting. However, local data may not allow for results to be generalizable to other settings or patient populations. For example, if the intervention occurs in a rural setting or typically sees certain types of patients that are not representative of the state, region, or country, the results may only be applicable to rural settings with similar patient populations.

More general data often involve national, literature-based, or policy-based estimates. Depending on the situation, these estimates would be obtained from a national database or report or as the result of a literature summary on heart failure-related hospitalizations or a large representative study. These estimates may increase the generalizability of the analysis, but they may not reflect the real benefit experienced at the local facility where the intervention takes place. The appropriate choice of which type of data to use will depend on the situation, what data are available, and the goals of the analysis.

Microcosting Versus Gross Costing

In addition to deciding from where to pull the information for the monetary estimates, you should also determine how best to compile them. The method of calculating the average cost of all heart failure-related hospitalizations at the local facility described previously is referred to as "gross costing." It relies on the average being an accurate representation of a typical or usual encounter (note: You could similarly obtain estimates of the variability to use in sensitivity analyses).

Alternatively, one could also employ "microcosting." Instead of lumping everything together and averaging, microcosting involves identifying each of the individual elements that are typically involved in a heart failure hospitalization and adding them together. These individual elements might include room charges, typical laboratory tests, staff time, facility resources, durable medical equipment, etc., that when summed together represent the charges one could expect for a typical heart failure hospital stay. When deciding which method to employ, consider what information you have available, the scope and perspective of your analysis, and the populations and settings you intend to generalize your results to (if any).

Extracting Monetary Information from Published Literature

As with extracting estimates of rates and changes in quality or health from the literature, obtaining monetary estimates from the literature follows a similar procedure: Identify relevant studies, compare the specifics of the study, patient population, timing, and setting to your own situation, and abstract and summarize the relevant information for use in both your base case and sensitivity analyses.

4.3.3 Estimating Non-MMA Benefits

Once MMA benefits have been identified and quantified, it becomes necessary to determine how best to address benefits that fail to meet at least one of the three criteria of being measurable, monetizable, and directly attributable to the intervention. Now, we will explore the most common types of these benefits, in no particular order.

4.3.3.1 Increased Revenue Potential

When compiling benefits to a care provider or healthcare system, there is the potential for improvements in either patient care or efficiency to increase the opportunity and/or likelihood of additional revenue. These may take the form of increased reimbursement from risk pools or performance-based reimbursement, increased capacity to/availability of care for other patients, or newly identified sources of revenue streams. Sometimes, it may be possible to directly estimate the amount of the increased revenue, but often it will require some approximation or extrapolation to arrive at a reasonable estimate. For example, it is true that improved patient experience may result in higher HCAHPS scores, which influence performance-based reimbursement from Medicare. However, estimating the amount requires that one estimates the potential impact to HCAHPS, relative improvement in the performance-based quality program, and the estimated payment, all of which may be elusive to establish with any sort of precision.

In a summary, it may be preferable to simply point out the opportunity for increased revenue from this source and provide some context (like what the facility received previously or what the average reimbursement was for facilities with slightly higher HCAHPS scores, etc.). You would point out the opportunity so that the reader would be aware of the potential but would not have to fully buy into whatever assumptions or approximations that would be needed to arrive at an exact estimate.

Estimating the potential increased revenue opportunity from increased capacity or availability faces similar challenges. It first requires that one can accurately extrapolate current demand to a future state that involves increased capacity, which can be difficult. Put more bluntly, having extra beds available does not guarantee that you are going to fill them at the same rate that you fill your current beds. Also, often, while improving efficiency and increasing capacity in one area are beneficial, there may be unintended impacts in other areas (e.g., records, billing, etc.) that may be difficult or impossible to predict or anticipate, let alone estimate. This, too, is often an opportunity that is best left to the hypothetical. Acknowledge for the reader that there exist opportunities to increase revenue from additional capacity or availability and provide some context (e.g., "based on current volume, the ability to increase patient load by just 5% could potentially add an additional $X in revenue each quarter…"). Whatever choice you make, be sure not to ignore the potential for unforeseen problems that can result from simply increasing volume.

In addition to increased revenue from risk pools, improved performance, and increased volume, the potential for new revenue streams exists. This source of increased revenue will typically be identified in retrospect; however, given the right situation, one may be able to predict new revenue streams during the proposal stage. In fact, some organizations seek to implement a new kind of care model in part because of the opportunity it may provide to market new services. For example, a healthcare system that becomes known for exceptional rehabilitation care may consider whether there will be new opportunities to partner with other institutions or community organizations to fill a need in long-term rehab for more than just their own patients.

4.3.3.2 Patient Experience

You can use a variety of tools to measure patient experience or satisfaction, but these results may be difficult to monetize and/or to attribute directly to an intervention. In part, this results because the patient experience can be influenced by so many things, including several outside of the control of payers or providers. For example, studies have shown that patient satisfaction can differ by their underlying level of health and by certain patient characteristics. Involving surveys and the potential bias they can introduce, if not applied appropriately, can add a layer of complexity to an already complex situation.

Nonetheless, quantifying and improving the patient experience is an important goal and one that is receiving increased attention. It may be a measure that is collected for purposes of assessing quality, but in any calculation of value it may be omitted if it cannot be suitably monetized. This closely mirrors the struggle to measure or monetize a facility's "brand" discussed earlier; patients' impression of a facility, a provider, or a healthcare system will color their perceived experience and influence not only how they respond to a survey but also how they talk about their experience on social media, which can have untold impacts on the reputation and impression of the healthcare system.

4.3.3.3   Staff Satisfaction

Like the patient experience, staff satisfaction (or buy-in, or loyalty, or burnout, etc.) is important (and possible) to measure and improve but can be difficult to monetize. One option for dealing with this is: Select measurements that are more easily monetized or even directly linked to finances, like staff retention (e.g., the percent turnover, the average time on staff, etc.). One potential problem with this approach is that often quality improvement opportunities are selected not for their fiscal impact but for their importance in improving care quality and facility culture. Therefore, it may be necessary to explore the possibility of including multiple aims: to improve staff sat-isfaction *and* demonstrate to the administration that there can be a positive monetary return to justify the cost of the intervention. That is, even though the primary goal is not staff retention, it may be an outcome that provides the necessary justification from a financial point of view and therefore is worth measuring in addition to more direct representations of staff satisfaction.

Finding the balance in this type of situation can be challenging. However, it is likely that for quality goals that are driven by these larger priorities like culture and quality of life, the calculated financial return is not going to make or break the decision to proceed, unless of course, it demonstrates such a huge financial risk as to make the activity unwise. These types of analyses may be more likely to involve slightly more extrapolation or less well-founded assumptions, but it may also be that the reader will be likely to give you a little more leeway in these areas because the focus is on the improvement in quality, not value.

It might be possible, for example, to survey staff after the intervention and ask them directly about the likelihood of them staying on staff for some given period of time ("Before this intervention, if asked, what would you have said was the likelihood that you would still work here twelve months down the road? And now [after the intervention] what would you say that likelihood is?"). Or it might be possible to estimate the amount of time directors and administrators deal with staff issues and to equate potential reductions in that time to cost savings. This can be tricky to do, but there are ways to approach it that can offer information that will provide some general estimates that can be monetized and attributable to the intervention, if necessary.

4.3.3.4 Other Benefits

Improvements in organization or department "culture" are frequently sought by providers, staff, and even administrators. Increased feelings of togetherness, helpfulness, and collaboration, as well as an atmosphere that is perceived to be less punitive, can all be measured to some degree through surveys or direct reports by staff. Additionally, depending on how it is defined, culture can include aspects like coordination, buy-in, and even innovation. These can be powerful benefits to measure and laud when they are successfully improved, but links to monetary returns are difficult to establish. Even so, aspects related to attitude, feelings, impressions, intentions, or pattern of interactions are important and should not be overlooked if there can be a credible process to estimate their value.

4.3.3.5 How to Measure and Monetize Non-MMA Benefits

It may seem counterintuitive to explore methods to measure or monetize benefits we have previously classified as *not* being MMA, but if it is possible to gather data or evidence that they add value, they can be presented in some form in the sensitivity analysis. Additionally, a little more leeway is associated with estimates in the sensitivity analysis, because it is understood that it is an exploration into "what ifs" and/or "best-case" scenarios. Therefore, it is worthwhile to explore some of the tools that can be used to either measure or monetize these benefits.

Surveys

Surveys are mentioned as having the potential to measure things like patient experience, staff satisfaction, culture, general attitudes, intentions, and impressions. However, it can be somewhat challenging to obtain information that can be monetized. There may be indirect measurements of patient experience, some of which may be more easily monetizable, whether it increased patient–provider face-to-face time, fewer complaints, fewer skipped appointments or last-minute cancelations, reduced administrative time-resolving issues, etc.

Expert or Knowledgeable Opinion

This resource, too, was mentioned previously as a way to gather information and gain understanding of aspects of the situation and intervention. Just as this resource can help establish estimates for incidence, prevalence, and event rates, there may also be information to glean regarding benefits that are harder to measure and quantify, let alone monetize. For example, physicians who work on the front lines of the hospital may know how much time would be saved if a new protocol was implemented that eliminated their need to navigate a certain section of the EHR interface. Or, those in human resources may be able to estimate how much time and resources are consumed every time there is turnover.

Administrative Data

In all likelihood, facility or administrative information probably exists regarding costs, resource use, the amount and frequency of repairs, etc., that could aid in your estimation of how improvements in quality or efficiency might translate into dollars. The difficulty may be in obtaining enough detail to be able to attribute it to the intervention. For example, maybe there are administrative records that detail exactly how much was spent last year on repairs, water, or electricity, but it may not provide enough information to determine how much was due to a particular activity or piece of equipment; therefore, it may not help with an estimate of how much savings would be realized through making the activity more efficient or updating the piece of equipment.

Many facilities and healthcare systems use relative value units (RVUs) as a measurement of individual physician productivity. RVU data may be useful as a way to measure and monetize physician activity and effort (since RVUs are commonly used for reimbursement), but, as with anything, they are not perfect. RVUs often fail to reflect contributions of individuals with more administrative or leadership duties since they reflect only activities billed for patient care.

Contingent Valuation

Contingent valuation is a method where individuals are asked to consider hypothetical situations and their willingness to either pay for a service not currently offered or accept payment in lieu of a current service no longer being offered. For example, if trying to assess the monetary value that patients in an ED waiting room placed on reduced wait times, one could ask something like,

> Imagine that the next time you needed to visit the ED you could choose to limit your wait time to no more than 20 min, but you have to pay for that service directly; how much would you be willing to pay for this?

Often, establishing either willingness to pay (WTP) or willingness to accept (WTA) compensation is done to estimate the demand for a product or service. That said, it can also be used to measure the value that patients place on certain aspects of care. In the latter case, WTP is sometimes used to identify which improvement activity should be pursued when the facility or organization has multiple alternatives to select from (i.e., they do not have the time or resources to do them all, so they need to determine which improvements would provide the biggest value for patients).

Unfortunately, there are a variety of challenges to using contingent valuation effectively. They include inherent biases in how individuals respond and that respondents know that they will not actually be asked to pay anything for a hypothetical situation, so their answers may not be a good reflection of true value. Additionally, sometimes patients find it difficult to fully grasp what they are being asked to assign value to or what constitutes a reasonable amount because they lack knowledge regarding health-care costs or prices. Further exploration of the topic of contingent valuation can be found in the chapter on expanded topics.

4.3.3.6 Attributing Benefits to the Intervention or Activity

In previous sections, we discussed ways to attempt to ensure that benefits are directly attributable to the intervention, including controlling what you can, using random-ization, thinking strategically about data sources and data collection, and even con-sidering alternative measures. There may also be circumstances, however, where it is appropriate to estimate a proportion of the benefits that results from a particular intervention.

For example, perhaps multiple interventions are occurring at the same time or changes in policy or practice guidelines are taking effect at roughly the same time. An option for estimating the proportion of the benefit that can be attributed to the intervention is to ask those who are directly involved and have specific knowledge of the intervention and the benefits. That is, providers who have been working on the front lines before, during, and after the intervention are often well positioned to estimate, in a general sense, how much of the improvement is due to different sources. Even if the estimated contribution is relatively small by most accounts, it can add monetary value to the benefits and improve the ROI. Therefore, if used with caution, it can be a useful method.

4.3.4 Calculating Benefits (Formulas)

Once measured, monetized, and attributed to the intervention, calculating benefits is relatively straightforward. However, it is still a good idea to include formulas in any reporting of a ROI analysis so that the reader can quickly see and understand where the calculations come from. For instance, one of the most commonly calculated monetary benefits from quality improvement projects is cost avoidance due to lower disease burden or fewer adverse events. This is done by calculating the number of affected individuals, estimating the number of events avoided, and then multiplying that number by the estimated cost of each event to produce the total cost avoidance.

For example, let us assume that there is an attempt to reduce infectious compli-cations after surgery, which are estimated to prolong length of stay by three days and incur additional costs of $3500, on average. Let us also assume that there are 80 individuals in the intervention who have a pre-intervention risk of infection of 15% (i.e., it is expected that roughly 12 individuals would develop an infection), and the goal is to cut this risk in half (to 7.5%, or six individuals post-intervention) (Table 4.10).

The associated monetary benefit due to cost avoidance would be calculated as follows:

Table 4.10 Example of estimating the monetary value of a benefit (hypothetical data)

Step in the process of estimating benefit
Each infection incurs costs of $3500
Prior to the intervention, 80 individuals have a 15% risk of infection = 12 individuals
The goal is to cut this in half or to reduce the total number of infections by six
Avoiding six infections that each cost $3500 results in a savings of $6 \times \$3500 = \$21,000$

(Expected number with infection before intervention

− Expected number after) × cost savings per event avoided

$$= (12 - 6) \times \$3500 = \$21,000$$

It is advisable to include both the formula and the raw calculations at least once when reporting an analysis to clearly demonstrate to a reader or audience how the dollar value of the benefit was generated. For other types of benefits that require similar types of calculations, additional formulas and explicit calculations are needed to retain a clear and transparent process for those who will be evaluating the analysis.

4.4 Discounting

Any time costs and benefits will occur over multiple years, monetary values should ideally be discounted to allow for more appropriate comparisons. The basic concept is that a benefit of $100 that will not be realized until a year from now is worth less than $100 today. How much less depends on the chosen discount rate, which is commonly between 2 and 4%. A somewhat more intuitive way of understanding the need for discounting involves the consideration of the opportunity cost associated with an initial investment in the intervention. If the funds needed for the intervention (say, $10,000) were instead invested in an account that earned interest (say, 2%), in a year the initial investment would be $10,200. Therefore, when invested in the intervention, the benefits realized in year two would need to be at least 2% higher than in year one to be "worth" the same amount to the investor as what they would have received from the alternative investment with the guaranteed rate.

Discounting is a relatively straightforward process and is done the same way it would be done for a financial asset. Typically, future costs and benefits are discounted to provide the present value of those future monetary values. Once an appropriate discount rate is chosen (typically between 2 and 4% annually), the general formula for converting monetary values is simply:

$$PV = FV \times (1 - \text{Discount Rate})^t \tag{4.1}$$

where PV indicates "present value," FV indicates "future value," and "t" is the number of years between PV and FV. Using this formula and a discount rate of 3.5%, a benefit of $10,000 realized in year two (the FV) would have a value in year one of $9650 (the PV). To see this, plug in $10,000 for FV, 3.5% for the discount rate, and 2 for "t" in Eq. 4.1.

In a prospective analysis, this allows one to calculate the present value of continued cost avoidance for an improvement that occurs over multiple years. Consider an intervention that assumes benefits in the form of cost avoidance of $2500 for the current year and each of the next two years. While the raw benefit would be calculated as 3 × $2500 = $7500, the discounted amount (using a discount rate of 3%) would be arrived at by calculating:

- Current year benefit = $2500
- Next year benefit = $2500 × (1 − 0.03) = $2425
- Following year benefit = $2500 × (1 − 0.03)^2 = $2352.

The present value for the first three years of benefits = $2500 + $2425 + $2352 = $7277, which is less than 3 × $2500 = $7500 and allows for a more reasonable comparison to the investment that is necessary in the current year to achieve those benefits.

If there are ongoing costs in future years, those would be discounted in the same way. So, to extend this example, if the intervention involved an initial investment of $4000 and estimated ongoing costs of $1500 in each of the next two years, the present value for the first three years of costs would be:

$$\text{PV of costs} = \$4000 + \$1500 \times (1 - 0.03) + \$1500 \times (1 - 0.03)^2$$

which equals $4000 + $1455 + $1411 = $6866, which is less than the raw amount of $7000.

Even though in this example we are discounting both costs and benefits, the results will produce different values for the ROI than when using the raw values. To see this, we can calculate the ROI each way:

$$\text{ROI using raw values} = (\$7500 - \$7000)/\$7000 \times 100\% = 5.98\%$$
$$\text{ROI using discounted values} = (\$7277 - \$6866)/\$6866 \times 100\% = 7.14\%$$

The difference between ROI using raw and discounted values will be a function of how the costs and benefits are distributed over the evaluation time frame. If most costs are incurred up front while most benefits accrue in later time periods, then discounting will decrease present value benefits more than costs which will lower the calculated ROI. Additionally, since costs are in the denominator, any decrease in those values will increase ROI, even if the net benefit does not change much due to discounting.

As an aside, an important distinction to make is the difference between a "discount rate," which we just discussed, and an "interest rate," which is also commonly used in

Table 4.11 Comparing discount rate to interest rate

Situation	Type of rate set = 3.5%	Result
Calculating what $10,000 realized in year two is worth in year one	Discount rate	$9650 (using Eq. 4.1)
Calculating how much we would need to invest in year one for it to be worth $10,000 in year two	Interest rate	$9661

PV and FV calculations. Note that in the example introducing this section, an initial $10,000 investment earns *interest* of 2% so that in two years it is worth $10,200. If you wanted to determine how much money you would have to invest (at 2%) in the present in order for it to be worth a certain value in the future, then you would approach it slightly differently. In that case, you would select a future value and a time period and calculate the amount needed in the present as: $FV/(1 + r)^t$, where r is the interest rate. This is not equivalent to Eq. 4.1, which calculates the present value of a future benefit or cost as $FV \times (1 - \text{discount rate})^t$.

The difference stems from the use of a *discount rate* as opposed to an *interest rate*. You can use either formula as long as you are clear about what type of rate you are using. If using an *interest rate* of 3.5% and the corresponding formula, the amount needed in year one to be worth $10,000 in year two is $9661. It is instructive to compare that value with the $9650 calculated using Eq. 4.1 and a *discount rate* of 3.5% (Table 4.11).

It is possible to determine what *interest rate* equates to a particular *discount rate*,[7] but typically you would just choose a method and stick with it.

When pulling cost and/or benefit information from multiple sources (published literature, online sources, etc.) that report monetary values using dollar values from different years, it is generally expected that one will convert the values into "constant dollar" or "current dollar" values using price indices. The steps to perform this operation are as follows:

1. Select the common year you want to convert all dollar values to (e.g., 2019).
2. Identify the appropriate index for 2019, as well as for each of the years' values that need converting. This is most commonly done using either the consumer price index (CPI) or one of the eight major groups of the CPI that reflect different industries, including the medical care CPI. An online search for any of these will allow you to quickly find indices you can use and apply to your values. This will provide also more information regarding how the indices are developed if you are interested.
3. Multiply the dollar value you want converted by the ratio of the index for 2019 (your selected base year) to the index for the year of the converting dollar value.

---

[7] Through algebra, we can show that if the *interest rate* is set equal to $d/(1 - d)$ where d is the *discount rate*, then the two formulas would produce the same result for PV; in our example of a discount rate of 3.5%, that formula indicates that an interest rate of 3.627% is roughly equivalent.

In practice, if a published paper reported a cost or benefit from activities in 2012 of $5000, and we wanted to convert it to 2019 dollars, we would do the following:

$$\$5000 \times (2019 \text{ Index}/2012 \text{ Index})$$

When repeated for each cost and benefit obtained, the result is a series of values all in 2019 dollars.

4.5 Summary

Identifying and quantifying costs and benefits often involves multiple steps. Working within the framework established by the chosen scope and perspective, one can determine which costs are relevant and work to monetize them into quantities that can be applied to the ROI calculation. When identifying relevant benefits, one should evaluate each benefit to identify which are measurable, monetizable, and attributable to the intervention. These benefits will provide the most defendable monetary return. Once those benefits have been quantified, other types of benefits can be explored for potential inclusion into the analysis. There may be several methods for estimating the financial benefit of these other benefits. Finally, discounting of costs and benefits that occur in different years will provide the most equitable representation of the return.

4.6 Key Concepts

- To determine costs, one must traverse several steps: identifying cost sources, estimating and monetizing costs, and aggregating them into relevant categories or time-related buckets.
- Of all the benefits that may be realized, only some will be measurable, monetizable, and attributable to the quality improvement activities.
- Unmeasurable benefits may be those where no measurement exists (e.g., increased engagement, improved culture, etc.) or those either unavailable or outside of the scope of the current analysis.
- Some benefits that are measurable may not be monetizable; those not directly linked to changes in care utilization, staffing, expenses, or efficiency may be difficult or impossible to monetize.
- Even if a benefit is measurable and monetizable, if it is not directly attributable to the intervention, it may not be appropriate for inclusion in the analysis; there may be several reasons why a benefit may not be directly attributable, including confounding, bias, preexisting trends in outcomes, or too much distance between the intervention and the benefit.

- To estimate the monetary value of benefits that are measurable, monetizable, and attributable, the necessary steps are similar to those required for determining costs: identifying benefit sources, estimating the monetary value, and aggregating into relevant categories.
- When pulling information from published literature regarding benefits in the form of reduced incidence, prevalence, or adverse events, be careful to ensure that the reported information is relevant to the current analysis; rates per time at risk are best, while percentages or hazard ratios can provide misleading or unusable information.
- If necessary, there may be instances when benefits that are not measurable, monetizable, or directly attributable can be estimated for inclusion in a ROI analysis; several methods and tools allow for reasonable estimates to be made.
- Costs or benefits that will accrue over multiple years should be discounted to reflect a constant-year currency; this can be achieved using relatively simple formulas and/or published indexes of equivalent values.

References

1. Spetz J, Brown DS, Aydin C (2015) The economics of preventing hospital falls: demonstrating ROI through a simple model. J Nurs Adm 45(1):50–57. https://doi.org/10.1097/NNA.0000000000000154
2. Boustani M, Azar J, Solid CA (2020) Agile implementation: a model for implementing evidence-based healthcare solutions into real-world practice to achieve sustainable change. Morgan James Publishing, New York
3. Sashegyi A, Ferry D (2017) On the interpretation of the hazard ratio and communication of survival benefit. Oncologist 22(4):484–486. https://doi.org/10.1634/theoncologist.2016-0198

Chapter 5
Performing Base Case and Sensitivity Analyses

5.1 Prospective Versus Retrospective ROI Analyses

The goal of the base case and sensitivity analyses in a prospective analysis is to demonstrate the range of possible returns that a project or initiative will generate and to provide some context and guidance about what the most likely outcome(s) will be and why. This requires a full exploration of all relevant assumptions and estimates, including supporting evidence for not only why they apply to the proposed situation, but why certain estimates are chosen for the base case or sensitivity analysis. When reading a proposal, those evaluating its merits will decide whether they consider the assumptions, estimates, and projections to be realistic and whether the reasoning is sound. Therefore, it is essential to be transparent, comprehensive, and objective. Many opportunities will arise to inject suppositions or speculations in the sensitivity analysis to follow. If presented as part of the base case, they could hurt credibility if the reviewers do not share the opinion or agree with the logic.

In contrast, the base case in a retrospective analysis should attempt to be the most accurate representation of what actually occurred and what was observed over the given time period. The sensitivity analysis can then be used to: (1) identify observed results that deviated from what was anticipated and the resulting impact on the realized return, (2) explore what return would have been realized under different circumstances, and (3) provide context to assist in any attempts to generalize the results for another population, setting, or situation.

In the details that follow, it will often be clear whether the concepts refer to a prospective analysis, a retrospective one, or both. If it is not clear from the context, it will be stated. Ultimately, the goal for either type of analysis is to explore the role played by uncertainty and variation in order to better understand drivers of return to aid in the evaluation of financial feasibility and inform future activities or pursuits (Table 5.1).

© Springer Nature Switzerland AG 2020
C. A. Solid, *Return on Investment for Healthcare Quality Improvement*,
https://doi.org/10.1007/978-3-030-46478-3_5

Table 5.1 Goals of the base case and sensitivity analyses in prospective versus retrospective analyses

	Prospective analysis	Retrospective analysis
Base case	Demonstrate the most "likely" outcome	Accurately reflect what happened
Sensitivity analysis	Explore what could happen if certain assumptions or estimates vary	Examine why return was higher or lower than expected, what main drivers of return were, or what would have been realized in certain circumstances

5.2   Developing the Base Case Scenario

The base case scenario represents the primary starting point for any interpretation of the financial return of a quality improvement intervention. Therefore, should be constructed with sound reasoning and based on values that will stand up to scrutiny (Fig. 5.1).

5.2.1   General Considerations for the Base Case

5.2.1.1   For a Prospective Analysis

As just mentioned, the base case analysis in a prospective analysis should represent the most likely or most reasonable outcome, and therefore return, of a project or initiative. An important distinction is that the "likely" or "reasonable" outcome will not necessarily be the same as the lowest or most conservative outcome. The base case should be based on estimates and assumptions that can be considered the most credible and defendable for the particular issue, setting, and situation.

Identifying which estimates and assumptions meet these criteria may or may not be straightforward. Presumably, those preparing the proposal have done their due diligence to obtain relevant information from published literature, consulted experts

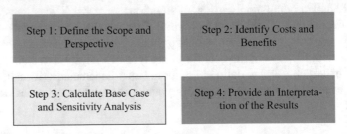

Fig. 5.1 Step 3 in the ROI process

in the field, collected preliminary data when possible, etc. Hopefully, they have also amassed a set of estimates for the key aspects of the project, including the associated costs and benefits. Some estimates will be used to construct the base case. Others will be used in sensitivity analyses, and others may not be used at all. In selecting estimates for the base case, one should consider:

1. The strength or credibility of the source
2. The similarity of the source's circumstances to the proposed project
3. The recency and range of available estimates.

The Strength or Credibility of the Source

Randomized trials and well-designed research studies as well as large or even national surveys are often sources that contain strong and robust evidence for a particular estimate or set of estimates. Additionally, estimates obtained from publications or data produced by federal or national agencies, like the Census Bureau or the Department of Health and Human Services are likely to be seen as very credible. There are also independent associations, groups, and nonprofits that focus on a particular clinical topic or setting of care—think: the American Society of Clinical (*fill in the blank*) or the National (*insert disease or condition*) Foundation; these groups will often pull information from credible sources and provide a summary or fact sheet.

Consider not only what you deem as credible but also what the intended audience would view as credible. You may have previous experiences (e.g., pilot studies) you can pull from that you believe produced credible data and results than are reasonable to use in the current analysis. However, be sure to clearly relay the details of such studies or projects, especially if they do not appear as peer-reviewed publications. Readers may be critical of these types of studies and assume that you may be biased in your assessment of their robustness and generalizability due to your close relationship with them.

The Similarity of the Source's Circumstances to the Proposed Project

The following are the most direct examples of when estimates may be applicable to your project due to key similarities: pilot studies or in previous experience with the same population or within the same setting as that of the proposed intervention. That is, a pilot study at a local nursing home is likely to provide good information for what could be expected in terms of reach and effectiveness in a larger intervention at the same location.

However, some situations where interventions are performed elsewhere can be excellent resources for needed estimates. This is especially the case if those interventions are performed on a similar population, in a similar setting, or that leverage a similar intervention to the one being planned. For example, a telehealth program at a rural hospital may produce estimates for the reach and effectiveness of telemedicine programs of multiple forms that are applicable to rural settings across the country, not just the one where it was performed. Or, the time and resources required to fully implement a new triage process at a large urban ED may provide reasonable estimates for what other large urban EDs could expect if they were to employ a similar process.

Determining what is relevant and can supply you with reasonable estimates will rely on your knowledge and experience in the field and of the literature. While you should refrain from "reaching" or simply providing information you hope reviewers will see as relevant, remember that the credibility of you and your team can lend credibility to the information you present as relevant. It can be difficult to be objective, but if you can demonstrate a working knowledge of the topic and provide reasoning for why the information is pertinent to your project, then it is reasonable to use it.

The Recency and Range of Available Estimates

When multiple credible and similar sources are identified, other criteria can help determine which estimates to use for the base case and sensitivity analyses. For example, more recent estimates, especially those that may have occurred after the start of a national monitoring program or after a major shift in policy, may be the most reasonable to use for a present analysis.

Another option would be to calculate a new estimate by combining information provided from multiple sources. That is, if a long-term care center has previously performed multiple pilot studies they could draw from, instead of just using estimates from the most recent pilot, it may be prudent to consider the effectiveness of each pilot study and develop an estimate that reflects all of them, like the mean or median effectiveness.

There often can be more than one reasonable value to use. As long as the one chosen is justifiable and reasonable, it can be used for the base case.

An Example

When determining which estimates of prevalence, incidence, effectiveness, etc., to use, those for which the strongest argument can be made will be supported by sound evidence and applicable to the project being proposed. Again, these may not be the most conservative estimates.

For example, let us pretend that published literature reports that educational interventions on infection prevention reduce hospital-acquired infections anywhere from 10 to 40%, depending on the characteristics of the intervention, the setting, and the time frame. From those studies, perhaps one example in particular closely reflects the intervention you are proposing in terms of its population, setting, and time frame, and which resulted in a 16% reduction in infections. One could likely make a reasonable case that a 16% reduction is the most appropriate estimate to use for the base case, even though it is not the most conservative estimate (10%) nor is it midway between the highest and lowest estimate obtained (which would be 25%). Most reviewers would understand the logic behind using 16% for the base case scenario.

The fact that 16% may represent the most reasonable estimate for the base case does not imply that the range of estimates from the published literature should be discounted. On the contrary, it would be wise to address, either in text or in analysis, the entire spread in the published rates of success of education-based interventions (10–40%) since variability equates to uncertainty, and without proper context a reader may be concerned about the likelihood of your assumed result.

In our example, perhaps the study that observed a 40% reduction is unique in some way (e.g., it was performed in an uncommon staffing situation or had a high baseline value providing a large improvement opportunity, etc.) or is not credible in your opinion (e.g., small sample size, unclear methods, etc.). This type of exploration not only provides reasoning for the chosen estimate, but it also demonstrates to those evaluating your proposal that you have knowledge of the subject area and have considered all possibilities. Table 5.2 displays how this type of exploration may look to justify the estimate of 16% as being the most relevant to the base case.

5.2.1.2 For a Retrospective Analysis

When calculating the base case ROI retrospectively, the appropriate values to use for the rates, reductions, and impacts are those that were observed over the course of the project. It will be likely that some or even all of the values observed during the activities will differ from what was anticipated (or hoped for), but for the base case it is usual to simply present the return that was actually realized.

The exception might be if there is not a comparison group or if data from that group are unavailable or unusable to viably help determine change or improvement, thereby making a value determination difficult or impossible. This could happen if (1) there were no data collected prior to the intervention and there was no control group or (2) something unattributable to the project changed during the intervention as to make a comparison to any pre-intervention or control group tenuous. Perhaps significant changes occurred to the patient population in some characteristic that are known to influence outcomes, for example. Or maybe external forces existed that were thought to introduce bias or uncertainty during your intervention. Changes in health policy, reimbursement, practice guidelines, and even the local and/or physical environment may reasonably affect the observed outcomes in a way that complicates or compromises the ability to make a reasonable comparison. In these circumstances, if comparison data are not available, it may be reasonable to use values from other sources like published literature or expert opinion, similar to when performing a prospective ROI analysis. Ideally, one would gather information from multiple resources and select the most reasonable, just like when amassing estimates for a prospective analysis.

Table 5.2 Example of rationale for determining the most appropriate estimates from published literature to use for the base case (hypothetical data)

Study description	Estimate of infection reduction (%)	Comments
A single training session where physicians and nurses received specific education about best practices	10	Only one educational session; in the limitations, it was noted that not all staff members were able to attend
Two training sessions separated by two months, plus the adoption of an infection prevention bundle	16	The most similar to the project being proposed in terms of: population (central-line infections in those aged 65+), setting (urban, acute care hospital), and intervention (multifaceted including educational sessions and infection prevention bundle)
A series of training sessions with role-play and Q&A sessions; three total sessions over six months	22	Slightly more intense educational sessions that are being proposed in the current project
Infection prevention bundle plus EMR-based reminder to remove catheters after a certain number of days	23	Our study does not involve EMR-based reminders
Focused on elderly patients' post-operative infections (all kinds) in a hospital-based ambulatory surgical center	40	Initial infection rates were twice as high as any of the other studies, suggesting that there may have been more opportunity or "low hanging fruit"

The decision to use 16% for the base case is a result of considering the similarity of the source study to the proposed project

5.2.2 Identifying Usable Estimates

5.2.2.1 Use Measurable, Monetizable, and Attributable (MMA) Values

As explored previously, in almost any quality improvement activity, a variety of impacts could represent improvements in quality or value. However, not all are measured (or measurable), quantifiable, or can be translated into monetary values. These types of elements can pose particular challenges when attempting to assess the value of associated improvement activities. Identifying estimates that are usable and applicable to value are obviously important for successfully evaluating value and financial return.

Table 5.3 Types of benefits to use in the base case and sensitivity analyses

Benefit types	Base case	Sensitivity analysis
Measurable, monetizable, and directly attributable to the intervention	Yes	Yes
Those not fully MMA: • Not fully measurable • Difficult to monetize • May only be attributable in part or tangentially to intervention	No	Maybe

While intangible benefits or more general impressions of value may be reasonable to explore in text or the sensitivity analyses, the base case should typically be limited to those benefits that are measurable, monetizable, and directly attributable to the intervention. This will result in a ROI estimate of the tangible fiscal return and will therefore represent the strongest "business case" for the project or initiative. After presenting the base case and interpreting the results, either in written form or when presenting your results in person, the discussion of additional benefits that lack one or all of those attributes will strengthen the argument for the viability and fiscal responsibility of the proposed project.

For a retrospective analysis, it is still best to limit the base case calculations to those benefits that are MMA; however, that may encompass a different set of variables or measures than were available during the proposal stage. During the project, it may have become possible to measure or monetize outcomes that did not previously have information to form a reasonable estimate, or others that were completely unanticipated. For example, perhaps when a project to improve laboratory efficiency was proposed, the analysis focused on benefits related to staff time, the reduced likelihood of errors, and the increase in potential reimbursement (e.g., billing) for laboratory results. However, perhaps after efficiency increased, the administration observed lower turnover of laboratory techs and support staff. Upon further investigation, maybe there is good reason to believe that this was a direct result of the intervention (e.g., maybe there is direct feedback from employees suggesting that the intervention improved their working experience and increased the likelihood that they would stay for another three years). This type of benefit, which was not anticipated prior to embarking on the targeted improvement, can be a powerful addition to any analysis and can also serve as a learning experience for future projects and others who seek to effect similar changes at their facility or organization (Table 5.3).

5.2.3 Applying the Perspective and Scope to the Base Case

5.2.3.1 Whose Perspective

In a prospective analysis, the most likely perspective chosen for the base case ROI will be the individual's or group's from whom funding is sought. That may be an outside entity like CMS, or it could be an internal department as well. It makes no difference in terms of the goal of the proposal, which is to convince those with the available funding that the project has merit. To do that, the proposal must demonstrate the effectiveness and relative value of conducting the project or intervention; therefore, you must demonstrate to the funding source that it will be money well-spent, in addition to any clinical improvements that will be realized.

While the funding source may be the most important perspective to consider (in terms of pure financial return), it may be helpful to also present the anticipated return for other key players and stakeholders that reflect benefits realized by patients and the larger community. For many organizations and external funding agencies, these types of benefits can influence business decisions. That is because in most cases funders are interested in the overall impact of the intervention to improve care quality and value for all involved. When appropriate, these additional calculations can help provide context during the interpretation phase (see the next chapter), but one needs to be careful not to mix or confuse returns for these different perspectives with that of the funding source. In most cases, calculating ROI for different perspectives should be done separately but presented in tandem.

The same is true when calculating the ROI in a retrospective analysis: The most important perspective to calculate return for is the group that ultimately funded the project. However, just as in the prospective analysis, explorations into the financial return for other key individuals and stakeholders have merit for the same reasons as previously described.

5.2.3.2 What Scope and Time Frame

The most appropriate scope and time frame for the base case will be situation dependent. Sometimes, the most appropriate scope and time frame will be limited to the targeted population and for only the duration of the intervention. Other times, a time frame of several years across multiple settings and populations may be appropriate. When selecting the scope and time frame, you should consider the timing of when costs are incurred and benefits are realized; many costs may be incurred prior to the intervention starting in order to fund the development, planning, or ramp-up phases.

If the timeline in each panel of Fig. 5.2 represents a typical intervention where a specific start and end date to the intervention exists, we can represent the time frame for the evaluation (i.e., the time frame for when costs and benefits are examined) as a shaded area; any costs or benefits that occur during a point in time covered by that area are then included in the ROI calculation. Determining the appropriate time frame, then, is akin to determining the appropriate location and size of that shaded area. The three panels represent three different time frames and the implications they have on the relevant cost and services. In the middle panel, the shaded region is shifted left of where it resides in the top panel, and therefore includes costs that occurred during the pre-intervention period and captures less of those that occur during the sustainability time frame than in the top panel. In the bottom panel, the time frame is narrower, so that it only overlaps the period between when the intervention started and ended. It is

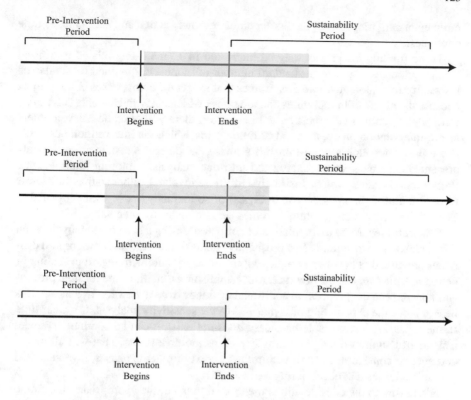

Fig. 5.2 Selecting the appropriate time frame for evaluation

easy to imagine that as its location and size is adjusted and covers different portions of the timeline, different cost and benefit amounts would be included and thereby affect the resulting ROI.

The goal of a sound analysis is not to determine how to draw the shaded area to maximize ROI, but instead it is to capture the most appropriate information to inform decisions that will be made as a result of the analysis. Often, simply extending the shaded area further to the right will increase ROI by including more of the ongoing benefits realized over time, but this may not be appropriate.

Costs needed to create materials, train staff, and establish the framework for collecting feedback and results should be included in calculations of return, regardless of when they occur. Similarly, activities needed to terminate or shut down the initiative if it produces unexpected harms or poor performance as well as to analyze and interpret collected data also represent costs related to the implementation and ideally would be included, too. Benefits, on the other hand, may begin to be realized immediately upon project initiation or may take weeks or months to begin to accumulate. Sometimes, these are due to the nature of the measure of interest (e.g., 30-day readmission, etc.), but other times there is simply a learning curve or natural ramp up of activities where benefits accumulate slowly at first and accelerate as time continues.

Those funding the project may be interested in a time frame related to a fiscal year or calendar year or for a standard number of months or quarters. It can also be instructive to explore multiple time frames that reflect different phases of the project because the nature of the activities and the rate at which costs and benefits accrue can differ significantly. In the most basic breakdown, there will often be a development or pre-intervention phase, a period of time during which the intervention occurred, and a post-intervention or sustainability phase. Whether the results are ultimately presented separately or are aggregated into one analysis, exploring multiple time frames independently can be instructive for those involved, either so that they know what to plan for (in a prospective analysis) or so that they know what happened to assist them with planning future activities (in a retrospective analysis).

Be careful regarding extrapolation or spill-over during a base case analysis, even if it is reasonable to assume. In a prospective analysis, several assumptions and estimates are already likely to be employed; introducing more with regard to scaling or potential spill-over can only detract from establishing a credible and feasible process and may expose the proposal to additional critiques from reviewers. In general, it is best to leave the expounding of "what ifs" to the sensitivity analysis. If a clear time frame reflecting a reasonable base case does not exist, it can be common to select a standard length of time, like a single year, as the time frame. That will allow the audience to consider the return within the context of other expenses, revenues, and general activities that occur during a given year.

In addition to the considerations mentioned thus far, the appropriate time frame for a retrospective analysis will also consider the timing of the analysis; is it occurring a month after the intervention or a year after or more? As with a prospective analysis, it may be instructive to explore multiple time frames, if only to enhance the understanding of how the associated costs and benefits manifested over the course of the intervention. Regarding scope, in a retrospective analysis it may be more reasonable to include some benefits related to spillover or unanticipated opportunities if it is possible to attribute some or all of those outcomes to the project or intervention. You should pursue this cautiously, however, to avoid appearing as though the estimated return is being "padded" or bolstered by unexpected benefits realized in settings or individuals outside of the intended group or setting.

If the inclusion of these benefits is the difference between a positive and negative return (or an acceptable and unacceptable return, however those are defined), it can actually detract from the merits of the intended intervention or may reveal an omission or insufficiency in the original planning or design.

5.2.4 A Base Case Example

Here, we continue the example of a proposed intervention to reduce hospital infections (see Table 5.2), where the calculations will involve both costs and benefits, with necessary estimates and assumptions throughout.

Table 5.4 Example of inputs for cost calculations (hypothetical data)

Cost source	Initial investment	Monthly cost
Development of infection prevention bundle	$2500	$200
Training sessions for staff	$1500	$300
Staff time for training	$4500	$1500
Etc.	(Additional costs)	(Additional costs)
Total	$11,000	$3000

The relevant costs are likely to include expenses for developing any materials and training identified as the method for preventing or reducing infections, as well as the staff time required to attend training and get up to speed. If there are monthly costs for maintenance, they may be related to additional training, maintenance of relevant supplies, oversight and tracking of progress, etc. These amounts will be heavily influenced by the complexity of the materials developed and the number of staff included. Table 5.4 displays a simple template that might be a good start.

The total costs are easily calculated as the total initial investment plus the total monthly cost times the number of months being evaluated. For example, the total cost for the first six months of the program would be:

$$\text{Costs} = \$11,000 + (6 \text{ months} \times \$3000 \text{ per month}) = \$29,000$$

Calculating benefits requires a little more effort and involves a few more inputs. Specifically, the magnitude of the benefits will be a function of several things:

- The number of patients affected
- The baseline (pre-intervention) infection rate
- The effectiveness of the intervention (i.e., the rate reduction)
- The time frame
- The associated cost avoidance for each infection avoided.

Table 5.5 describes these with hypothetical values to illustrate how they would be accrued.

The total fiscal benefit will be simply the number of infections avoided (3.59) multiplied by the cost avoidance associated with an infection.

Note that while there are several calculated values, they are based on multiple assumptions regarding the number of patients, their length of stay, what the infection rate in this population would be if we did not pursue the intervention, and the level of impact the intervention would have. Also note that the chosen time frame affects both the benefits and costs so that a longer time frame would incur more costs but would also accrue more benefits.[1]

---

[1] In interventions where all, or most, of the costs are front-loaded (i.e., prior to or at the beginning of the intervention with little to no ongoing costs), extending the time frame may only impact the amount of benefits accrued. In these situations, one needs to be careful not to manipulate the results simply through a time frame extension.

Table 5.5 Hypothetical values for base case scenario

Input	Type	Notes
200 patients per month	Estimate	Likely based on historical volume
6-month time frame	Scope	A specific choice that could be adjusted
8.5 days at risk per patient	Estimate	Also likely based on historical data regarding average length of stay
10,200 days at risk	Calculation	Multiply the first three rows to get this number
2.2 infections per 1000 patient days	Assumption	Hopefully, this is a value that is known based on historical data; listed as an "assumption" because this is what we are assuming the rate would be during the six-month evaluation period if we did not perform the intervention
22.44 total infections	Calculation	Multiply the days at risk by the assumed infection rate if nothing is done
16% reduction in infection rate	Estimate/assumption	As described earlier in the chapter, this is the rate that was determined to be the most applicable to this situation and thought to be the most reasonable estimate; it assumes that the study from which it was pulled is representative of the proposed project
1.848 infections per 1000 after intervention	Calculation	This represents a 16% reduction from the infection rate of 2.2 per 1000 patient days
18.85 total infections after intervention	Calculation	Multiply days at risk by the reduced infection rate
3.59 fewer infections	Calculation	The difference in the number of infections during this time period

At this point in the process, we should assess the calculated values that are a direct result of the assumptions and estimates that have been employed. Do these calculated values make sense? Are they feasible? If not, then we must re-examine the relevant assumptions and estimates to see what may be driving the calculated values beyond the realm of what is realistic. Often, calculated values are a function of multiple estimates, and while no one estimate is unreasonable, when compounded they produce results that seem unrealistic. In the previous example, the final value of 3.59 fewer infections is a function of the following estimates or assumptions:

- A volume of 200 patients per month
- A time frame of six months
- An estimate of 8.5 days at risk per patient
- A baseline infection rate of 2.2 per 1000 days at risk
- A 16% reduction in the rate of infections.

Changes to any one of these will produce a different base case value for the number of infections avoided. Uncertainty and variability for each of these will compound when they are multiplied together and result in significantly more uncertainty for the final value. A close examination of each of these values will allow those planning the intervention and performing the ROI analysis to make adjustments so that they are comfortable with the final result. As they are currently presented, they allow for a calculation of ROI as long as we establish a dollar value for the cost avoidance of an infection. If we assume that each infection costs, on average, $4500 to treat, including extended days in the hospital, medications, follow-up, etc., then we can calculate the benefits and the resulting ROI assuming we will accrue $29,000 in costs calculated earlier.

$$\text{Benefits} = 3.59 \text{ infections avoided} \times \$4500 \text{ per infection} = \$16,155$$
$$\text{ROI} = (\$16,155 - \$29,000)/\$29,000 \times 100\% = -44.3\%$$
$$\text{BCR} = \$16,155/\$29,000 = 0.557$$

At six months, we expect the ROI to be negative and to have recouped a little over half of our investment. Here is where a calculation of the payback period may be beneficial: The initial costs represent a sizeable portion of the total costs, and our monthly expenditures are more than covered by each additional infection prevented, so we would hope that it is just a matter of time until we begin to see a positive return. However, we expect to see, on average, less than one infection prevented per month while we will continue to incur monthly expenses, so our calculation of payback period is slightly more complicated. Specifically, each additional month after month six we will incur $3000 in costs and expect to reduce infections by an average of $3.59/6 = 0.598$ infections per month, which equates to $0.598 \times \$4500 = \$2693$ per month. Therefore, the monthly benefit we expect to realize is less than the monthly cost, meaning that given current values, this intervention will never produce a positive ROI.

At this point, we should consider whether these results reflect an acceptable return. While the expected improvement represents a significant relative reduction (16%, by assumption), in real terms and in monetary terms, it is too small to demonstrate a sufficient financial return for the project. Here, again, we encounter an example of why we should perform the prospective ROI analysis while the quality improvement activities are still being planned and developed. In this case and using the provided estimates, we can adjust certain assumptions or estimates, such as the proposed time

Table 5.6 Determining the needed efficiency for an initial cost of $18,000 plus monthly costs   of $3000 if each infection avoided produces $4500 in benefits (hypothetical data)

Percent reduction	Number of infections avoided per month	Monthly savings	Payback period
16% (Base case)	0.598	−$307	Never
20%	0.75	$375	48 months
27%	1.0	$1500	12 months
33%	1.25	$2625	6.9 months

frame or the underlying infection rate, to determine what would be necessary to produce a level of improvement that is likely to result in a financial gain. That is, we know, or are assuming, the cost-avoidance associated with each infection avoided.

Given our proposed costs, we can determine that we need to avoid at least seven infections to cover our costs in the first six months. Or, we can understand that on a monthly basis we need to achieve benefits that exceed our monthly costs of $3000 in order to eventually recoup our investment. Given that each infection avoided earns us $4500 in benefits, we can figure out how many infections we would need to avoid each month on average to produce a reasonable payback period (Table 5.6).

For example, we can see that avoiding 0.75 infections per month (a 20% reduction from baseline) would produce a payback period of four years; avoiding a full infection per month would reduce the payback period to one year. We can also work backward to figure out how many infections we need to avoid to achieve a certain payback period. For example, if we would be satisfied with a payback period of 24 months, then we can calculate the total costs: $18,000 + (24 months × $3000) = $90,000. That equates to $90,000/$4500 = 20 total infections avoided, or an average of 20/24 = 0.83 per month. These types of explorations are helpful to determine how to adjust the proposed activities or when to decide that the goal is not feasible and abandon the intervention until a financially feasible one can be developed.

As we can see, when we have both initial costs and recurring costs, this exercise is more complicated than if costs were limited to those for the development and start of the initiative. Extensions in the time frame in order to accrue more benefits in the form of avoided infections also carry with them additional costs to maintain the program. Obviously, in a retrospective analysis, this exercise is moot. The observed costs and benefits are established, and the base case simply presents that information as accurately as possible. In a prospective analysis, however, this type of exploration allows for potential adjustments to the planned activities. If and when a feasible base case is established, we must next explore and demonstrate how the inherent uncertainty and variability in the intervention could produce different returns.

5.3 Sensitivity Analysis

5.3.1 General Considerations for the Sensitivity Analysis

Typically, a sensitivity analysis for a prospective analysis includes, at a minimum, best- (or better-) and worst- (or worse-) case scenarios, although there may be circumstances that warrant an exploration of even more possible outcomes, as we will see. Constructing the best- and worst-case scenarios is as much an art as it is a science. This is because accurately demonstrating the potential for variability and the subsequent impact are the essence of the exercise, but doing so credibly requires weaving together possibilities, assumptions, and expectations.

For a retrospective analysis, the sensitivity analysis may be more nuanced. In all likelihood, the realized return is a fixed and determined value. Exploring what *could have* happened if certain values had been different or what *might* happen in the future or in different settings or populations can quickly devolve into what appears as a rationalization of a poor return or unreasonable fantasies of "what might have been." But, make no mistake, to understand the true drivers of costs and benefits it is responsible and necessary to explore aspects where observed results (e.g., recruitment, effectiveness, the magnitude of certain costs or benefits) differed significantly from what was anticipated. This not only helps to identify and explain why the realized return was higher or lower than originally proposed, it also provides the reader with a full picture of what occurred and how the activities translate into value.

5.3.2 Creating Best- and Worst-Case Scenarios

Establishing a reasonable spread of best- (or better-) and worst- (or worse-) case scenarios in a prospective analysis necessitates considerations of the assumptions being made, the risks involved, and any possible alternatives or contingency. Depending on the situation and the setting, there may be assumptions being made regarding patient recruitment and participation, the effectiveness of the intervention, or the ability to implement it in the speed and thoroughness needed to achieve the desired results. Whether to vary these items in tandem or individually may depend on the severity of their resulting impact and the seriousness of the consequences if the base case estimate is inaccurate.

For example, if a key driver of the realized return is achieving a certain effectiveness in the intervention (which is also a key component of demonstrating improvements in quality), it may be reasonable to explore the sensitivity of just that one value while holding all of the other values constant. This can directly speak to the robustness of the intervention, because if it is possible to demonstrate that the intervention is likely to produce a positive, or acceptable, return either universally or in all but

Table 5.7 Example of how
sensitivity analysis   can
demonstrate project
robustness (hypothetical data)

Scenario explored	Resulting ROI (%)
Effectiveness is 20% higher than anticipated	45
Effectiveness is 10% higher than anticipated	34
Effectiveness is as anticipated	23
Effectiveness is 10% lower than anticipated	13
Effectiveness is 20% lower than anticipated	5

the worst-case scenarios, it can be a powerful argument for the financial viability of pursuing the project (see Table 5.7 for how this could play out).

In the example in Table 5.7, the results demonstrate that even if the intervention performs significantly worse than anticipated, the resulting ROI is likely to be positive. This can go a long way toward convincing a prospective funder that the project is a good investment. And frankly, if the actual effectiveness ends up being more than 20% lower than anticipated, one could argue there are bigger problems with how the intervention was planned and executed than the expected ROI.

There may also be assumptions that are contingent upon circumstances outside of the control of those conducting the intervention. Recruitment and participation can be influenced by a number of factors, as can the time required to collect and analyze data. Anyone who has participated in this type of design can attest to the fact that these, and other aspects, are notoriously difficult to predict with accuracy.[2] Best practice is to be honest about what happens if one or more key drivers of the project's success completely implode or disintegrate. This exercise is as much for those proposing the project as it is for those who are being solicited for funding. Exploring the possible uncertainties and their implications allow those designing the intervention to understand where challenges may be encountered and identify how they will be addressed. If after identifying the major potential pitfalls you can show how the intervention can remain effective and still produce a reasonable return, you will have gone a long way toward ensuring some level of success and in turn demonstrating the merit of the initiative or intervention.

5.3.3   Identifying What to Vary in the Sensitivity Analysis

Knowing what to vary and how to vary it is essential for a thorough sensitivity analysis. Particularly in a prospective analysis, numerous assumptions and estimates

---

[2]Here, too, it is worthwhile to point out that if the outcome measure or value measure of interest is also subject to influence from circumstances outside of your control, that may impede your ability to demonstrate value, even when value is generated.

are made, some of which may be vital for the success of the intervention and to demonstrate financial viability. Varying them individually as well as together can help paint a picture of the possible outcomes to allow all involved to assess the risk and determine how best to proceed. Retrospectively, knowing which estimates to vary and how much to vary them can help identify what factors were the main drivers for the financial success or failure of the intervention and how best to structure future endeavors to ensure an acceptable return.

5.3.3.1 Varying Recruitment and Participation

The level of expected recruitment and participation is a key component of prospective analyses to adjust. In addition to the difficulty of accurately estimating what is reasonable, uncontrollable factors could influence the ability to recruit and qualify the necessary number of participants. As stated previously, part of the goal of this type of exercise is to determine which assumptions are robust to variability and which are not. This will allow you to determine which are the most important ones you should ensure you achieve (i.e., deserve the most resources) and allow the reader to gain a level of confidence with the feasibility and viability of the economic benefits of your proposed intervention. Keep in mind that in addition to recruitment for the start of the intervention, there are also issues related to attrition, lost-to-follow-up, or the need to later exclude participants who are no longer eligible for a variety of reasons.

5.3.3.2 Varying the Effectiveness of the Intervention or Level of Improvement

The effectiveness of the intervention will often be the key component that determines the overall success of the project. Before beginning you should come up with some reasonable estimate of how much quality can be expected to improve *during the period of time when it will be evaluated.* Not all components of quality will experience a linear or immediate shift; often improvement occurs gradually and follows a nonlinear path that reflects things like steep learning curves, gradual acceptance or understanding of changes, or a delay in when results can be observed. Therefore, several things may influence the impact of the effectiveness of the intervention, including the intensity with which the intervention can be implemented and the level of personal "buy-in" from staff and participants required to produce and sustain change.

In Fig. 5.3, we see three examples of patterns of how benefits may accrue over the same six-month period. The example in the top row demonstrates a situation where perhaps there is a learning curve, so that benefits increase each month as staff learns how to incorporate a new process or as a new system is slowly diffused to more and more patients. In the second row, this pattern reflects a situation where there is a large benefit in the first two months, and after that benefits drop off significantly. The bottom row displays a situation where the intervention produces a consistent benefit

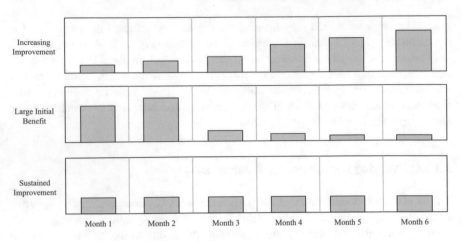

Fig. 5.3 Examples of different patterns of benefit accrual

each month. When deciding how to vary the effectiveness of the intervention and the level of improvement, consider not only the absolute amount but what that may mean in light of what the pattern of benefit accrual is likely to look like.

You must examine the range of estimates being considered in light of the specific situation. In the example presented previously, there was noticeable variability in the achieved reduction in infections (10–40% reduction) from the published literature of similar interventions. An appropriate sensitivity analysis would explore reasons for this large gap and assess what portion of this range is reasonable to apply to the best-case and worst-case scenarios of the project. As previously mentioned, perhaps it is not reasonable to apply the 40% estimate to your intervention; you may instead select one that is slightly lower.

Variations in the effectiveness may affect the magnitude of realized benefits but may also influence costs or the desired time frame (e.g., perhaps you determine that four training sessions are required instead of three).

5.3.3.3 Varying Associated Benefits

There may be variability in how improvements in quality translate into monetary benefits, either in the form of cost savings, cost avoidance, or revenue gains. This is common for measures of quality that reflect reductions in utilization or adverse health events. For example, the estimates one may have compiled regarding the cost associated with a serious fall will most likely be averages. The actual cost savings may be higher or lower due to differences between characteristics of the current project and those where the estimates were pulled from, or they may vary simply because averages fail to encompass the full breadth of what can occur (i.e., natural variability). Understanding statistical variability, relative likelihood, and the influence of rare events can help determine the most appropriate values to examine

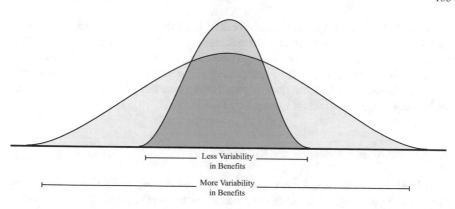

Fig. 5.4 Understanding that variability can inform how to vary values for the sensitivity analysis

during a sensitivity analysis. If there is more inherent variability in the associated benefits (Fig. 5.4), then it would be prudent to explore a wider range in the sensitivity analysis than would be necessary if there was less variability.

5.3.3.4 Varying the Time Frame (Short-Term vs. Long-Term)

Under certain circumstances, varying the time frame can produce noticeable changes in the realized financial return of a project. Part of the decision regarding the applicable time frame is related to the immediate goal and acceptable level of risk: Namely, is a short-term loss acceptable if there is likely to be a long-term gain? Certain quality outcomes may become more or less common over time; and sometimes there can be a cumulative effect of the intervention (especially those that employ multiple simultaneous or sequential strategies). In these cases, extending the time frame disproportionally increases the realized benefits (i.e., doubling the length of the time frame during which you evaluate costs and benefits more than doubles the realized benefits). Regardless of what is deemed to be the most appropriate for the given situation, these kinds of explorations are useful in helping us understand the dynamics of how costs and benefits accrue over time.

As already mentioned, one may believe that a characteristic of a successful quality improvement intervention is that it is sustainable long after the intervention has ended. Therefore, a successful intervention can often be shown to eventually produce a positive return as long as the time frame for evaluation can be reasonably extended until accumulative benefits exceed the initial investment plus on-going costs. Selecting the appropriate time frames for the sensitivity analysis requires the discipline to not overreach or be unreasonably optimistic.

Remember that the further into the future you project, the more unanticipated changes can occur which may derail or at least alter the benefits associated with an intervention from a fixed point in time. As a reasonable alternative, reporting how different metrics like the payback period behave when other factors are varied can provide the necessary context for a reader. For example, if you can demonstrate that varying prevalence rates and the effectiveness of your intervention result in the payback period potentially ranging from one year to three years, it may not be necessary to calculate the ROI at one year or three years (in addition to your base case). You already know from the other analyses under what circumstances the ROI will be 0% at those individual time points (Table 5.8).

5.3.3.5 Example of Sensitivity Analysis

Revisiting the infection reduction example and the corresponding table describing the estimates, assumptions, and calculations, one can quickly identify all of the values that could be varied, either individually or simultaneously. Varying the effectiveness from the base case value of 16% would likely be prudent, especially given the variability seen in the estimates from the literature. But, other values could also impact ROI, including the number of patients affected and their average length of stay. Both of these factors influence the total time at risk. Additionally, alternative time frames will also alter the total time at risk, which will impact the number of infections avoided and therefore the associated monetary benefit.

A full sensitivity analysis would examine each one of these variations individually to understand how they each impact the result, in addition to examining what happens when they all vary simultaneously. However, for illustration purposes, we can calculate changes in benefits and ROI for both the worst- and best-case scenarios.

Table 5.10 repeats the base case calculation from Table 5.5 (assuming costs of $29,000) and uses the inputs from Table 5.9 to calculate the best- and worse-case scenarios.

This analysis shows us that even under the best conditions this intervention is likely to produce a financial loss after six months. Together with the base case analysis,

Table 5.8 Common attributes varied during sensitivity analyses

Attribute
Recruitment and participation
Intervention effectiveness or level of improvement
Associated benefits
Time frame

Table 5.9 Hypothetical best- and worse-case scenarios

Inputs to vary	Base case value	Values for sensitivity analysis
Volume per month	200 patients	180–220
Baseline infection rate	2.2 per 1000 patient days	1.8–2.6
Intervention effectiveness	16% reduction	12–20%

Table 5.10 Hypothetical sensitivity analysis

Inputs	Base case	Worst-case	Best-case
Volume per month	200	180	220
Total days at risk	10,200	9180	11,220
Baseline infection rate per 1000 patient days	2.2	1.8	2.6
Baseline infections (*Row* 2 × *Row* 3)	22.44	16.52	29.17
Relative reduction in infection rate	16%	12%	20%
Total infections avoided (*Row* 4 × *Row* 5)	3.59	1.98	5.83
Associated benefits (*Row* 6 × $4500)	$16,155	$8923	$26,255
ROI (*Row* 7 − $29,000)/$29,000 × 100%)	−44.3%	−69.2%	−9.5%

this provides a more complete picture of the likely return because of the inherent variability in the assumptions and estimates used, and the fact that the financial return is a function of all of them.

5.3.3.6 A Final Caution

It may be necessary to extend the sensitivity analysis to occasionally use estimates that lie outside of the range of those previously experienced or observed. However, doing so requires a credible justification, *especially* if the estimate represents an improvement over what has previously been realized. Even best-case scenarios need to be viewed as feasible and credible. For example, if published studies report a range of post-intervention rates of post-operative infections from 4 to 12% and observed results demonstrate a rate of 5%, this does not mean that sensitivity analyses cannot explore what would happen if the rate could be reduced to, say, 3%. The reasonableness of this extension would depend on the situation and how far past the known boundaries it attempts to go.

When performing sensitivity analyses, the goal is to provide a full picture so that the reader understands how the different assumptions impact the potential costs and benefits. We also do this to (hopefully) demonstrate that our intervention is likely to result in a positive return even if not everything goes to plan. However, every assumption we make is another leap of faith the reader is asked to take, and we must take care not to ask them to leap too far too many times or they may begin to feel shaky about our project. In short, we must be creative, but not confusing; practice optimism, but also prudence.

5.3.4 Adding in Non-MMA Benefits

As previously mentioned, when establishing the base case, it is often best to limit ourselves to MMA benefits. In the sensitivity analysis, however, it is reasonable to prudently add them into further explore the possible realized return. Obviously, if benefits are strictly not measurable nor monetizable, their inclusion may be in concept alone, or through the language contained in the interpretation, either written or spoken. How this is achieved will depend on the type of benefit and how much information is available that may allow you to infer the potential value.

For example, it may only be possible to speak in terms of ranges or orders of magnitude. However, it may also be possible to leverage information from other sources. A statement such as, "While we didn't measure the impact on medication adherence, a similar study done at XYZ University found that this type of intervention increased adherence by 20%, resulting in 30% fewer avoidable health encounters for uncontrolled hypertension. If this occurred in our study, it would represent more than 250 additional dollars of benefit per patient per month in the way of attributable reduced utilization."

Benefits that are measurable and monetizable but not directly attributable, in whole or in part, may be discussed with caution. They key concern for these measures is the potential to mislead the reader or appear to make too far a leap from the sturdy standing of the base case. Clarity and transparency are paramount; if the reader or audience senses even a hint of hand-waving, it can result in serious demerits regarding the credibility afforded the overall proposal. There is a risk in unintentionally conveying a notion that without such leaps of faith the project will be in danger of producing an inadequate return. As the author or presenter, the level of confidence you project regarding the merits of the project and ROI greatly impact your ability to influence or convince.

5.3.5 Adding Other Forms of Value

Inevitably, when performing ROI analyses, there will be outcomes and results that produce value for some parties that are simply not captured by financial means. A common question is when, if ever, it is reasonable to include these types of value. For example, when performing a retrospective analysis on a CMS-funded project for improving nursing home care, those running the analysis will want to show the return on the original investment realized through lower utilization and fewer adverse events that translate into fewer CMS-paid reimbursements; but those who performed the intervention will want to also laud the improvements in patient experiences, staff satisfaction, and the general excitement and sense of accomplishment shared by those involved. There may even be value in terms of overall health, quality of life, or additional gains in years lived. Including these or other benefits or value-adds can be effective and certainly merit mention, although the formal ROI analysis may not be the most appropriate location. However, as mentioned several times throughout this text, ROI is but one piece of a larger conversation about value, which is often presented in tandem with improvements in quality or efficiency.

Those preparing the summary report will need to determine which of the additional forms of value should be added and where; some argue that as part of the value conversation they are appropriate to include in some sensitivity analysis to provide a

Table 5.11 Examples of benefits that are often not MMA

Benefit	Reason
Patient experience	Difficult to monetize
Staff satisfaction	Difficult to monetize
Facility brand or reputation	Difficult to measure and monetize
Reduced caregiver burden	Difficult to monetize and attribute
Improved communication	Difficult to measure and monetize

full picture. Others argue that diluting the quantifiable and measurable fiscal impact with less tangible or indirect benefits muddies the waters, and that a ROI analysis is more effective if it is limited to benefits that are more acutely and precisely identifiable (Table 5.11).

5.4 Uncertainty and Alternatives

For both base case and sensitivity analyses, you must acknowledge uncertainty associated with any estimates or assumptions, and to examine how the possible variability from this uncertainty could, or did, affect the realized results. This entire exercise is about being transparent, but it also provides useful feedback for those performing the analyses by forcing an examination of all aspects of the intervention and its potential costs and benefits.

5.4.1 Identifying Key Assumptions

The first step in addressing uncertainty is to identify the assumptions and estimates that have been made, especially those related to key components and determinants of project success. In a prospective analysis, these will include estimates related to participation or recruitment, the ability to implement the intervention, the impact of the intervention, its sustainability, and the degree to which key metrics can be measured, monetized, and attributed to the quality improvement activities. Fewer assumptions are employed in a retrospective analysis, and therefore, not all of these may be applicable retrospectively (Table 5.12).

Table 5.12 Common key assumptions

Assumption
Participation or recruitment
Ability to implement intervention (feasibility and intensity)
Impact of intervention (effectiveness)
Sustainability of improvement
Ability to measure, monetize, and attribute benefits to intervention

5.4.1.1 Assumptions Regarding Participation or Recruitment

Obviously, the number of patients, providers, and/or facilities involved in the intervention will have a large effect on the costs of implementing the project (including potentially data collection, if they involve resource-intense methods like chart abstraction or one-on-one interviews) as well as the potential benefits. Typically, recruitment costs will be structured as some fixed cost plus a variable amount depending on the scope and breadth of recruitment activities. However, benefits are often realized on a per-person basis, so lower participation or slower recruitments reduce potential benefits faster than they reduce costs. When determining what to vary, consider the assumptions being made regarding the ability to identify, reach, and qualify participants. These assumptions may relate to the time and effort needed to recruit a certain number, or they may concern the number who will participate and the frequency with which they will drop out or end their enrollment.

5.4.1.2 Assumptions Regarding the Ability to Implement the Intervention

Often, assumptions are made regarding how quickly training can be performed or how long a new workflow will take to be fully integrated. Consider which assumptions may be subject to more or less uncertainty and whether there are any that are key to the success of the project. Then, identify what potential challenges could emerge and what kind of impact they may have. If leveraging a new technology, for example, there can be unforeseen barriers to incorporating it into existing systems and unanticipated difficulties in usability or functionality that are unique to the setting or situation. The ability to apply the new techniques, systems, or technologies in the time frame allowed and with the intended intensity and penetration will directly affect the intervention's effectiveness and ultimately value.

5.4.1.3 Assumptions Regarding the Impact of the Intervention

Even if an intervention is implemented with the appropriate speed and efficiency, sometimes the impact it has on the desired outcomes differs from what was originally expected. Realized value is derived from improvements in quality, so the impact of the intervention is a key driver of how much value is realized. Any time there is an expectation of effectiveness, it should always be included in the sensitivity analyses to determine how much variability the project can withstand and still be deemed a success.

5.4.1.4 Assumptions Regarding Sustainability

Most agree that a successful quality improvement intervention not only evokes change but can be successfully sustained without significant additional burdens on costs or resources. Similarly, often benefits are assumed to accumulate over time— if the achieved improvement deteriorates over time, so will the associated benefits with that initial improvement. The rate at which benefits accumulate, the necessity of ongoing investments in time or resources, and the possibility that staff turnover or fading excitement for the intervention could reduce long-term benefits are all aspects that could be explored.

5.4.1.5 Assumptions Regarding the Ability to Measure, Monetize, and Attribute to the Intervention

In some circumstances, there may be reasons why there is some level of uncertainty associated with the ability to measure key metrics, to translate them into monetary benefits, or to fully attribute benefits to the intervention. One example may include primary data collection activities that take longer than anticipated, resulting in less data collection (e.g., chart abstraction takes twice as long as it should, depleting the budget for data collection before the desired sample size is achieved). In another situation, perhaps an unanticipated change in policy or practice guidelines occurred during the intervention, confounding the results so that it is difficult to know how much of the observed improvement is due to the intervention versus the new policy or guidelines.

5.4.2 Assessing How Much Key Assumptions Could Vary

Once the key assumptions and estimates have been identified, the next step is to establish which ones are the most uncertain or have the greatest possible variability. The level of uncertainty or variability may be driven by the quality of evidence that supports their value or the range of identified estimates. That is, perhaps it was difficult to identify sources that provided strong evidence or that closely resembled the proposed intervention in a meaningful way so that there is uncertainty regarding how applicable those estimates will be to the proposed situation. Or, perhaps there was a wide variety of possible estimates identified (multiple similar studies that produced varying results, etc.), so that there may be several estimates that may seem reasonable, and there is no clear indication of which might be the most accurate. In these cases, it is prudent to explore a wider variety of possibilities than if there was more certainty in the estimated values.

5.4.3 Estimating the Potential Impact of Assumptions and Estimates

Key assumptions or estimates are often identified as such because of the potential impact they can have on the observed results. For example, the level of effectiveness of the intervention will obviously have huge implications for the amount of improvement seen in quality and therefore the amount of value that is realized. For assumptions that hold significant influence over the project's outcome, even small deviations from the estimated quantities of these key assumptions can have major implications on the results of the impact; therefore, the impact of all key assumptions should be explored.

However, if assumptions or estimates involve a lot of uncertainty or potential variability, the impact can be even more dramatic. If a worst-case scenario occurs with one of these estimates, will it completely sink the project? Would the other estimates have to compensate so much as to make a positive return completely unlikely? Such values deserve special consideration, or at a minimum should be called out as critical to the success of the project. In addition to these questions, you may also want to consider whether there will be any compounding effects if multiple assumptions or estimates simultaneously underperform or underdeliver; if recruitment is lower than anticipated *and* the intervention is not as effective as hoped, consider what compounded impact that could have on the realized return.

In addition to examining how variability can affect the realized return for the chosen perspective, consider as well if there may be implications for the costs or benefits realized by other perspectives. For example, if the intervention cannot be implemented as quickly or intensely as planned, could it impose additional costs on participating sites and providers that have to spend more time and resources on the intervention than originally planned, in addition to potentially reducing the return realized by those funding the project? If so, then sensitivity analyses should explore how variability may impact those who have agreed, or will be asked, to participate and what the implications of those impacts may be.

5.4.4 Exploring Alternatives to Assumptions

In addition to exploring all of the potential ramifications associated with the uncertainty and variability in the project, you should offer possible alternatives that would address and hopefully mitigate the effects. That is, a project that is unlikely to produce a positive return if the targeted enrollment is not achieved will likely be less appealing to those being asked to take on the risk associated with providing funding. Projects shown to be more robust to variability by having specific contingency plans are more likely to be funded. These alternatives are put in place to reduce the perceived risk of pursuing the opportunity and can go a long way toward demonstrating the necessary knowledge and acumen to handle unforeseen circumstances to reviewers. During this process, if the risk of disastrous results is relatively high and there are no feasible alternatives, it may be necessary to re-evaluate the intervention itself to determine whether it can be pursued or adjusted to reduce some of the uncertainty or variability.

In a prospective analysis, when providing alternatives to mitigate potential variation, you must distinguish which scenarios are within your control and which ones are not. For example, if recruitment at the specified sites (which may be in your control) occurs more slowly than anticipated, perhaps there are options to dedicate more resources to recruiting participants or even to add a site to jumpstart recruitment. If, however, there are rumors of major policy changes, it may not be possible to propose an adequate contingency given that they are completely out of your control.

In a retrospective analysis, an exploration of alternatives will involve an evaluation of where the values and results observed during the course of the intervention differed from the original estimates, often to determine where the driving forces were and why they occurred. Which assumptions were accurate or inaccurate, and how did they affect the return?

It may also be prudent to explore what would have happened if certain key assumptions that turned out to be inaccurate had been closer to what was originally estimated. Perhaps there were unanticipated circumstances that are unlikely to occur again. Some of the benefit provided by this exercise for a retrospective analysis will be to place the observed results in a greater context of what was expected, but it can also serve to inform future projects. It is appropriate to identify key lessons learned and how you would revise certain estimates if you were to repeat the intervention. Also of interest will be how the observed process and results affect your ability to generalize the return to other settings or situations, if that is your goal.

5.5 Summary

The base case and sensitivity analyses are at the heart of any ROI analysis, whether it be prospective or retrospective. Properly compiling costs and benefits and calculating the appropriate measures allows for a thorough assessment of the merits and performance of the associated quality improvement activities. Understanding how to approach various scenarios and acknowledge and explore the relevant uncertainty contribute to a full picture of what did or can occur.

5.6   Key Concepts

- What are included in base case and sensitivity analyses will differ depending on whether the analysis is prospective or retrospective; a prospective analysis will attempt to show what is likely to happen and quantify the uncertainty inherent in a project that has not yet occurred, while a retrospective analysis will present what happened and explore variability to identify key drivers of costs and benefits.
- In a prospective analysis, the base case should include the most relevant and credible estimates, not necessarily the most conservative ones.
- It is good practice to limit the base case benefits to those that are measurable, monetizable, and directly attributable to the intervention; other benefits may be introduced in the sensitivity analysis.
- The selected scope (including the time frame) and perspective can significantly affect the magnitude of the costs and benefits included in the analysis and should be chosen carefully.
- The sensitivity analysis allows for an exploration of how variability and uncertainty affect the realized return and place the base case results in a larger context.
- Prospectively, the sensitivity analysis often provides best- and worst-case scenarios so that the value of the intended activities can be evaluated in light of what might happen.
- Retrospectively, the sensitivity analysis can help determine key drivers of realized return, attempt to estimate what could have happened under different circumstances, and provide valuable information that can be used to plan future interventions.
- Typically, several aspects of the analysis can be varied during the sensitivity analysis and explored either individually or together; selecting what to vary and how much to vary them will depend on the situation, the intended goals of the analysis, and the available information.

Chapter 6
Interpretation and Presentation

6.1 Exploring the Background and Project Motivation

As with any good report or presentation, appropriately setting the stage for the intended audience is paramount to effectively communicating the results and interpretation. There are several keys to providing the appropriate amount of information and lead-in so that your reader or audience can understand what follows. This is a balancing act: Too little information will leave them uncertain or unable to follow your later logic; too much information can either bore them or overload them so that they are unable to focus or process the key points.

Appropriately setting up the presentation of any type of results can be a challenge, in part because as project participants, we are immersed in every detail and iteration and can lose sight of how someone newly learning of the situation will interpret the information we provide. There are dozens of ways one could effectively accomplish the task of preparing the reader or listener for what is to come, but in my experience, a few methods can help if you struggle with this process.

6.1.1 Methods for Providing Appropriate Background

6.1.1.1 Describing the Motivation

Origin Story: The first method can be referred to as the "origin story." This technique involves taking the reader or listener through the steps that led to the initiation of the project. This typically begins by describing some challenge or issue and describing why it was important to address it. The next step is to lay out the intermediate steps (excluding what is either not directly relevant or not totally necessary) and what you hoped this project would accomplish. By doing this, you allow your intended audience to share the experience with you a bit and to see things from your point of view, and hopefully, they will understand the motivation and goals of the project.

© Springer Nature Switzerland AG 2020
C. A. Solid, *Return on Investment for Healthcare Quality Improvement*,
https://doi.org/10.1007/978-3-030-46478-3_6

An example is presented in Chap. 7 as part of the hypothetical scenario of attempting to reduce serious falls in nursing homes:

> Over the last several years we have had the great privilege of working with several nursing homes (NHs) in our local community and surrounding region. In all, we have partnered at various times with six individual NHs on various projects to improve the quality of care for residents. During this time, we have gotten to know both administrators and the dedicated staff of these facilities and have listened when they have confided in us regarding aspects of quality that they feel are important and achievable. Almost universally, one of the quality topics that that administrators and staff bring up is that of patient falls. As described elsewhere in this proposal, our preliminary work with two NHs produced encouraging results in terms of the reduction in falls that require medical attention ("serious falls"), and we have come to believe that a more widespread effort can be effective and economically feasible. By leveraging proven tools to reduce serious falls, we feel strongly that we can have significant impact on the quality of NH resident care that will produce a net financial benefit for CMS through a reduction in healthcare utilization associated with serious falls.

The danger of this method is its tendency to become an epic instead of a brief story. As integral players in this drama, we have emotional sentiments to certain plot points along the way and will tend to include them, even if they are not necessary for the audience. There is a fine line: Countering the desire to ensure that the audience understands the motivation behind the project, which often involves things that evoke emotions (improving care for patients, reducing caregiver burden, etc.), is the possibility of going too far or assuming too much about what the audience may perceive about the importance of the issue we have chosen to address. Some ways to ensure that the narrative is a reasonable length and includes only appropriate elements include:

- Have a neutral party read it and ask him or her to ruthlessly suggest cuts to material they do not feel is necessary. You probably will not end up cutting everything that is suggested, but it will likely slim down the narrative significantly and may even prompt you to reframe or abbreviate certain points.
- Think of it as a story or movie plot and only include things that "move the story forward." Maybe you were sidelined at some point during the planning stage because another project required your full attention for some period of time. It is likely that was a significant point of stress for you and that you experienced enormous relief when you were able to return to planning, but it may not warrant any mention at all in setting up the situation.

When done well, the "origin story" method of presenting the background can be an effective way to clearly enumerate all of the motivating factors behind the project and allow the reader to fully understand its implications if successful.

Starting with the end in mind ("desired future state"): This method begins by describing what you hope to accomplish. This may be appropriate in situations where the motivation is obvious (e.g., a federal agency tasked you with improving care in a certain area, giving you no choice) or can be effective in retrospective analyses to let your audience "look back" from the current state.

The Collaborative Care Model example in Chap. 7 includes a background section that uses this method:

Twenty-four months ago we implemented a collaborative care program intended to improve care for patients with multiple chronic conditions (such as diabetes, cardiovascular disease, depression, etc.) and provide the necessary education and support for them and their informal caregivers. Our facility cares for roughly 250 patients per year who have two or more of the targeted conditions, and historically the costs to care for each patient have ranged from $15,000 to $20,000 annually or between $3.75 million and $5 million in the aggregate (in 2019 dollars).

After considerable time and effort to develop the program and determine how to implement it within our system, we now have the benefit of examining two years of real costs and benefits to evaluate the financial viability of this program for continued use.

Certainly, there are other methods for providing the necessary background and motivation for the project and the ROI analysis. In general, whatever method is employed, demonstrating the need and potential benefit of a successful intervention is crucial for framing the subsequent exploration into associated costs and benefits.

6.1.1.2 Identifying the Demand for an Improvement

Just because there is an opportunity for improvement does not mean that there is universal demand for it to be addressed. This may be counterintuitive, but the point here is not that there might be individuals actively pushing against improving care, but that unless you can identify, or secure, true demand, you may struggle to obtain the buy-in from staff or the commitment of necessary resources from administrators or key stakeholders.

Most of the estimates you will base your ROI calculations on in a prospective analysis assume a certain level of effort, time, and resources will be available and employed to try to improve care. Nothing will derail an intervention faster than the discovery that the administration does not consider it a priority, or that fellow staff do not believe it to be necessary or that the chosen intervention is the correct one. The process of identifying or securing demand might simply be a matter of getting verbal or written commitment from the appropriate individuals and having contingencies in place if those commitments are not met.

6.1.1.3 Describing Aims and Defining Concepts

In addition to providing insight into the project motivation, the appropriate background also requires that the aims of the project are clearly articulated and that any necessary definitions are presented and discussed. One should never assume that the reader already knows or understands the aims; nor should one leave the reader to discover the aims on her own through the context of the remaining analysis. Clearly defining the aims at the outset allows for a focused evaluation of the merits of the project to achieve those aims.

Part of this process will be to define key terms. This ensures that those who read or view the subsequent analysis have the same understanding of what the calculated values represent and can follow the logic of the interpretation. When describing the aims under the auspice of the inherent vagaries of terms like "value" and "return," you should specifically describe what you hope to (or had hoped to) accomplish. This may involve real quantities: "We wanted to determine how to keep costs under $35,000 and achieve a ROI of at least 20%," or it may involve more general statements: "We want to demonstrate that in addition to improving care quality, this project will produce an acceptable return for the funding agency."

When more general statements are used, like in the latter example, it becomes necessary to clearly define thresholds so that there are targets and benchmarks to which the projected or observed results can be compared during the evaluation. In addition, this is the time to discuss what would constitute an acceptable ROI. As mentioned previously and described later in this chapter, there is no standard for what is acceptable for quality improvement, and there may be instances when a cost-neutral project or one that produces a slightly negative financial return would be acceptable if there are concurrent improvements in quality. Therefore, this discussion is really about providing the appropriate context through a discussion of alternative activities, similar interventions, or links to other types of investments that allow the reader or audience to understand why a particular ROI is or is not acceptable for the given situation.

Also note that because ROI is closely tied to the time frame, discussions that propose what would be an acceptable ROI can only occur while also describing the time frame: "We believe that a return of at least 10% over the first year would be sufficient to justify this investment…," for example (Table 6.1).

If you fail to define what constitutes an acceptable ROI, for example, you will struggle to place your results into any sort of context and will instead muddy the interpretation of whether the predicted or realized ROI is "good" or "bad" or something in between. For example, the achievement of a ROI of 8% can only be interpreted in light of the larger context: What was the motivation for the project, what have previous projects produced, what would alternative investments produce, what were you expecting given the topic, the setting, the patient population, and the constraints?

If you do not provide any context, your audience will evaluate your ROI using whatever information they have available, either from their experiences, what they have read or seen elsewhere, or perhaps something else. Effectively weaving the financial results into the context of the overall value associated with the project anchors the subsequent results in real terms as they apply to practical considerations and constraints that payers, providers, and administrators face.

Table 6.1 Steps involved in providing the appropriate background

Steps
Describe the motivation for the project and the demand for a solution
Describe the aims of the intervention
Define terms and key concepts
Provide some context for what represents an acceptable return

6.2 Interpreting ROI Analysis Results

As mentioned, the scope and perspective of the analysis are crucial aspects to consider and should be defined as part of any introduction to ROI interpretation. Most likely, discussing aspects of the scope and perspective will naturally fit throughout the introductory portion. For example, after describing the desired future state of the hospital's administration and those concerned with the long-term financial viability of the facility, it is natural to describe how the analysis will be performed from the perspective of the hospital administration. Similarly, after detailing challenges your providers have experienced trying to provide effective collaborative care for patients and their family caregivers, it is natural to describe the type of patients and families who will be, or were, included in the project's scope (Fig. 6.1).

Interpreting your results will depend on the context within which you carry out the project or intervention and the specifics of that situation. However, each calculated metric of your results has a specific interpretation to consider. These interpretations of different metrics will naturally overlap, and when presented together, they will provide a comprehensive picture of the project, its impact, and its implications. But, before we can examine how the interpretations compliment and compound each other, we will first need to explore interpretations of several metrics individually.

6.2.1 Interpreting ROI Values

The definition used for ROI in this text produces a percentage. However, the range of possible values is not limited to 0–100%. In fact, there is really no theoretical limit for its value. The only inherent threshold in this metric is 0%, which represents the break-even point: Less than 0% (negative percentages) reflect situations where the costs exceed the benefits (at least during the time frame specified for the calculation), and greater than 0% (positive percentages) reflect the opposite situation. Obviously, a positive return is the desired outcome, but before we explore in more depth what positive values of ROI might constitute "good" or "acceptable" levels, we should explore what it means to achieve the break-even point where ROI is 0%.

When ROI is 0%, this represents a cost-neutral situation. That is, not performing the intervention results in the same net benefit as performing the intervention, and financially you are just as well off whether you implement the

Fig. 6.1 Step 4 in the ROI process

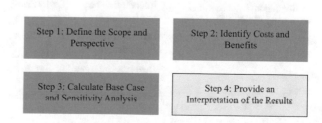

Step 1: Define the Scope and Perspective

Step 2: Identify Costs and Benefits

Step 3: Calculate Base Case and Sensitivity Analysis

Step 4: Provide an Interpretation of the Results

process/change/intervention or not (after discounting values, if appropriate). In most industries, this may be seen as the threshold for whether to undertake the activity. However, in health care, one should make additional considerations before making this determination.

First, keep in mind that even if undertaking the project produces the same net monetary benefit as not proceeding, there will likely be improvements to quality. So, given that idea when comparing these two situations—not doing the project = worse quality versus doing the project = better quality (see Table 6.2)—undertaking the project is clearly the better choice because you will have essentially improved quality at no (net) cost. Extending this idea, in some situations a negative ROI is acceptable when viewed in light of the associated improvements in quality or even benefits to other perspectives (Table 6.3). When this happens, metrics like net savings per patient (which would either be a negative savings or simply relabeled as net cost per patient) can provide the necessary context to allow for an interpretation of the financial costs to achieve the associated quality benefits. Said another way: It may be that a certain net cost per patient is worth the improvement to care and outcomes that are observed.

As we will see in the case with positive ROI, there is no set standard for what threshold is acceptable; it will be entirely situation dependent. But, one can imagine any number of scenarios where a provider, a payer, and even a patient may be willing to experience a negative ROI to achieve improvements in quality and even outcomes.

As a corollary to the first consideration is a reminder that not all benefits are monetizable. Under the circumstances of a zero or negative ROI based on monetizable

Table 6.2 Potential trade-offs involved in evaluating a cost-neutral (ROI = 0%) intervention

	Level of quality	Financial situation
Intervention not implemented	Lower	Same
Intervention implemented	Higher	Same

In a cost-neutral situation, it is often clear that performing the intervention is preferable to not performing it, since it is possible to attain a higher level of quality without any negative financial implications

Table 6.3 Potential trade-offs involved in evaluating an intervention with a negative return

	Level of quality	Financial situation
Intervention not implemented	Lower	Better
Intervention implemented	Higher	Worse

When an intervention produces a negative ROI, one must determine whether the financial loss is worth the improvement in quality, considering nonmonetizable value may help establish the merits of such a project benefits (and where quality is improved), the addition of nonmonetary benefits will provide further support that the project was "worth it" even if it did not produce a net monetary gain.

The final consideration is that the time frame identified for a ROI analysis has significant implications for the resulting ROI value. As mentioned several times up to this point, a good quality improvement intervention is sustainable, so that even if ROI is negative in the short term, the project may produce a positive return when viewed over a longer time frame.

It is clear from these considerations that the interpretation of ROI is not black and white. Obviously, a positive return is preferred, but in some situations, cost-neutral results or even a negative return is acceptable.

6.2.1.1   What Is a "Good" ROI?

One of the most common difficulties organizations face when interpreting an esti-mated or realized ROI is determining what constitutes an "acceptable" or "good" return. For example, if presented with the information that the anticipated ROI is 8%, those around the table may look at one another and struggle to identify relevant benchmarks or thresholds with which to compare.

Other authors have addressed this issue in an attempt to provide some guidance. Buzachero et al. [1] offer the following possibilities:

1. Use what other industries shoot for: 15–20%.
2. Compare what could be obtained from other investments.
3. Use a break-even value.
4. Let the funder set the minimum acceptable ROI.

In lieu of other criteria, these suggestions offer a backdrop for some possible approaches to establish the rate of return acceptable to stakeholders for a particu-lar project. For example, in some situations it might be reasonable to compare the ROI to what could be obtained from other investments. These alternatives may be investments in infrastructure or durable medical equipment or simply some other intervention (that is, perhaps only enough funds are available to support one of two possible interventions and ROI will be used to help determine which one to pursue).

The investment may also simply be a hypothetical one based on a standard dis-counted rate or rate of return. That is, all else being equal, projects with ROIs less than 4–6% may be a hard sell for their business case alone (but, as just mentioned, gains to quality and nonmonetizable benefits may more than make up for it). How-ever, these provide only general guidance; the nuance of a particular project may override any attempt to apply a standard rule of thumb or industry standard to it.

If one were to use the break-even value (a ROI = 0%) as the threshold, he or she would encounter some of the challenges described previously regarding when or under what circumstances, if ever, negative returns are acceptable. But the consid-eration of this threshold also raises another point: the time frame. For a sustainable intervention where cumulative benefits will eventually exceed the initial costs of the intervention, almost any ROI can reach the break-even value of 0% if the time frame is extended out long enough. Perhaps the more appropriate way to consider this type of criterion is to frame it in terms of the payback period. That way, instead of simply looking at whether the ROI will reach or exceed 0%, you will look at *how long it will take* before that break-even point is reached. There may be practical implications for how long a time frame the funder is willing to endure, or it may be simply a matter of feel (e.g., there may be instances when a payback period of 20 years is acceptable, but there are probably many instances when it is not).

The idea of allowing the funding party to determine the minimum acceptable ROI may be applicable in specific circumstances. As a general practice, however, it is typically in the best interest of those seeking funding or justifying a recently completed intervention to provide arguments for what an acceptable ROI would be for a given situation. The complexities of healthcare delivery services combined with the uncertainties associated with diagnoses and treatments simply exclude the possibility of a one-size-fits-all benchmark for what constitutes an acceptable level of ROI. It is likely that each unique situation can have an argument made for a different level of ROI. The burden of determining the effectiveness of the intervention lies with those seeking funding or approval—so should the burden of defending why the expected or realized ROI is acceptable.

Beyond the four methods of establishing an acceptable ROI just presented, there is another way to establish a benchmark for an acceptable level for ROI—namely, what has been obtained previously. Within healthcare quality improvement, many of the key quality areas (ED efficiency, patient safety, excess utilization) have been addressed numerous times by various parties and in a variety of ways. Previous ROI analyses can provide explicit benchmarks for what could be expected in future studies, provided any glaring differences in methodology do not prohibit a reasonable translation of the previously realized ROI to the proposed situation.

Additionally, to *estimate* what the ROI of previous studies *would have been,* you may only need to use the information presented on changes in clinical outcomes or utilization; this is the case as long as the associated costs and benefits can be reasonably approximated. In these situations, one attempts to monetize the improvement realized by the study, estimate the costs, and calculate an approximate ROI for the project. As explored in a previous chapter, you can often find studies that provide enough information to estimate the associated costs and benefits, and therefore ROI. Let us review an actual example to see how this works.

Estimating ROI of a Published Study

A study published in 2015 details a patient hand-hygiene protocol in an adult cardiovascular medical ICU to reduce hospital-acquired infections. Within the text, the authors describe the intervention and provide information on the number of patients affected and the resulting rates of infections [2]. The study offers no cost data or information on the monetary value of benefits, but using the information provided,

Table 6.4 Key results from a published study on a hand-hygiene protocol to reduce hospital-acquired infections

Key result	Before protocol	After protocol
Patients admitted (N)	2183	2326
Days in ICU (mean)	3.69	3.46
CAUTI rate (per 1000 catheter days)	9.1	5.6
Catheter utilization days	5190	4992
CLABSI rate (per 1000 catheter days)	1.1	0.5
Catheter utilization days	6447	5620

CAUTI catheter-associated urinary tract infection; *CLABSI* central line-associated bloodstream infections; *ICU* intensive care unit

we can demonstrate how one could estimate the monetary ROI this protocol produced. In addition to a 10-week protocol training period, data on catheter-associated urinary tract infections (CAUTIs) and central line-associated bloodstream infections (CLABSIs) were collected and reported per 1000 catheter days. The key data from the article are summarized in Table 6.4.

From those values, you can calculate the *number* of events observed in each time period using the following relationship:

$$\text{Infection Events} = \text{Infection Rate} \times \text{Utilization days}/1000 \qquad (6.1)$$

Using that equation, we calculate that the number of CAUTIs dropped from 47 events before the protocol to 28 after (a decrease of 19), and the number of CLABSIs dropped from 7 to 3 (a decrease of 4). If one can estimate the potential savings per infection avoided, it is straight-forward to calculate cost-avoidance associated with 19 fewer CAUTIs and four fewer CLABSIs:

$$\text{Cost Avoidance} = 19 \times (\text{Cost to Treat CAUTI}) + 4 \times (\text{Cost to Treat CLABSI})$$

Note that this is probably a conservative estimate of the monetary benefits because these types of infections often prolong lengths of stay, either in the ICU or for the overall hospital stay. However, information regarding how the infections affected length of stay is not provided. Even so, this basic calculation can provide a reasonable estimate of the financial benefits associated with this intervention.

As an aside, you might wonder whether it would be appropriate to use the decrease in the overall mean ICU length of stay as an additional monetary benefit since the mean number of days in the ICU dropped from 3.69 before the intervention to 3.46 after. You could multiply the difference between these values by the average daily cost of a stay in the ICU to obtain additional monetary benefit. The problem with doing this relates back to what we talked about previously in terms of determining whether benefits are attributable to the intervention. Depending on the information provided, it may not be reasonable to infer that the reduction in infections was directly responsible for the reduction in ICU days. Therefore, attributing the difference in the average length of stay of the *entire* ICU population of over 2000 patients per year as a result of 23 fewer infections may be too much of a leap. A more appropriate calculation would be to use the difference in length of stay between those with and without infections (if it had been reported), and then calculate the benefit as: [23 fewer infections × (additional ICU days due to infections) × daily ICU cost]. The product of the first two terms represent the utilization avoided by the fewer infections, which are then multiplied by the cost of that utilization to produce the ICU cost avoidance. There may be other benefits as well, but these values would provide at least approximate values for use in a ROI calculation.

Estimating costs in this case is slightly more complicated than estimating the associated monetary benefits. To accurately estimate costs, we would like to have information such as:

- The number of staff involved in the intervention.
- The number of hours and resources used during the 10-week training period.
- The number of hours spent during implementation to incorporate the protocol and document the necessary actions.

Unfortunately, those values are not provided. However, those familiar with this type of setting may make some reasonable guesses based on the information provided about the facility: It was a 27-bed ICU within a 498-bed community hospital, with a mean annual ICU daily census of 22.2 patients and staffing ratios commonly of one nurse to two patients. With assumptions regarding the number of staff and the hours required during the training period and during protocol implementation, you could estimate the associated costs and then use them along with the estimated benefits to estimate a ROI for this intervention.

Once costs and benefits are estimated, the estimated ROI could be calculated using the usual formula. As shown here and previously, this process is certainly not an exact science. You should exercise caution in the interpretation of these values and the resulting ROI. But, if key results are provided within the text and you can make reasonable assumptions regarding the associated monetary costs and benefits, it can provide at least a starting point for the ROI that other interventions have produced in lieu of a specific ROI analysis. Once completed, the estimated ROI could serve as a benchmark for what would be considered an acceptable return for similar projects.

6.2.1.2   Presenting ROI Values

For obvious reasons, the ROI calculation will likely be included in any type of analysis of financial return. However, as we have discussed, ROI calculations can be significantly influenced by key estimates and assumptions as well as by the chosen time frame. Specifics of these, as well as their potential impact, should be included in the interpretation of ROI, as these will certainly influence a reader's interpretation of the numerical results. Ideally, in addition to including details of its calculation and interpretation, the ROI would be used in combination with one or more additional metrics. Often, the ROI is expected to be one of the metrics presented, as it is often explicitly requested by those who will be evaluating the project's merits; however, anyone experienced in these types of analyses know that providing only ROI can omit key information and insights that can help appropriately assess the projects feasibility and financial viability.

6.2.2 *Interpreting the Benefit-to-Cost Ratio (BCR)*

Other than ROI, the BCR is probably the most common metric used, in part because it is often (incorrectly) referred to as the ROI. Given that BCR is a ratio of two numbers, the key threshold for it will be a value of 1.0 which reflects a cost-neutral situation and corresponds to a ROI of 0%. Values less than 1.0 reflect a ratio where benefits are less than costs (a net loss or negative ROI), and values greater than 1.0 indicate that benefits exceed costs (a net benefit or positive ROI). The BCR and ROI are linked: A BCR of 1.4 reflects a ROI of 40%, for example. But, the BCR can be interpreted as "the benefit for each dollar spent": a BCR of 1.4 says that "for each dollar spent, a $1.40 in benefit was realized."

The BCR may also be presented as a true ratio; in the above example this would look like the following:

$$BCR = 1.4{:}1$$

While unnecessary, the advantage to this notation is that its interpretation may be more intuitive for some because it more closely reflects what would be stated in sentence form: "The project resulted in a ratio of $1.40 in benefits to $1.00 in costs." When the BCR is in ratio form, a reader is immediately aware that benefits exceeded costs and is spared any confusion regarding the appropriate value for the break-even point to use as a comparison (e.g., 0% for ROI versus 1.0 for BCR).

Because of its similarity to ROI, it may be unnecessary to report BCR and ROI together. However, in some situations the interpretation of benefit per dollar spent is very appealing and adds substance and context to the overall project interpretation. Many of the same caveats that will be relevant to ROI will be applicable to BCR, and much of the interpretation will follow from how the ROI would be interpreted. And, estimates of the BCR realized by previously published studies can be obtained through the same means as estimating the ROI since they use the same values in their calculations.

6.2.2.1   Presenting BCR Values

Given its similarity to ROI, the BCR can be used as often and in many of the same ways as ROI. Therefore, deciding when to use it may depend heavily on the intended audience and what they may prefer. Each metric will be more intuitive for some than for others. Sometimes, presenting them together can produce a better understanding of the same concept or can help drive home the results: "This project produced a ROI of 40%, so that for every $1 spent, a total of $1.40 in benefits were realized."

The BCR can also be more intuitive when the ROI is very large. Some projects will produce benefits that are hundreds or thousands of times higher than costs. For example, interventions to increase influenza vaccinations are relatively inexpensive to implement and maintain, but the cost avoidance associated with influenza-related hospitalizations and deaths may run in the thousands or tens of thousands of dollars for each event avoided, which can result in extraordinarily high values for ROI. Reporting that the flu-vac intervention produced $24 in benefit for each $1 spent (the BCR) is perhaps easier to interpret than reporting that it produced a ROI of 2300%. In such a situation, the immense value of ROI loses some of its effectiveness because it is difficult to conceptualize such a value, whereas the BCR provides a more tangible comparison for the reader or audience to consider.

6.2.3   Interpreting the Payback Period

Because the calculations of ROI and BCR both have costs in the denominator, the result is a relative value that is interpreted similarly regardless of scale. That is, the calculated number does not reveal on its own whether costs and benefits are a few thousand dollars or whether they range into the hundreds of millions. So even though a ROI greater than 0% is universally interpreted as a positive return, it lacks detail about the magnitude of the absolute benefit realized. This property can be useful when comparing returns across multiple activities or to some standard threshold (like a discount rate), but it can also hide some of the practical interpretations associated with an individual situation. Therefore, other metrics that explore the return over a period of time or per individual affected can be instructive and provide additional insights above those delivered by ROI and BCR. The first of these is the payback period.

Given that the chosen time frame plays a key role in the accumulation of both costs and benefits, the payback period is a nice compliment to ROI and/or BCR because it removes time frame as a part of the calculation (it is, instead, the result). That is, instead of selecting a particular time frame to examine, the payback period calculation returns a value that represents the length of time until the ROI reaches 0%.

This calculation is effective when costs either occur prior to the realization of benefits, or when some initial investment and potentially some ongoing maintenance costs occur while benefits accumulate (which are common situations). A key assumption, however, is that benefits continue to accrue (i.e., the intervention is sustainable) and will eventually exceed costs. Two examples are described in Table 6.5 (Fig. 6.2).

Table 6.5 Examples of interventions where payback period may be a useful metric

Intervention	Costs	Benefits
An EHR-based clinical decision tool is added to a pre-existing system to reduce unnecessary laboratory test orders	The bulk of the costs are up front to design and apply the tool to the current system, as well as some initial training for those who will use it	Assuming it is effective, over time the cumulative benefits associated with fewer unnecessary laboratories will eventually exceed the original investment
A provider training and education problem involves three sessions spaced two months apart; these sessions are intended to raise awareness of medication errors and reduce their frequency	The largest cost drivers will be the staff time and resources needed for the three educational sessions; perhaps there will be occasional costs if there are future refreshers or reminders	Here, too, the hope is that the improved knowledge about medication errors will produce small benefits that will accrue and accumulate to eventually exceed the costs of training

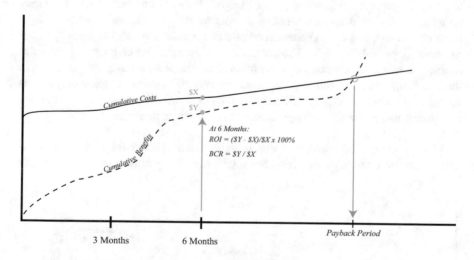

Fig. 6.2 Graphical representation of ROI, BCR, and payback period

The most common method for calculating the payback period is to assume or calculate the net benefit over a short period of time, such as a month or a quarter, and then divide the total cost of the intervention by that benefit-per-month (or quarter) to arrive at the number of months until the cost is covered.

For example, if the EHR-based clinical decision tool from Table 6.5 had an initial cost of $50,000 and was found to produce a total benefit in its first six months of use of $24,000, then the payback period would be calculated as follows:

$$\text{Net Benefit per month} = \$24,000/6 \text{ months} = \$4000/\text{month}$$

$$\text{Payback Period} = \$50,000/(\$4000 \text{ per month}) = 12.5 \text{ months}$$

So, if the analysis was being performed after month six, this would be an estimate that assumes that benefits will accrue similarly over the following six months. To see how this calculation can aid in the interpretation, we need only to look at what the calculated ROI would be at this same time point (month six):

$$\text{ROI} = (\$24,000 - \$50,000)/\$50,000 \times 100\% = -52\%$$

Without additional interpretation, this looks like it is financially disastrous. However, when presented alongside the payback period of 12.5 months, the conclusion is that the intervention will have paid for itself in another 6.5 months, which is likely to be much more acceptable.

In the current example, our calculation of the payback period assumes that an average benefit of $4,000 per month is reasonable for the subsequent time period. That may not be realistic, depending on the situation. Instead, it may often be the case that realized benefits occur in a nonlinear fashion: They may start out slowly, speed up to a steady pace, and then trail off as the marginal benefits are used up. Or, there may be some immediate lump-sum benefit with continued benefits accumulated over time at an ever-decreasing rate. The assumed rate of accumulation will ultimately affect the payback period (Fig. 6.3). The example from the previous chapter demonstrates a situation where benefits and costs continued to accrue on a monthly basis, and in the base case, costs exceeded anticipated benefits so that the payback period was technically infinite. This may still be helpful by demonstrating that the accumulated investment will *never* be recouped if benefits continue to be realized at the assumed rate.

The payback period calculation also assumes that the intervention will be sustainable at least until the payback period ends, which also may or may not be true. In the

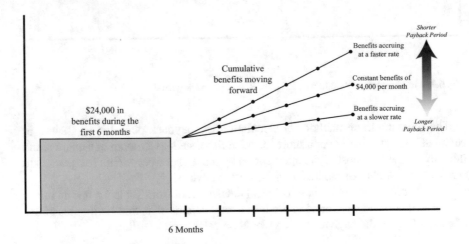

Fig. 6.3 Estimating payback period based on the assumed rate of benefit accrual

second example in Table 6.5, this would assume that the effectiveness of the education and training remains as strong months or potentially years after the intervention as it was immediately following the training series.

You may want to attempt to more accurately reflect the true pattern of costs and benefits over time either to add credibility or because you believe it will lead to more accurate prediction. There may be several methods to employ to do this, the complexity of which may be a function of choice and situation. As an example, one could assign different monthly values over time: Perhaps it is reasonable to assume that after the first six months benefits will reduce by approximately 10%. Or, if the calculation is being done retrospectively at month six, perhaps the current trajectory of monthly benefits over the six months (increasing, decreasing, etc.) is extended or extrapolated into future months.

If you choose to employ one of these more complex methods, consider and explore the real implications of uncertainty or variability. How much do these different estimation methods affect the estimated payback period? A lot or a little? Perhaps it is possible to describe multiple methods: Providing a range for the payback period is completely acceptable; "depending on the rate of benefit accumulation after the first six months, the payback period is estimated to be between 12.5 and 16.5 months."

You can also use more complex forecasting models based on time series and which can incorporate various factors and even seasonal fluctuations. The improvement in accuracy produced by these methods may not be worth the added complexity and effort needed to carry them out. Often, an intentional and thoughtful selection of what to vary in the sensitivity analysis is enough.

6.2.3.1 Presenting the Payback Period

This metric is excellent to use when ROI is, or is expected to be, negative for the initial evaluation period. Instead of simply pointing out a current negative financial return, it provides the additional information of *how much longer* it will be until the return starts to become positive. Given the ambiguity of what constitutes a "good" ROI, the payback period can also provide more concrete motivation for a proposed project: "The overall ROI at one year will likely exceed 80%; the payback period is only three months, meaning that after the first quarter we should be cost neutral for this project."

The additional information regarding the payback period may influence those on the fence about whether 80% is enough of a return in light of what else the investment could be spent on. Noting how quickly the project will be cost neutral may frame it as a situation where it could potentially be shut down in as early as three months with no negative financial ramifications, and therefore, evaluators may consider it to be of very little risk financially.

6.2.4   Interpreting Savings Per Patient

Savings per patient involves scaling the total net benefit to the population to which the intervention was applied. For multiple reasons, it is a metric to use intentionally and with some caution:

- Often an intervention produces costs or benefits on an aggregate or fixed-cost basis, as opposed to a per-patient basis; therefore, the measure itself is a little bit contrived.
- The same ROI or BCR in the aggregate will produce very different savings per patient based on sample sizes. The total costs and total benefits are the same whether they are divided over 10 patients, 1000 patients, or 10,000 patients.

This also has implications for interventions that may impact the number of patients involved: Increasing ED efficiency may increase patient load, which can ultimately "de-value" the savings per patient—not because there are fewer savings but because there are more patients. On the other hand, this metric can provide some much-needed context and scale for many of the same reasons:

- $10,000,000 in savings may look like a huge net benefit, but when it is spread over 20 million Medicare beneficiaries it loses some of its luster (net savings per patient = 50 cents).
- $30,000 in savings from stroke prevention may look like a meager amount, but in a rural setting that has only 20 stroke patients per year, it may produce a commendable savings per patient ($1500 per patient in this case).

Therefore, savings per patient is almost always used in combination with explicit descriptions of overall costs and benefits to provide the reader or audience the full breadth of the scale and scope of the project.

6.2.4.1   Presenting Savings Per Patient

Presenting net benefits on a per patient basis is warranted in specific situations, like those just described, and is almost never used on its own. It can provide some much-needed perspective, but usually alongside metrics that provide more aggregate information for those deciding whether an investment is (or was) worth it. As stated previously, it is typically used to provide a more relatable scale for the net benefits when dealing with either costs and benefits of large magnitudes or to appropriately scale the results to the size of the affected population.

6.3 Extrapolating and Generalizing Results

In a prospective analysis the metrics just described are used to demonstrate the fiscal feasibility of a project, but in a retrospective analysis, they may also be used to extrapolate or generalize findings to other situations. Let us explore how that might be done.

6.3.1 Generalizing to Other Settings

Extrapolating results to other settings requires careful considerations of the similarities and differences between those settings. In certain circumstances, such a leap is clearly inappropriate and would not provide usable information for the alternative setting. For example, certain aspects of care provided in rural areas are very different than what would occur in an urban setting. Most understand that rural facilities face challenges related to resources and patient populations that are unique to that setting. Applying results from a rural intervention to an urban setting would often be inappropriate and should be avoided.

In some cases, however, certain aspects of a project in one setting may be applicable to another. For example, while reducing infections in an ICU may have different benefits than reducing infections in other hospital departments, many of the costs associated with training and staff time may be similar. Therefore, one may be able to extrapolate the associated ROI or BCR by using the cost results from an ICU intervention and adjusting the benefits to more appropriately match what is likely in a general hospital setting. That is, perhaps it would be reasonable to assume that benefits would be higher or lower by some reasonable percentage, based on relative differences in hospital versus ICU costs. While still an approximation, it may provide some threshold or benchmark to strive for when conducting a similar intervention in a different setting.

6.3.2 Extrapolating the Effect of a Change in Scope

It is not always clear how the effectiveness and intensity of an intervention may scale to larger or smaller populations. However, metrics like savings per patient provide for an easy calculation when estimating the potential return for differently sized target populations. Sometimes, pilot projects are used to demonstrate the feasibility of an intervention and often utilize only a portion of the facility, staff, and patient population. If increasing the scope of the intervention can be thought to mean simply replicating the same intervention in multiple departments or locations, it is possible that one could assume a similar ROI or BCR, assuming that there would not be significant cost associated with overall oversight and coordination across the departments or locations.

It may also be possible that there would be economies of scale, so that fixed costs associated with the administration and monitoring of an intervention would be lower on a per-patient basis. That is because monitoring two locations versus one location may not require twice the resources and time. If done conscientiously, scaling results to apply to other scopes can help you effectively estimate the financial return.

6.3.3   Extrapolating the Effect of the Intensity of the Intervention

Using calculated returns to extrapolate for changes in the intensity of an intervention poses some challenges. Typically, the intensity of an intervention depends in part on the number of staff involved and the frequency with which certain actions are performed or avoided. For some types of interventions, it may be difficult to maintain a certain intensity when performed in other settings or on larger scales. For example, staff-intensive interventions have limitations because staff members typically are responsible for other duties, and scaling the intervention would require either that staff allocate more time for the intervention to reach more patients, or that more staff members are added, which invariably involves more logistic and administrative costs. However, if you can reasonably identify any potential efficiencies (which may reduce costs and increase benefits) or complications (which could do the opposite) stemming from this increased intensity, then it may be possible to adjust expected costs and benefits accordingly and use the adjusted values to calculate an expected return.

6.3.4   Extrapolating to Different Populations

To extrapolate the expected return of an intervention if applied to a different population of patients requires that (1) relevant results can be summarized and broken out by key population characteristics (e.g., age, comorbidity burden, stage of disease, etc.), and (2) one can estimate how costs or benefits may change (if at all) given the different population. It also assumes that these characteristics encompass the majority of the variability that may be associated with applying the intervention to another population, which may or may not be true. For example, cultural or language barriers may make it impossible to replicate an intervention for a particular patient population so that results regarding benefits and costs are no longer valid. Care should be taken when trying to extrapolate in these situations.

6.4 Developing a Full Report to Present Results

It can be difficult to know how best to present the results of a ROI analysis given that significant amounts of background, assumptions, and calculations often exist. Providing the appropriate amount of information on these aspects as well as on the interpretation involves striking a delicate balance. Offer too little information and the reader may struggle to understand the process or why certain assumptions were made or estimates used. Too much information can quickly overwhelm and even confuse the reader so that they may struggle to locate your key takeaways or understand how to use the provided information to evaluate the level of return reported.

6.4.1 Ensuring the Key Information Is Reported

In most reports, specific aspects of the project and associated ROI analysis need to appear. These include:

1. The necessary background or context
2. Key definitions
3. Major assumptions and estimates
4. Base case and sensitivity analysis calculations
5. Interpretation.

We will discuss each of these in turn.

6.4.1.1 Including the Necessary Background or Context

The amount of background and motivation you should provide for the project will vary depending on the situation. Often, if the ROI is part of a larger proposal or report, much of the relevant information regarding the background and motivation will likely be presented separately from the ROI analysis. If the ROI is intended to stand on its own, this information will need to appear as part of the reporting of the ROI results. At the beginning of this chapter we discussed the importance of exploring the background and motivation as a way to provide context for the reader for what follows as well as to justify the perspective and scope that has been selected for the analysis.

The background section of a ROI analysis interpretation will often not only include a discussion of the motivation but will also clearly lay out the aims of the project with as much specificity as possible. Instead of simply stating that the aim is to reduce blood pressure among uncontrolled hypertensive patients, it could say something like:

The overall aim of this project is to increase the percent of participating patients with controlled blood pressure by 5 percentage points and to simultaneously achieve a reduction of at least 10 mmHg in systolic and 5 mmHg in diastolic blood pressure for at least 75% of patients during the nine-month observation period.

This detailed description includes **specific metrics** and **thresholds** for improvement over a **precise time period**. If relevant to the intervention, it would also serve to add important elements regarding **patient characteristics** (those over the age of 65, those experiencing at least one prior cardiovascular event, etc.). By being explicit about the aims, it foreshadows the aspects that will inform the ultimate value and sets the stage for the definitions, estimates, and calculations that will follow. It may not always be necessary to include all of the specific information in one sentence. But, somewhere in describing the background for the project and the overall aim, it will be necessary to be specific about what is measured and over what time period. For example, in a retrospective analysis it may be enough to simply describe what has transpired and what the analysis that will follow attempts to accomplish, as in the hypothetical example of the collaborative care model (from Chap. 7):

The analysis that follows will examine the ongoing costs and benefits [of the collaborative care model that was implemented 24 months ago]... to provide an estimate of the expected return in future years if this program is to be continued.

Because it is a retrospective analysis, costs reflect data recorded or collected on staff effort during the 24 months of the program. Benefits, described shortly after, are realized through lower utilization and care costs (cost avoidance). There are multiple reasonable ways to adequately provide the necessary background for the reader, and these examples are certainly not exhaustive. In general, though, one should clearly state the main aim of the project and the goals of the ROI analysis.

Finally, for a prospective analysis it may be wise to further demonstrate the feasibility of the proposed project by mentioning the results of similar interventions and studies to achieve aims that are relatable to yours:

Previous attempts to increase blood pressure control in this population have successfully reduced systolic blood pressure levels by an average of 4.5 mmHg and diastolic blood pressure by an average of 12.4 mmHg.

If there are several studies, a table can effectively summarize multiple results that support the merits of your proposed project and add credibility to the aims being proposed (Table 6.6).

Together, these aspects provide information that helps the reader or audience understands the purpose of what is to follow. Clearly conveying the background and motivation establishes the groundwork and basis for the subsequent calculations and their interpretation.

6.4.1.2 Establishing Key Definitions

In every ROI analysis presentation, you should specifically and explicitly define every financial metric that will be used, such as ROI, BCR, and payback period.

Table 6.6   Example table summarizing previous studies (hypothetical data)

Study[a]	Description	Mean reduction in blood pressure
Smith et al. (2004)	Self-management program, 24 patients aged 75+	SBP reduced 6.5 mmHg
Jones et al. (2012)	Educational seminars on medication adherence, 55 community-dwelling seniors	SBP reduced 3.4 mmHg, DBP reduced 8.3 mmHg
Anderson (2018)	Physician education on masked hypertension	SBP reduced 5.5 mmHg, DBP reduced 16.2 mmHg

[a]Studies are not real

Never assume that the reader will know what definition you used, and never require them to deduce it from the text.

You must also define any clinical classifications or thresholds, like "in control" or "cardiovascular event." These definitions provide the framework for the measurement piece that is necessary to demonstrate improvements in quality and gains in value. Typically, these definitions will be standard to the clinical topic and obtained from the literature since there are often accompanying estimates that are used directly in calculations of monetary return.

In the example just presented, you could define the notion of "in control" within the statement of the aim, as in:

> …to increase the percent of participating patients with controlled blood pressure (systolic <140 mmHg and diastolic <90 mmHg) by 5 percentage points…

Or, it could also be described separately, which can be effective if more than one definition will be explored:

> Patients will be considered to be in control when their systolic blood pressure is <140 mmHg, although a subanalysis will be performed using the additional criterion of a diastolic blood pressure <90 mmHg.

There are numerous options for how to present the key definitions, but the main goal is to ensure that all of the relevant information is presented in one place.

6.4.1.3   Describing Major Assumptions and Estimates

Information regarding the assumptions made and estimates used are often presented alongside the key definitions, as they are a natural extension of the definitions. For example, once blood pressure control is defined in terms of systolic and diastolic blood pressure, it is natural to discuss the assumptions and estimates regarding the percent of patients currently achieving that threshold and the ability of the intervention to improve it.

Current estimates place the percent of patients with blood pressure control in our targeted population at 65%. If this is accurate, then we expect to be able to increase this level to between 70% and 75%. Such an improvement would reduce the risk of stroke for a total of 200 patients and theoretically prevent as many as 25 strokes...

As described previously, much of the calculated values in a prospective analysis rely on the interplay of multiple assumptions. Presenting the steps by which specific results are estimated allows the reader to understand how the assumptions build upon each other and ultimately form the underlying estimates of effectiveness and impact.

Similarly, when attempting to demonstrate the value of reducing falls that result in injury, it is logical to discuss assumptions regarding relative frequency expected for different fall-related injuries alongside the cost to treat each type of injury. From the hypothetical case study in Chap. 7:

We anticipate recruiting eight facilities with an average of 180 residents each for a total of (8 × 180) = 1440 residents. Prior to the intervention, the assumed rate of serious falls is 15 per 100 patient-years, which would correspond in the current population to 1440 × 9/12 years × (15 falls/100 patient-years) = 162 serious falls over the nine-month observation period.

In general, in a prospective analysis, several types of assumptions and estimates will be necessary to present and describe. These may include:

• The number of entities impacted by the intervention (patients, providers, facilities, families, or whatever is relevant given the situation)
• Baseline or "usual care" rates of a condition, event, or care utilization
• Effectiveness of treatment in reducing or improving the baseline or "usual care" rates
• Associated benefits (e.g., the reduction in stroke and heart failure risk associated with improvements in blood pressure control)
• Costs associated with the intervention
• Monetary benefits realized from the improvement in quality or patient outcomes.

Just as with the overall project aim, providing specific sources of information that supports these estimates will be crucial. This can be done either as text, "Avery et al. observed a reduction in stroke rate from 12.3 per 1000 patient years to 8.2..." or by including a table of several sources. It can also be helpful for the reader to translate those values into tangible values for the current project:

Such a reduction in our expected cohort of 850 patients would translate into 3.5 fewer strokes per year, or 2.9 fewer strokes during the nine-month observation period.

One of the challenges is that when the ROI analysis is done prospectively as part of a proposal, the assumptions and estimates can compound one another. In the case of the blood pressure example, an assumption is made about enrollment, another about the baseline rate, yet another about the effectiveness of the intervention, and still another about how that effectiveness translates into fewer adverse events that produce the benefit in the form of cost-avoidance.

Even if any one of the assumptions varies only slightly, confounding effects on the realized benefit can occur. Consider the situation in Fig. 6.4. Down the center are

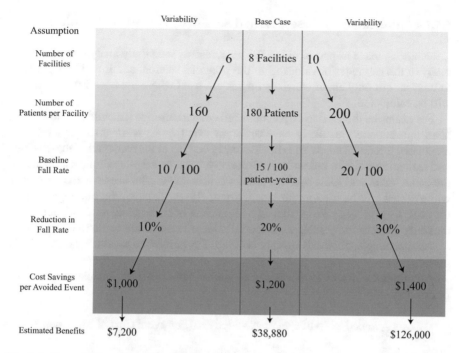

Fig. 6.4 Compounding effect of variability in assumptions that combine to build an estimate of the potential financial benefit of an intervention

the assumptions listed for the base case. On either side are values that may represent potential variability for each assumption, and you can see that each one pushes the ultimate benefit further away from the base case estimate. The result is a very large difference between the lowest and highest estimate of what *could* happen.

This is why it is critical to be transparent and ensure that the assumptions and estimates used are credible and reasonable and have data or expert opinion to back them up (Table 6.7).

Table 6.7 Common estimates needed for a prospective analysis

Estimate
Recruitment or population affected
Prevalence/incidence
Pre-intervention rates or likelihood
Effectiveness
Intervention costs
Associated benefits

6.4.1.4   Presenting the Base Case and Sensitivity Analysis Calculations

Calculations made as part of either the base case or sensitivity analysis will involve many of the estimates or values from the previous section, and it will be necessary to be clear not only about which estimates are used where but how different values will be calculated.

For example, the myriad of potential fall-related injuries (fractures, dislocations, head injuries, etc.) all likely have different event rates, relative frequencies, and associated treatment costs. You should clearly display to the reader all of these values and their source and/or rationale. Additionally, in some cases, multiple estimates for the same value will exist because certain estimates will be used for the base case while others will be used in the sensitivity analyses. This will be true regardless if the analysis is prospective (so that all of the values are estimated) or retrospective (so that only the sensitivity analyses potentially include estimated or alternative values).

As an example, Table 6.8 appears in Chap. 7 as part of the hypothetical case study on falls:

Additionally, it will be necessary to define how different calculations will be performed:

$$\text{Costs Avoided} = (\text{\# of Events Avoided}) \times (\text{Per-event Cost of Treatment})$$

It may seem like this calculation should be obvious, but best practice is to include any formulas somewhere in the presentation of the results, even if it is in an appendix or methods section.

Any discounting or adjustments should also be clearly described with the necessary calculations presented.

Fall result	Number of events avoided	Associated cost to medicare	Total cost avoidance
Hip fractures	16.2	$12,000	$194,400
All other fractures	24.3	$4000	$97,200
Head injuries	12.15	$2400	$29,160
Joint dislocations	8.1	$1500	$12,150
Other events	20.25	$150	$3038
Total			$335,948

Table 6.8 Estimated cost avoidance for hypothetical case study of nursing home falls (hypothetical data)

6.4.1.5 Providing an Interpretation of Results

No ROI analysis is complete without an interpretation of the results. In a prospective analysis, this will incorporate results from the base case and sensitivity analysis to provide a conclusion about the likelihood of a positive or "acceptable" return. The interpretation should also acknowledge and address uncertainty and describe any contingency plans if certain assumptions are not met or certain estimates end up being inaccurate. For a retrospective analysis, the interpretation of the base case will involve an examination about *why* the realized return was achieved and identify any unexpected or special circumstances that may have affected the return. Since the sensitivity analysis in a retrospective analysis often explore alternative scenarios, the interpretation can include suppositions about what might happen in future time periods or in other situations or settings if the intervention was to be replicated.

In general, the interpretation should address several questions:

In a Prospective Analysis

- What will be the financial return for this project during the selected time frame?
- Why is this an acceptable return?
- What are the main assumptions that may threaten this level of return, and what could happen if certain aspects of the intervention do not achieve the assumed levels?
- What are the contingencies in those situations?

In a Retrospective Analysis

- What was the financial return for this project during the selected time frame?
- Is that acceptable? If so, why?
- If not, why? Were there aspects of the intervention that did not go as planned? What were they and what was their impact?
- What were the main drivers of ROI, and what was learned that can inform future activities?
- Sometimes, how does this inform what the ROI would be if this intervention was performed in a different setting with a different population?

In each case, context will be key, and the interpretation may even include recommendations for next steps or future projects.

6.4.2 Effectively Presenting the Essential Information

After accumulating key information, gathering the necessary data, establishing the credibility of needed estimates, and calculating multiple relevant value metrics, you should synthesize all of the information into a coherent, understandable summary. The presentation of the information will have major implications for how effective it will be in informing, educating, and even persuading the intended audience.

6.4.2.1   Leading the Reader Through the Process

Although the ROI analysis culminates with the calculation of a few key metrics, much of the key information required for a full understanding of what those metrics mean is contained in the process that produced them. Ensuring that the intended audience can easily follow the steps to identify and establish the individual components (assumptions, estimates, methods, calculations) that contribute to the ultimate evaluation of value requires that you articulate those steps with sufficient detail.

Additionally, while you should interpret the results in the given context, you should also allow room for those reading or listening to the results to develop their own interpretation. Perhaps the best analogy is that of a peer-reviewed paper: The background and supporting information is presented, as are observed results and the authors' interpretation. However, information is shared objectively and with standard metrics (e.g., p values). Additionally, along with the transparency offered through stated limitations and alternative explanations, it will allow the reader to make their own determination regarding the strength of the evidence and form their own opinion regarding the conclusions and implications.

Providing Clarity

Having said that, often the amount of information gathered and examined in ROI analyses is immense and could easily overwhelm and confuse the intended audience. Therefore, whenever possible, you should seek to provide key information in a way that clarifies and simplifies. In written form, for example, include all of the primary model inputs in a single table that will allow the reader to see everything at once, quickly locate and refer to important values, and directly compare estimates used for the base case and sensitivity analyses.

Table 6.9 gives an example of how this could be done. Even though the individual values are likely already included throughout the text, having a central location

Table 6.9   Example table of inputs (hypothetical data)

Input	Estimate	Source[c]
Patients impacted	25,000 Medicare beneficiaries	Internal estimate
Impact of intervention	5% reduction in fractures[a]	Smith et al. (2004)
	2% reduction in fractures[b]	Nelson et al. (2008)
	7% reduction in fractures[b]	Tao et al. (2012)
Mean cost avoided per fracture (2019 US$)	$8500[a] $7500[b]	Billing claims
Reduction in FTE	10%	Preliminary data

[a]Used in base case calculation
[b]Used in sensitivity analyses
[c]These studies are not real

provides clarity and focus for the reader among what is likely to be a significant amount of information and data being presented.

This table provides a single location for the reader or audience to refer to as they work their way through the analysis to understand what was done and why. It allows one to quickly identify all of the inputs, which ones were varied as part of the sensitivity analysis, and to what extent.

6.4.2.2 Using Tables and Graphs

Tables can be used either to display a large amount of information in a succinct way (as in Table 6.9 in the previous section) or to highlight or emphasize key components of the analysis. They can also effectively demonstrate how assumptions and estimates are combined to produce calculated values that may be a function of several values. For example, to calculate the number of falls or infections that an intervention may prevent or avoid, arriving at that calculated value involves estimates of enrollment/participation, baseline rates, assumed reductions, post-intervention rates, and differences in raw counts.

A table like Table 6.10 can quickly lead the reader through the process of how certain calculations were performed. An expanded version of this can be useful in showing sensitivity analysis calculations. Adding columns with alternative values can highlight how specific changes in one or more values in Rows 1 through 9 ultimately impact the result in Row 10.

Graphs may be used more sparingly than tables, but their inclusion can add to the overall effectiveness of the presentation. Often, they are most useful to show the flow of costs and benefits over time, either to demonstrate where the cost-neutral time occurs (Fig. 6.5), or to demonstrate how variations in the sensitivity analysis affect long-term return (Fig. 6.6).

Table 6.10 Example of a table used to display steps of calculations (hypothetical data)

	Value	Description
Row 1	200	Estimated enrollment per month
Row 2	6 months	Time frame
Row 3	8.5	Estimated days at risk per person per month
Row 4	10,200	Total days at risk ($Row\ 1 \times Row\ 2 \times Row\ 3$)
Row 5	2.2	Estimated infection rate per 1000 days at risk
Row 6	22.44	Total infections, baseline ($Row\ 4 \times Row\ 5$)
Row 7	16%	Estimated reduction in infection rate
Row 8	1.848	Reduced rate ($Row\ 5 \times (1 - Row\ 7)$)
Row 9	18.85	Total infections, intervention ($Row\ 4 \times Row\ 8$)
Row 10	3.59	Reduction in total infections ($Row\ 6 - Row\ 9$)

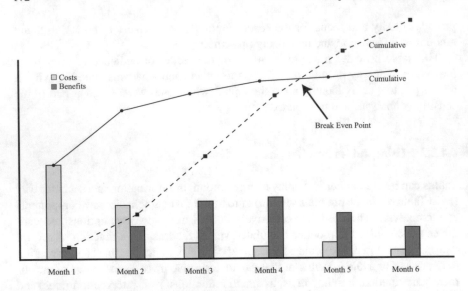

Fig. 6.5 Using a graph to show costs and benefits over six months

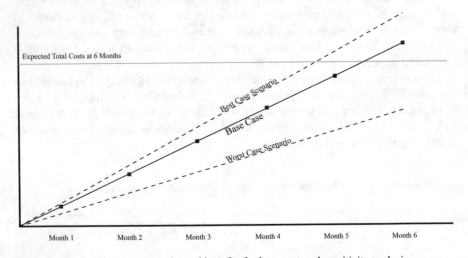

Fig. 6.6 Graphically represent estimated benefits for base case and sensitivity analysis

6.4.2.3   A Final Word About How to Present Results

Regardless of how the information is included, you should aim to provide a clear and transparent account of how the background information, assumptions, and estimates work together to produce the resulting financial return. By presenting a full picture of what was done and why, and leveraging tables and graphs in addition to texts, you can ensure that the reader or audience has the information necessary to make a valid assessment of the merits of the project or intervention.

6.5 Summary

The use of multiple metrics of value are an effective way to fully assess the value of a given project. Different ones may be more or less appropriate in different situations, and each may provide unique insight into key aspects of the project and its activities. When presenting the results of a value assessment, you should lead the reader or audience through the process so that they see it as credible and reasonable and so that they understand what the calculated metrics reflect. When put together, these results and the corresponding interpretation and presentation will provide a clear picture of the value of particular activities.

6.6 Key Concepts

- You must appropriately and effectively describe the background and motivation for the project, so that the discussion of value and ROI can be interpreted in a particular context.
- You must also clearly state aims and define concepts and metrics; do not assume that your intended audience understands ROI at the same level that you do.
- Each metric of the financial return has a specific interpretation; different metrics may be more helpful in certain situations, either alone or together.
- As a metric, ROI is common but may not tell the full story.
- There is no established benchmark for what constitutes a "good" or "acceptable" ROI; previous experience or the anticipated ROI of alternative activities may represent reasonable benchmarks.
- If using prior studies to establish a benchmark for ROI, you may need to extrapolate reported results into associated financial return to determine an estimate of the realized ROI.
- The BCR is as common a metric as ROI and offers an attractive interpretation for some because it is the ratio of benefits realized per dollar spent.
- Both ROI and BCR are calculated once a time frame has been fixed; in contrast, the payback period imposes no time frame and instead estimates the length of time until benefits equal costs.
- Savings per patient can be a useful metric when trying to scale down results in large populations and provide a more meaningful interpretation.
- You should exercise caution and care when attempting to extrapolate results to other settings, scopes, or populations.

- When presenting analysis results, in addition to providing the necessary background and defining key concepts and metrics, typically you should also present major assumptions and estimates, base case and sensitivity analysis calculations (with formulas), and an interpretation.
- You should lead the reader or audience through the process so that they see it as reasonable and credible; be thorough but do not overwhelm those who will see the results.

References

1. Buzachero VV, Phillips J, Phillips PP, Phillips ZL (2013) Measuring ROI in healthcare. McGraw Hill, New York
2. Fox C, Wavra T, Drake DA, Mulligan D, Bennett YP, Nelson C, Kirkwood P, Jones L, Bader MK (2015) Use of a patient hand hygiene protocol to reduce hospital-acquired infections and improve nurses' hand washing. Am J Crit Care: Official Publ Am Assoc Crit-Care Nurses 24(3):216–224. https://doi.org/10.4037/ajcc2015898

Chapter 7
Hypothetical Case Studies

In each of the hypothetical case studies that follow, I provide a little background regarding the motivation for the project and who the key stakeholders are, and I delineate whether the ROI analysis is part of a proposal (prospective) or a summary report (retrospective). The "referenced literature" for each case study is completely fabricated in the interest of time and to allow me to explore different scenarios I felt would be the most instructive. Additionally, *all the data presented in tables and graphs are completely fabricated for illustrative purposes.*

Throughout the examples, I have inserted commentary in the shaded sections within the narratives or highlighted things of note in the shaded blocks of text. If these were real-life reports, these additional pieces of commentary would not appear. Additionally, in each case I have tried to provide enough detail regarding the intervention or project to give sufficient context for the example. That being said, keep in mind that in a real situation these would be part of a larger application or report that would presumably cover additional detail regarding the activities.

I hope that these examples will allow you to more fully internalize the information we have covered up to this point, and in some cases maybe a case study will even serve as a template for part or all of your own proposal or summary report. Understand that these are not intended to be exhaustive in their scope or breadth but instead should be viewed as a way to showcase and demonstrate the concepts from the previous chapters.

7.1 Example 1: Reducing Nursing Home Falls

The Scenario: A nonprofit organization is applying for funding from CMS to initiate a program to reduce the number and severity of falls in a local nursing home. As part of the application process, CMS has asked for a ROI analysis to demonstrate the return CMS can expect if it chooses to fund the program. What follows could reflect that analysis.

© Springer Nature Switzerland AG 2020
C. A. Solid, *Return on Investment for Healthcare Quality Improvement*,
https://doi.org/10.1007/978-3-030-46478-3_7

Internal Decisions Made By the Nonprofit Organization Applying for Funding: The perspective will be that of CMS, although to booster the sensitivity analysis it would be prudent to include estimates of the benefits to providers, nursing home staff, patients, and their families. The intended intervention will be multifaceted and will include (1) specific exercise programs for patients to improve their stability, (2) two to three face-to-face provider trainings to improve staff knowledge and experience, and (3) posters to remind everyone of safeguards. This will be a pre-post-analysis and will include all nursing home residents, although a subgroup analysis could also be performed on those who experience a fall in the baseline period or who exhibit specific risk factors (issues with balance, gait, cognitive impairment, Parkinson's disease, etc.).

The organization will focus on "serious" falls, which they have defined as any fall requiring some sort of medical attention no matter how small. It will be assumed that prior to the intervention, the serious fall rate was roughly 15 falls per 100 patient-years (either from the literature or from previous experience or both). The intervention will be three months, with nine months of follow-up to collect information on fall events and the type and cost of the associated medical attention.

7.1.1 Sample ROI Analysis

7.1.1.1 Background

Over the last several years (*origin story method*), we have had the great privilege of working with several nursing homes (NHs) in our local community and surrounding region. In all, we have partnered at various times with six individual NHs on various projects to improve the quality of care for residents. During this time, we have gotten to know the administrators and dedicated staff of these facilities and have listened when they have confided in us regarding aspects of quality that they feel are important and achievable.

Almost universally, one of the quality topics that administrators and staff bring up is that of patient falls. As described elsewhere in this proposal, our preliminary work with two NHs produced encouraging results in terms of the reduction in falls that require medical attention ("serious falls"), and we have come to believe that a more widespread effort can be effective and economically feasible. By leveraging proven tools to reduce serious falls, we feel strongly that we can significantly impact the quality of NH resident care that will produce a net financial benefit for CMS through a reduction in healthcare utilization associated with serious falls.

The Overall Aim of this project is to reduce serious falls by 50% in the population receiving the intervention during the observation period. This level of reduction is based on our previous experiences with two local NHs. In the enclosed ROI analysis, we estimate the expected cost savings from reduced healthcare utilization from this reduction in serious falls and compare that savings to the total funding we believe would be needed to cover costs related to staff, training, materials, travel, data collection and analysis, and producing a results summary for this intervention. Costs and benefits will represent those incurred and realized by CMS (*this is the perspective*) and will cover the pre-intervention time frame through nine months after the beginning of the project (*time frame*).

Our previous experience indicates that a positive financial ROI for this type of project may not occur for one to two years, and that the ROI to CMS during the initial nine months may be negative. However, given the significant improvement in quality and patient experience from this project, we believe that these improvements are sustainable and will ultimately produce a net financial benefit for CMS (*here they are providing context for the calculations that are to follow*).

For this analysis, we will define metrics as follows:
ROI is defined as:

$$(\text{Benefits from Reduced Serious Falls} - \text{Costs of Intervention})/\text{Costs} \times 100\%$$

Benefit-to-cost ratio (BCR) as:

$$(\text{Benefits from Reduced Serious Falls})/(\text{Costs of Intervention})$$

Savings per patient as:

$$(\text{Benefits from Reduced Serious Falls} - \text{Costs of Intervention})/(\text{Number of Patients})$$

Payback period as:

$$(\text{Costs of intervention})/(\text{Savings per Month})$$

7.1.1.2 Recruitment and Baseline Serious Fall Rate

We anticipate recruiting eight facilities with an average of 180 residents each for a total of $(8 \times 180) = 1440$ residents. Prior to the intervention, the assumed rate of serious falls is 15 per 100 patient-years, which would correspond in the current population to:

$$1,440 \times 9/12 \text{ Years} \times (15 \text{ Falls}/100 \text{ Patient} - \text{Years})$$
$$= 162 \text{ serious falls over the nine-month observation period}$$

Table 7.1 Prevalence of serious fall results and associated costs

Fall result	Percent of serious falls (%)	Cost to Medicare per event	Sources[a]
Hip fracture	20	$12,000	Smith (2012)
All other fractures	30	$4000	Anderson (2014)
Head injury	15	$2400	Liu (2009)
Joint dislocation	10	$1500	Johnson (2018)
Other medical attention	25	$150	Claims analysis

[a]These studies are not real

The financial benefits of reducing serious falls stem from the cost avoidance associated with fewer care visits and lower levels of care utilization. Table 7.1 provides the estimated relative frequency of serious fall results and their associated cost to Medicare.

It may not be necessary to have individual categories like those presented in Table 7.1; it may be possible to find literature or information that would suggest an overall "average cost" per serious fall across all types of injuries that will allow you to estimate the cost avoidance from reduced falls. Having more granularity simply allows you more flexibility both before you begin the intervention and after it is completed when determining how your actual results differed from your estimates. That is, breaking this out as we see in Table 7.1 will allow you to see how closely your actual incidence of each type of event compared to what you estimated and the effect that had on your results. For example, perhaps you ended up having more or fewer hip fractures than anticipated—that will quickly change your associated benefits since they are so expensive to treat. Without that level of granularity, you may not be able to identify the reason why an observed result differs from your estimates. Additionally, doing it as above allows for more flexibility in the sensitivity analysis.

As stated above, we anticipate reducing serious falls by 50%, which would reduce falls by the amounts displayed in Table 7.2 over nine months.

Clearly, the numbers in the third and fourth columns of Table 7.2 are a function of at least two assumptions. The first assumption is the effectiveness of the intervention, and the second assumption is the relative frequency of each of the

Table 7.2 Estimated change in serious fall associated events

	Pre-intervention	Post-intervention	Difference
Rate of serious falls	15 per 100 pt-yrs	7.5 per 100 pt-yrs	
Number of serious falls	162	81	−81
Number of hip fractures	32.4	16.2	−16.2
Number of all other fractures	48.6	24.3	−24.3
Number of head injuries	24.3	12.2	−12.2
Number of joint dislocations	16.2	8.1	−8.1
Number of events requiring other medical attention	40.5	20.3	−20.3

Pt-yrs = patient-years

subsequent events that can stem from a serious fall (not to mention our assumed recruitment of 1440 NH residents). You can see how quickly uncertainty or variability in estimates or assumptions can compound. You can also see how doing this in Excel or some other software will allow you to play with some of these inputs and examine how they affect your ultimate estimates of the reduction of events.

Using these estimates, the total monetary benefit associated with this reduction over nine months can be calculated by determining the total cost avoidance:

$$\text{Cost Avoidance} = (\text{Events Avoided}) \times (\text{Per Event Cost to Treat}) \qquad (7.1)$$

The total estimated cost avoidance is $335,948, as displayed in Table 7.3.

Table 7.3 Estimated cost avoidance

Fall result	Number of events avoided	Cost avoided per event	Total cost avoidance
Hip fractures	16.2	$12,000	$194,400
All other fractures	24.3	$4000	$97,200
Head injuries	12.15	$2400	$29,160
Joint dislocations	8.1	$1500	$12,150
Other events	20.25	$150	$3038
Total			$335,948

Table 7.4 Cost estimates

Cost sources	Pre-intervention	During intervention
Staff time	$125,000	$420,000
Materials	$50,000	$35,000
IT support	$35,000	$20,000
Facilities to provide training	$40,000	$15,000
Data collection/analysis	$0	$65,000
Presenting results	$0	$25,000
Total	$250,000	$580,000

Total costs are estimated to be $830,000

If using an average cost per serious fall as the estimate instead of a breakdown of separate events, a table is likely not necessary. Instead, you can simply state the estimated benefit as "for each serious fall avoided, the average associated savings would be $X,XXX; if the intervention is successful in reducing the number of serious falls by 81, that would equate to a total monetary benefit of $81 \times \$X,XXX = \$XX,XXX$."

The costs of the intervention are described in Table 7.4.

The breakdown in Table 7.4 may or may not be appropriate in this part of the application. It is likely that elsewhere this organization has had to detail their expected costs to justify the level of funding/award they are requesting. But, for completeness we include here at least some exploration of the total costs.

7.1.1.3 Base Case Estimates

Our base case estimate of the ROI is calculated as follows: Among 1440 patients with a baseline serious fall rate of 15 falls per 100 patient-years, a 50% reduction over the nine-month observation period would result in 81 fewer serious falls. Assuming the base case distribution of the frequency of resulting events, the total cost savings from avoided healthcare expenditures would be $335,948.

This produces a ROI for the first 9 months of:

$$(\$335,948 - \$830,000)/\$830,000 \times 100\% = -59.6\%$$

The BCR would be equal to 0.404, which means that for \$1.00 spent, there is a \$0.40 in benefit realized.

The savings per patient would be equal to:

$$(\$334,948 - \$830,000)/1,440 = -\$373.79 \, \text{per Patient}$$

It is hard to know whether the (negative) savings per patient is useful here. On the one hand, it is negative, further highlighting the fact that this project will cost CMS more than they will save during the first nine months—and savvy policy makers probably know how much they already spend on a per-patient basis and may consider this cost in light of that value. On the other hand, spending \$343 per patient may not "sound as bad" as being almost \$500,000 in the red nine months into a project (the raw net cost is estimated to be \$495,052), especially if you were to present the cost per patient on a monthly basis: \$343 over nine months equates to about \$38 per month. Whether to present this metric may be a matter of personal choice.

Although these indicate a substantial loss during the initial nine months, it should be noted that the total benefit equates to an average benefit of \$37,327 per month. Assuming the intervention is sustainable, this would result in a payback period of \$830,000/\$37,327.50 = 22.2 months from the beginning of the intervention, or just over a year after the intervention ends (13.2 months after the original nine months).

At this point, we have not adjusted any dollar amounts to a constant year. This could be accomplished in a number of ways, although probably the most common would be to discount any costs and benefits occurring after the first year. This, too, requires some assumptions and approximations, which will need to be described and explained for the reader.

To arrive at a more accurate estimate of the payback period, we will apply a discount rate of 4% per year to benefits occurring after the first year (all of the costs are assumed to be incurred in the first year). Therefore, the monthly benefit of \$37,327 would be equal to a discounted value of:

$$\$37,327 \times (1 - 0.04) = \$35,834$$

In each month of year two and:

$$\$37,327 \times (1 - 0.04)^2 = \$34,401$$

In each month of year three (if needed for the payback period calculation). Therefore, the cumulative (discounted) benefits will surpass the total costs of $830,000 sometime between months 23 and 24:

$$\text{Through Month } 23 : (\$37,327 \times 12) + (\$35,834 \times 11) = \$804,777$$
$$\text{Through Month } 24 : (\$37,327 \times 12) + (\$35,834 \times 12) = \$840,611$$

> This calculation also assumes that benefits will be realized at a constant rate throughout the payback period, which may or may not be reasonable.

7.1.1.4 Sensitivity Analysis

Of all the estimates and assumptions we have made, we have identified those associated with our total patient recruitment and the estimated effectiveness of our intervention to be the most uncertain (*simply for illustrative purposes*). Also, given the large cost per event for hip fracture, we have also explored how varying the likelihood of that event (versus other types of fractures) could impact the results. Table 7.5 presents information on the variability considered in the sensitivity analyses.

Table 7.5 Base case and sensitivity analysis inputs

Input	Estimate	Source	Used for
Patients recruited	1400	Internal estimate	Base case
	1200	Internal estimate	Sensitivity analysis
	1400	Internal estimate	Sensitivity analysis
Intervention effectiveness	50% reduction in fall rate	Smith et al.[a]	Base case
	40% reduction	N/A	Sensitivity analysis
	60% reduction	N/A	Sensitivity analysis
Fracture frequency	Hip: 20%, other: 30%	Anderson et al.[a]	Base case
	Hip: 15%, other: 35%	N/A	Sensitivity analysis
	Hip: 25%, other: 25%	N/A	Sensitivity analysis

[a]These studies are not real

Varying those values and performing sensitivity analyses produce the results presented in Table 7.6.

The top row has the base case and the following rows show calculations when recruitment, intervention effectiveness, and hip fracture prevalence are varied. We can see that resulting estimated cost savings range from $223,965 (when both recruitment and effectiveness are at their lowest) to $447,930 (when recruitment and effectiveness are at their highest). It should be noted, however, that these analyses are limited

Table 7.6 Results of sensitivity analysis

Scenario	N Fall reduction	Hip Fx reduction	Other Fx reduction	Head Inj reduction	Joint Dis reduction	Other reduction	Cost savings
Base case (1440 Pts, 50% fall reduction)	81	16.2	24.3	12.15	8.1	20.25	$335,948
Less effective (40% fall reduction)	64.8	12.96	19.44	9.72	6.48	16.2	$268,758
More effective (60% reduction)	97.2	19.44	29.16	14.58	9.72	24.3	$403,137
Worse recruitment (1200 Pts)	67.5	13.5	20.25	10.125	6.75	16.875	$279,956
Better recruitment (1600 Pts)	90	18	27	13.5	9	22.5	$373,275
Less effective and worse recruitment	54	10.8	16.2	8.1	5.4	13.5	$223,965
More effective and better recruitment	108	21.6	32.4	16.2	10.8	27	$447,930
Fewer hip fractures (15%)	81	12.15	28.35	12.15	8.1	20.25	$303,548
More hip fractures (25%)	81	20.25	20.25	12.15	8.1	20.25	$368,348

Fx = fracture; Inj = injury; Pts = patients

to the nine-month period post-intervention. Assuming that the results are sustainable, these scenarios produce monthly cost savings between $24,885 (worst case) and $49,770 (best case), which result in estimated payback periods of 33.4 months and 16.7 months, respectively, when costs are $830,000 (*again, discounting would prolong these slightly*).

Clearly, we could vary other inputs and we would see different results. In a real situation, you would likely spend significant time examining the impact of varying more than two or three inputs (as well as the time frame). However, you want to be careful not to overwhelm the reader, so you will have to determine how best to present the results. Perhaps you would not need to show all the reductions in the number of falls and subsequent events but simply the resulting calculated cost savings. In that case, you may consider whether you should include an appendix (if allowed) that could contain large spreadsheets.

Also, in addition to the danger of overwhelming or confusing the intended audience (i.e., the funding agency or CMS in this case), you run a risk in sensitivity analysis of overwhelming yourself or your own organization. Whatever you do, clearly document it and organize the calculations so that someone else could easily understand what you did. This is especially helpful when you return to your calculations months or years later, either because you secured funding and completed the project and are now wanting to compare the estimates with what was actually observed, or because you are pursuing another activity where the calculations, or at least their format, may be useful.

Notice that in the text immediately following the table the authors recalculate payback periods but do not recalculate ROI or BCR. We certainly could, but in this case they will still be negative and therefore we may decide that payback period is a more relevant metric for the reader. As with anything, this will depend on the situation as well as personal preference.

Finally, a word about tables versus figures: If there are a lot of rows in a table like this, it can be difficult for readers to directly compare the associated cost savings in a meaningful way. One option would be to summarize the information (either instead of or in addition to the table) in a figure like Fig. 7.1. Here, the reader can immediately see the relative effects of variability in effectiveness versus recruitment and how together they impact the best- and worst-case scenarios. This is just an example; different situations call for different approaches, and you will have to determine what you feel would be the most effective way to convey the results of your sensitivity analysis.

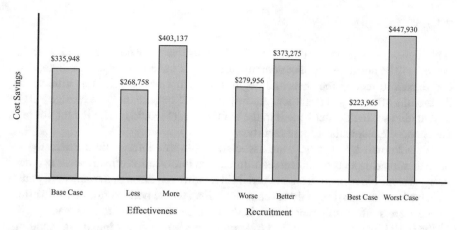

Fig. 7.1 Base case and sensitivity analysis results on cost savings

In addition to the monetary benefits just described, if we successfully reduce serious falls by our estimated amount, other benefits will result. First, serious injuries such as fractures and joint dislocations can pose a significant detriment to residents' quality of life and psychological health. Avoiding these adverse outcomes will result in additional cost savings to Medicare given the literature on the increased healthcare utilization associated with quality of life and psychological well-being (Jones 2008; Liu 2012). Additionally, those who experience a fracture are X% more likely to have another fracture in the next 12 months compared with those without a first fracture (Anderson 2015). Finally, we note that reducing serious falls that result in fractures and the need for health services will reap benefits in the form of mental and emotional well-being of patients, their families, and for the staff who care for them. These benefits are significant but are not easily quantified in monetary terms for inclusion in the ROI calculation.

While it is good to point out the benefits to NH residents of avoiding fractures and falls, whenever possible we want to bring it back to benefits that may be realized from the original perspective. That is, we can say that not only will residents receive a benefit from this intervention that is not included in the ROI calculations, but there are likely monetary benefits to CMS we are not capturing because there will be additional cost avoidance down the road from improved overall health. While one could attempt to estimate these costs, it can be a slippery slope. However, if you can identify strong literature or evidence that may allow you to quantify (even loosely) what that monetary benefit may be, it is certainly reasonable to include it in a sensitivity analysis.

7.1.1.5   Interpretation

Although we anticipate that the ROI to CMS during the initial nine-month observation period will be negative, we have demonstrated that if our estimates are accurate, CMS can expect to recoup the costs and begin to realize a net benefit in as little as 18–24 months after project initiation. Additionally, we believe that this change will be sustainable so that the net benefit in the coming years would be significant, for both CMS and the residents at these facilities.

We acknowledge that risks are associated with this intervention. Primarily, we have identified aspects of subject recruitment and intervention effectiveness as potentially susceptible to uncontrollable variability. However, through our sensitivity analyses we have demonstrated that even in situations where both recruitment and effectiveness are significantly worse than in the base case, the estimated payback period of the initial investment is still just over two years after project initiation. Additionally, given the demand for improvement in this area as reflected by the unsolicited requests of NH staff, we believe that our base case estimate of recruitment may be conservative so that the overall impact could likely be greater than estimated in our base case scenario.

We also acknowledge that serious falls represent only a subset of all falls. NH falls that do not result in serious injury or require medical attention are still important events to address and reduce. While the proposed intervention does not specifically target these types of falls, we anticipate that the activities intended to reduce serious falls may also reduce the likelihood and frequency of noninjurious falls. However, this project will not be able to quantify that impact or the associated monetary benefits (if there are any).

If successful, this intervention could be generalized to other NHs in different geographical areas. Nothing about our intervention is specific to this area or set of NHs, so there is no reason to believe that it could not be generalized or scaled to many more facilities.

> The interpretation should be thorough but brief. You have already stated much or all of this information previously and are simply summarizing it all into a single location. We have just touched on the results of the base case and sensitivity analysis, the potential risks and limitations, and the generalizability or scalability of the project. Given that this is intended to be part of a larger application, the goal is not to sell the reader on the intervention itself but to satisfy them that it is financially feasible and reasonable.

7.2 Example 2: Improving the Discharge Process

The Scenario: Like falls, the process of hospital discharge is often a topic of interest in federal quality monitoring programs. However, let us assume that this opportunity is initiated by hospital administrators who see it as a way to provide better care and improve coordination with community partners; let us also assume that these hospital administrators want to examine whether it could also result in an improved bottom line by reducing 30-day rates of readmission that can impact hospital reimbursement. In this case, hospital administrators need to be convinced that activities to improve the discharge process are worth pursuing instead of using available time and resources in other areas (the purchase of equipment, spending on facility improvements, additional staff, or quality improvement in other specific areas).

This example would be applicable either in the case where an administrative body wants to determine its own best course of action or where an outside organization wants to recruit the facility to participate in activities that have already been funded. This example, too, can serve as representative of a variety of process-improvement examples (increasing vaccination rates, improving handoff procedures for shift changes in a psychiatric facility, reducing door-to-needle time, etc.).

Decisions Made by Hospital Administrators Exploring this Opportunity: The perspective of this analysis will be that of the hospital because the administrators are trying to determine whether there is a business case for this project in addition to the benefits associated with improved care and coordination. While the administrators anticipate that they will be able to pay for the intervention with existing resources, for the analysis they will also examine ROI if they need to borrow money to fund some of the associated costs at an interest rate of 3%. They do not have any *a priori* thresholds for what they would consider to be an acceptable ROI; they acknowledge that a slightly negative ROI would be acceptable assuming they would recoup the investment within a reasonable time frame. They have already determined that hospital staff members are amenable to the proposed intervention and will willingly participate in the proposed activities to try to improve the discharge process.

7.2.1 Sample ROI Analysis

7.2.1.1 Background

Over the past five years, our facility has discharged an average of approximately 12,000 patients annually. During that time, our 30-day readmission rate has ranged from 12.4 to 18.4%, depending on the condition and year; the overall readmission rate in the last year across all conditions was 16.3%. For three of the last five years, we have fallen below the federal average and have experienced a reduction in reimbursement of approximately 0.25% each year, which equates to approximately $85,000 in penalties per year. In the other two years, we were within the range where there was no impact on our reimbursement.

The overall aim of this project is to improve the discharge process by implementing procedures demonstrated to be effective at other, similar facilities. We intend to provide patients with the necessary information to successfully navigate aftercare and the transition to home and take steps to ensure they understand and follow discharge instructions. As detailed elsewhere in this proposal, this intervention will include (1) a redesign of how discharge instructions are relayed to patients and in what format, (2) the addition of community resources available tailored to the individual patients' circumstances, and (3) one follow-up call by a nurse within 30 days to inquire about medication adherence and any outpatient appointments.

Costs will reflect those initially incurred to develop and implement the changes as well as ongoing costs associated with sustained changes (like the follow-up call). We anticipate a three-month period to develop materials and train staff in the new process, at which point we will launch the new process and collect information regarding readmissions for the 12-month period following initiation. Estimated monetary benefits will reflect the *estimated* change in readmission penalties associated with the decrease in readmission rate.

For this analysis, we will define metrics as follows:
ROI:

$$(\text{Benefits from Reduced Penalties} - \text{Costs of Intervention})/\text{Costs} \times 100\%$$

Benefit-to-cost ratio (BCR):

$$(\text{Benefits from Reduced Penalties})/(\text{Costs of Intervention})$$

Where you decide to put the metric definitions is up to you. We could have just as easily put the definitions just stated in the more technical sections that follow, but I have chosen to put them here because we need to provide some general indication of how we are going to measure costs and benefits in this scenario. Instead of using estimated changes we could use *actual* changes in penalties to assess this intervention, but often those penalties are calculated months later and subsequent adjustments to reimbursements occur a year or more after the care was originally provided. Using estimated values will allow the facility to get feedback regarding the success of this program sooner than that and is a reasonable substitute for actual changes in this situation.

If this ROI analysis is not part of a larger report that provides details on the intervention and the motivation for it, you would likely include more details when providing the background on how the intervention was designed and developed, including supporting information or published studies of previous endeavors. Here, I'm assuming that the ROI analysis is part of a larger application where much of those details appear elsewhere and here we need only to describe the pieces of the intervention that have costs associated with them.

7.2.1.2 Assumptions and Estimates

Given the success of similar programs, we estimate that we can lower our readmission rates by roughly 2–3 percentage points (by condition), so that in general they range from roughly 10–15%, depending on condition. Similar facilities have observed one-year decreases in readmission rates ranging from 0.4 percentage points to 5.3 percentage points (Smith 2009; Johnson 2012; Anderson 2014; Lee 2018), although these studies represent a variety of conditions. Additionally, while these examples focused on a single intervention, we intend to employ a multifaceted approach to maximize the impact in a short time frame. Therefore, we believe a 2–3 percentage point reduction is reasonable.

There is a lot going on here. You can imagine that even going through the exercise of crafting this paragraph, those designing the project and writing this proposal are made aware of all the potential challenges and barriers. Upon reviewing the information just presented, a critic might argue that more needs to be considered before landing on the estimate of 2–3 percentage points. In this example, the effectiveness of the intervention to reduce readmissions is the main driver of realized benefits; that is, while in the previous example there were other variables like the frequency distribution of the type of medical attention required after a fall and the associated cost of treating each one, here the benefits are subject only to the relative performance in readmission rate of this facility versus its peers as evaluated by the federal program calculating penalties. Therefore, this assumption is the lynchpin that if not credible will likely derail the entire proposal. This also assumes that the authors can attribute any and all improvements in readmission rate to this intervention. That will definitely be something we will need to address in the sensitivity analysis and interpretation section.

One option for internal staff to assess the feasibility of such an improvement is to put it in real terms. That is, this facility has roughly 12,000 discharges per year, an average of 1000 per month; if 18% are readmitted within 30 days, then prior to the intervention, one could expect roughly 180 readmissions. Reducing a readmission rate from 18 to 15% equates to avoiding 30 readmissions per month (i.e., maybe that means eight fewer heart failure readmissions, six fewer acute myocardial infarction readmissions, etc.). Staff may have opinions about whether that is reasonable given their personal experiences.

Some readmissions are likely not avoidable, while others may clearly be a result of poor medication adherence, a failure to connect to an available community service, or some other aspect that could be addressed by improvements in the discharge process. This can also be a good strategy if one is unsure of what level of effectiveness to target; breaking it down into real counts of each condition may allow those planning the intervention to estimate what is reasonable. Additionally, if trying to convince internal administrators to fund this initiative, that type of information may be especially convincing. Here, however, we will stick to the current estimates in the form of percentages.

Table 7.7 displays the estimated monetary benefits associated with different reductions in the average readmission rate. The overall estimate reflects an average across conditions.

Table 7.7 Estimated monetary benefits of reduced readmission rates from reductions in federal reimbursement penalties

Post-intervention overall 12-month readmission rate (%)	Estimated benefits from reduced penalties[a]	Justification for estimate of benefit
16	$25,000	Penalized, but less so
15	$45,000	Penalized, but less so
14	$85,000	No penalty
13	$85,000	No penalty
12	$110,000	Bonus received

[a]These values reflect the estimated relative standing our facility would have if we achieved the associated readmission rate, and the relative improvement to our current performance (e.g., the $85,000 savings for rates of 14 and 13% reflect the likelihood that we would fall into the group of hospitals that receive neither a penalty nor a reward)

This is done here for the sake of simplicity. That is, even though readmissions for heart failure and acute myocardial infarction are going to be more common than those for a broken hip or influenza, in this application the authors have ignored that and are shooting for an overall reduction. One could just as easily make assumptions about each individual condition to allow for the fact that perhaps the intervention is likely to have more of an effect for some conditions. Then, the sensitivity analysis could include explorations into how the ROI changes when those individual assumptions change. Or, this entire analysis could be limited to one, or a small number, of key conditions—maybe those targeted by most federal programs. The process would be the same, however, so for simplicity we will use the overall average readmission reduction. Note that the estimated benefits here really reflect estimated reduction in penalties. That is, achieving 14 or 13% means that they will not be penalized, which would be an improvement of $85,000 compared to what would happen if there was no improvement. Similarly, the benefit of $110,000 reflects no longer incurring a penalty of $85,000 plus receiving an actual bonus of $25,000.

Estimated costs are described in Table 7.8 for each period of the intervention and by implementation activity. These costs are based on internal estimates and conversations with current staff.

Table 7.8 Total estimated costs

Implementation activity	Cost sources	Pre-intervention (3 months)	Post-intervention (12 months)
New discharge instruction format	Staff time	$5,000	$8000
	Materials	$10,000	$2000
	Training	$15,000	$1000
	IT support	$2000	$500
Community service information	Staff time	$5000	$0
	Materials	$3000	$1000
	Training	$2000	$0
Nurse follow-up call[a]	Staff time	$0	$2500
	Materials	$2000	$0
	Training	$5000	$2000
Totals		$49,000	$17,000

[a]This assumes roughly 200 calls per month lasting an average of 30 min

It would be okay to break this down into monthly costs, but then the total cost would need to be presented either in another set of columns or in the text. You might as well have the table reflect the total costs, and you can insert the monthly breakdown in the text if you feel it is necessary to demonstrate how it falls out on a per-month basis. One reasonable alternative is: Leave the pre-intervention displayed as is but report the post-intervention costs on a per-month basis, since presumably these costs will be incurred on an ongoing basis for as long as this process is employed (i.e., beyond the 12-month evaluation period, assuming it is effective). Also, "staff time" may need to have several rows depending on how many or what type of staff is needed at each stage.

The total estimated cost associated with developing the necessary materials and training the necessary staff during the pre-intervention period and implementing the process during a 12-month period is $66,000.

7.2.1.3 Base Case and Sensitivity Analysis

Conservatively, we believe that we can expect the overall readmission rate to decrease to at least 15% and to fall to as low as 12 or 13%. In Table 7.9, we present the base case calculation of ROI and BCR using the just mentioned estimated costs for a variety of post-intervention overall readmission rates.

We can see that only if we achieved the minimum amount of improvement expected (readmission rate is only reduced to 15%) would the return be negative. In that scenario, there would be a total of ($66,000 − $45,000) = $21,000 not recouped in the first 12 months. However, over the following 12 months, if we perform no worse (15% readmission rate), by the end of year two we would realize a positive return, even after incurring another year of program costs of $17,000. That is, we would begin the second year with $21,000 in losses and incur another $17,000 in program costs but would realize $45,000 in benefits from *not* incurring the poor performance penalty, for a net positive return of $7,000:

Table 7.9 Base case analysis

Post-intervention readmission rate (%)	ROI (%)	BCR
15	−31.8	0.68
14	28.8	1.29
13	28.8	1.29
12	66.7	1.67

$$(-\$21,000 - \$17,000 + \$45,000) = \$7,000.$$

You will notice that we did not do a formal calculation of the payback period. It is not always necessary. Often, the notion of how long until funds are recouped can simply be described in the narrative, as in this situation. In fact, to introduce an additional metric may just make the presentation more convoluted. How you do it will be a matter of personal choice and whatever the situation calls for.

Also, when we extend these calculations for another year we are reaching a bit for a couple of reasons. First, we have not discounted (we also have not taken into consideration that we may be borrowing 80% of the funds up front, but we will tackle that soon). Second, negating a penalty in the current year is one thing, but trying to extend the avoided penalty as a benefit too far into the future may not always appear credible to your audience.

A reviewer of your proposal may ask things like, "How do you know the trend wouldn't have decreased due to some other factor by that point?" (You don't, but by the same token it may be reasonable to assume that if nothing is done it may even go up!) Or, "How do you know that the costs of your intervention won't change? What if you decide to alter the process…wouldn't that incur additional costs?" (Yes, it would, and whether you choose to alter the process, have staff turnover, lose staff morale for the process, or any number of other of things will depend on your situation and facility, so it's hard to say here.) The point is that you cannot just extend costs and benefits indefinitely. You still need to consider them as reflecting real-world situations, and therefore if they are not specifically controlled for, they are subject to be changed, terminated, adjusted, etc.

We understand that if administrators choose to fund this project, they may decide to borrow money to cover the pre-intervention costs (roughly 80% of the total cost) at an annual interest rate of 3%. In that case, the true cost at the end of 15 months (the three-month pre-intervention period and the 12-month follow-up) would be:

$$\left[\$49,000 \times (1.03)^{1.25}\right] + \$17,000 = \$67,844$$

This would not appreciably change the ROI or BCR calculations. Therefore, we will continue using the original cost estimate of $66,000 for simplicity.

Table 7.10 Sensitivity analysis

Post-intervention readmission rate (%)	Costs 15% lower		Costs 15% higher	
	ROI (%)	BCR	ROI (%)	BCR
15	−19.8	0.80	−40.7	0.59
14	51.5	1.52	12.0	1.12
13	51.5	1.52	12.0	1.12
12	96.1	1.96	44.9	1.45

In addition to variability in the effectiveness of the intervention, the possibility of variability in the estimated costs exists. As a sensitivity analysis, we have repeated the ROI and BCR calculations if costs are either 15% lower or 15% higher than expected (Table 7.10).

This table demonstrates that even with significant variability in the costs, the main driver of whether there is a positive return on this investment is whether we can reduce overall readmission rates to 14% or lower.

Finally, we also recognize that in addition to natural variation in readmission rates from year to year, other factors can affect the frequency of readmission. Therefore, it may be unreasonable to attribute all changes to readmission rate to this intervention. Under the conservative assumption that only 75% of the change in readmission can be directly attributable to this intervention, it still remains true that all but the minimum level of expected improvement will still produce an acceptable ROI: Reducing the readmission rate to 12% would produce a ROI of 25% (BCR of 1.25), while improvements to rates of 14 or 13% would result in roughly a cost-neutral situation as reflected by a ROI of −3.4% (BCR of 0.97).

In this situation, the base case and sensitivity analysis are basically presented together instead of in separate sections. As with many things, this is a matter of personal preference and what the situation calls for. Here, there are very few things that can vary, and really only one affects whether the result is a positive ROI. Therefore, it seems prudent to present everything together to allow the reader to review it all at once. Finally, the percent of the decrease that can be reasonably attributed to our intervention is not supported by any documented evidence. The goal in this example is to demonstrate how it might be incorporated, and the actual percentage we use for the calculations is immaterial in that demonstration. However, if this were a real analysis we would need to provide more evidence of why we believe that is a reasonable percentage or explore other possible percentages.

7.2.1.4 Interpretation

The analysis just presented demonstrates that as long as we can improve (reduce) the overall readmission rate by at least the minimum we believe possible, this project will produce a positive ROI within 12 months after implementation. In the worst scenario explored (where costs are 15% higher than expected and readmission is reduced only slightly, to 15% overall), the 12-month ROI would be −40.7% (and would be slightly lower if any money was borrowed to fund this project). Even in this scenario, we would have introduced a discharge process that improved patient care and resulted in better patient outcomes and quality of life and would likely reduce future penalties associated with readmission rates. We believe it is likely, in this scenario, that costs would be fully recouped within two to three years.

We acknowledge that risks are associated with this intervention. First, we are assuming that staff will participate fully and "buy-in" to the new discharge process. Additionally, we are assuming that the intervention will be sustainable for at least 12 months. If either of these assumptions turn out to be false, the initial investment of $49,000 could be a sunk cost, although terminating the intervention early would avoid the first-year implementation cost of $17,000. However, given the success of similar programs at similar facilities, we believe that these assumptions are valid and reasonable.

We also recognize that care received by patients outside of our facility or the healthcare system that we operate within may not be captured by our data collection, and therefore we may underestimate true readmission. However, as detailed elsewhere, we can use historical data to estimate the proportion of all readmissions (from federal program data) that we can capture (from our internal records), so that we feel confident in our ability to estimate the true readmission rates using our observed rates.

Finally, even if we do not attribute a sizeable portion of the expected improvement in readmission to our intervention, our calculations demonstrate that it is likely we will receive a return that will make our efforts at least cost neutral in the first year.

In the majority of reasonable scenarios, we explored the return was significantly positive within the first year. As long as overall readmission falls to 14% or lower, the anticipated return may range from 12% to as high as 96%, any of which represent substantial monetary gains over such a short period. Additionally, this type of improvement would motivate staff to pursue other interventions and would likely position us to have funds available to spend on either quality improvement or other staff and facility needs.

In this type of a ROI analysis where success is driven by one factor (i.e., the effectiveness of the intervention), it is not a bad idea to reinforce your faith in the effectiveness and mention the upside as well as the downside.

Clearly, this is a simplified version of this type of ROI analysis, but it is illustrative, in part, to drive home the point that you should let the scope of the analysis drive the complexity of the report. There is not that much to show for this ROI, so do not feel like you have to pad it with unnecessary metrics or too much speculation about what could happen. As it stands, it demonstrates what it needs to: that the return is largely driven by the success of the intervention, even if expected costs vary substantially. When presented within a larger proposal that extols the virtues and demonstrates that the intervention is very likely to produce results better than the minimum expectations, this analysis provides the reader credible evidence that the project is unlikely to lose money for the institution, which is exactly the goal in many cases.

The part about attributable benefits is tricky. It is certainly reasonable to mention and explore, but depending on the available evidence, if there is any, it may be difficult to make any concrete claims about how much of the benefit will be directly attributable to our intervention. One could even argue that a good intervention would mitigate negative external or uncontrollable factors and would accentuate positive ones. If that were true, then achieving a decrease in readmission rates to "only" 15% might actually reflect *more* benefit than we are giving the intervention credit for because perhaps if we had done nothing, things would have gotten much worse, instead of staying static. It is difficult to know. All you can do is try to think about every reasonable possibility and attempt to apply credible logic to examine and explore the variety of outcomes.

7.3   Example 3: Introducing a Collaborative Care Model

The Scenario: Some published literature demonstrates that care for those with multiple chronic conditions can be difficult to coordinate and that patients often struggle to manage their disease burden adequately without additional assistance, especially if they also suffer from a psychological disorder. Some are now exploring the effectiveness of collaborative care that incorporates regular contact with a healthcare provider, such as a nurse, to check control of common clinical indicators (HbA1c, lipids, blood pressure, etc.). In this scenario, the provider is also called upon to assess current disease management related to symptoms and medications as well as education for improved self-care and even support for family caregivers.

If a physician or healthcare system were to implement care that incorporated the key aspects of these collaborative models, it would likely be necessary to demonstrate to multiple parties its financial viability. Here is another example where it may not be necessary to demonstrate a positive ROI if one also highlights the significant improvements in outcomes and quality of life for patients and caregivers; but the realities of the business of health care dictate that it cannot be a huge financial loss.

This type of analysis can be difficult to conceptualize because whenever one considers the benefits in the form of avoiding costs associated with providing care, one needs to be cognizant that some or most of the costs will likely be reimbursed by a private or public payer. So are they really "costs" in the traditional sense? Also, some of the costs associated with providing care in an inpatient facility are fixed (rent, utilities, administrative costs, etc.), which would be incurred regardless of how many patients are cared for and to what extent. This, too, should be considered and discussed as appropriate given the situation. This example will serve as a model for interventions intended to change the standard of care and/or a series of processes associated with patient care, well-being, and experience.

The perspective of this analysis will be that of the healthcare system where the care program has been instituted. We will assume that this analysis is occurring two years after initiation as a retrospective exploration of what happened as a way to establish its merit going forward. This type of analysis could also be presented to policy makers to persuade them to adjust policy to help fund such programs.

7.3.1   Sample ROI Analysis

7.3.1.1   Background

Twenty-four months ago, we implemented a collaborative care program intended to improve care for patients with multiple chronic conditions (such as diabetes, cardiovascular disease, depression) and provide the necessary education and support for them and their informal caregivers. Our facility cares for roughly 250 patients per year who have two or more of the targeted conditions, and historically the costs to care each patient have ranged from $15,000 to $20,000 annually or between $3.75 million and $5 million in the aggregate (in 2019 dollars).

After considerable time and effort to develop the program and determine how to implement it within our system, we now have the benefit of two years of real costs and benefits to evaluate the financial viability of this program for continued use.

The analysis that follows will examine the ongoing costs and benefits separate from the initial investment in order to provide an estimate of the expected return in future years if this program is to be continued.

All costs reflect salary and fringe benefit expenses adjusted to reflect the proportion of each staff member's time spent working on this program and to care for patients within the program.

Benefits reflect the change in patient utilization of healthcare services (inpatient, emergency department, and outpatient) from the year prior to the implementation of the intervention. All costs and benefits are expressed in 2019 dollars.

7.3.1.2 Costs and Benefits

Table 7.11 details the annual costs to administer the program and care for patients involved in it.

These staff categories typically reflect effort from multiple individuals. Over the last two years, we have had cardiologists, endocrinologists, psychologists, pharmacists, geriatricians, and others participate in some form. Additionally, the RN role is staffed by five different nurses who contribute anywhere from 0.10 to 0.50 FTE each to the program. These costs do not reflect those incurred by other facilities or organizations when patients are referred for additional care (e.g., inpatient psychiatric treatment, kidney dialysis, long-term nursing care, etc.).

Notice that the number of patients who participated differed between years one and two. During year one, fewer patients than expected were enrolled due to the learning curve of staff regarding identifying and enrolling patients. Therefore, the effort distribution differed and the cost of the program per patient differed noticeably.

Table 7.11 Annual staff costs (salaries and fringe benefits), 2019 US $

Staff member	Year 1		Year 2	
Staff	FTE	Cost	FTE	Cost
Physician[a]	1.0	$248,000	1.25	$310,000
RN	1.75	$105,000	1.5	$90,000
Social worker	0.8	$60,000	1.0	$75,000
Admin	1.2	$40,000	1.5	$50,000
Total		$453,000		$525,000
N patients	158		262	
Cost per patient		$2867		$2004

[a]Multiple specialties (cardiology, endocrinology, psychology, pharmacy, etc.) contribute small portions of time for consult and coordination of care

As mentioned previously, monetary benefits are calculated as reduced utilization costs from before to after the implementation of the collaborative care program. Table 7.12 displays costs by category for each of the two years the program has been in effect in addition to the year prior to the program's initiation. All costs are in 2019 dollars.

Numbers in the aggregate are in $100,000 units, so total utilization in the year prior incurred $2.5 million, and for years one and two of the program, the total utilization expenditures were $1.3 million and $1.9 million, respectively (Fig. 7.2).

However, only 158 patients were enrolled in the program during the first year, due to the reasons enumerated previously. Therefore, the aggregate values for year

Table 7.12 Healthcare expenditures by year, 2019 US dollars

	Source	Year prior	Year 1	Year 2	Prior—Year 1 difference	Prior—Year 2 difference
Aggregate[a]	Inpatient	$1448	$769	$1120	$719	$368
	ED	$650	$219	$264	$432	$386
	Outpatient	$340	$265	$504	$75	−$164
	Total	$2479	$1253	$1889	$1225	$590
Per patient	N	243	158	262		
	Inpatient	$6125	$4867	$4277	$1258	$1848
	ED	$2677	$1385	$1009	$1292	$1668
	Outpatient	$1398	$1678	$1924	−$280	−$526
	Total	$10,200	$7930	$7210	$2270	$2990

[a]in $100,000 s

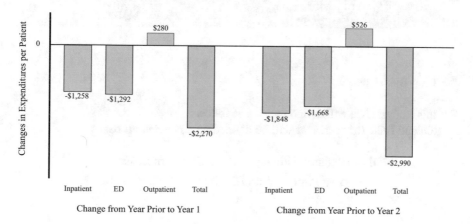

Fig. 7.2 Change in healthcare expenditures from year prior, per patient

one of the program are lower than for the year prior in part because they reflect fewer patients. This suggests that to truly assess the return of the project we should examine the per-patient values. The last row of the last two columns represents the per-patient benefits as reflected in reduced healthcare utilization expenditures of between roughly $2300 and $3000 per patient.

Also, while inpatient and emergency department (ED) expenditures after the initiation of the collaborative care program were reduced, outpatient expenditures in each year of the program actually increased. This reflects the increase in the number of outpatient visits by these patients. We believe the increase is due to the improved care management in the form of better clinic appointment attendance and more preventive and proactive care in this setting. In short, it appears that there was a shift in some care from the inpatient and ED setting to the outpatient setting.

Anytime you have a table with a lot of information in it, do not assume your reader will fully decipher it and pull from it what you are intending. This table requires some explanation and includes some important points you do not want the reader to miss, including that there were significantly fewer patients in year one than in either year two or the year prior, and that there was a shift in care setting to outpatient care. This is another reason why the figure may be useful to the reader.

Also, while the intended audience will likely understand the use of per-patient metrics for evaluating return, they will likely also be interested in the aggregate values since they reflect overall utilization, regardless of the reasons. That is, while it is true that lower enrollment in year one reduced the associated utilization, this truth reflects the messiness inherent in many of these projects, and whether it was anticipated, it has very real effects on the bottom line and the financial return of this project.

7.3.1.3 Base Case

For this analysis, we will define metrics as follows:
ROI and BCR for each year will be defined on a *per-patient* basis:

$$\text{ROI} = (\text{Reduced Utilization Expenditures from the}$$
$$\text{Year Prior} - \text{Yearly Costs})/\text{Yearly Costs} \times 100\%$$

BCR = (Reduced Utilization Expenditures from the Year Prior)/(Yearly Costs)

where in each case the reduced utilization expenditures and the yearly costs reflect the per-patient values in the previous table.

> By presenting the aggregate values, you allow the reader to examine the program's impact on an aggregate level if they so choose. But, as the one conducting this analysis, it is your job to help the reader interpret the analysis, and part of that means guiding them logically through the process and demonstrating to them why it makes sense, in this case, to focus on the per-patient values.

Table 7.13 displays the ROI and BCR calculations for each year of the program. While year one demonstrated a greater aggregate benefit, we have noted previously that this was partially due to fewer patients being included, and when calculated on a per-patient basis, the ROI is actually worse than in year two where the aggregate benefit was actually less than in year one.

The positive return in year two reflects the per-patient net benefit of $986 ($2990 − $2004) or roughly $1.49 in reduced utilization expenditures for every $1.00 in costs to run the program.

In addition to the ongoing costs, we also invested $125,000 into the development of the program including necessary materials, education, and training. Even though this was a one-time cost (a "fixed cost"), to assess return on the total investment to this point we need to consider the cumulative costs and benefits.

> The economic concept we are addressing here is the distinction between fixed and variable costs, and specifically, since we are talking about values on a per-patient basis we are referring to average fixed costs (AFCs) and average variable costs (AVCs). This is important because while the AVC will continue year after year, the AFC will slowly decrease as we spread that one-time cost over more and more patients who participate in the program. So, after the first year, the per-patient cost of that initial investment was $791.14, after two years it was $477.10, and it will just continue to decrease each year as its cost is spread over more patients.

Table 7.13 ROI and BCR per patient for Years 1 and 2

Metric	Year 1	Year 2
ROI per patient	−20.8%	49.2%
BCR per patient	0.79	1.49

The goal of the analysis is to demonstrate the ongoing financial viability of the program, which on a yearly basis will only include the variable costs. Therefore, it makes sense to examine ROI and BCR in Table 7.13 using only those costs. However, it is also prudent to present ROI using the total costs up to this point, which include the $125,000 initial investment. Depending on the scenario and the goals of the analysis, there may be an argument for excluding the one-time investment, but the safest route is to present the information both ways to allow the reader to make up their own mind about what is reasonable.

The first two years of the program included $158 + 262 = 420$ patients; the ongoing costs totaled $978,000 so that when added to the initial investment we obtain a total cost of $1,103,000 or $2,626.19 per patient. The total benefits in the form of reduced utilization expenditure during those same two years equal $2,719.14 per patient, for a total ROI after two years of 3.5%.

7.3.1.4   Sensitivity Analysis

On a yearly basis, the financial viability of this program relies on the amount of staff time required to perform the necessary duties and the ability to maintain the reduction in care utilization that we have observed up to this point. Therefore, we should examine how those values impacted the returns during the first two years in order to better anticipate future needs.

If the staffing costs were increased by 10 and 20%, the yearly return (excluding the original investment) would remain positive assuming a per-patient benefit of $2719 (Table 7.14). Additionally, if we could incorporate efficiencies that would reduce the time required by physicians (the most expensive labor category) through higher utilization of the less expensive RNs and social workers, it would positively impact financial return.

The redistribution of staff time proposed in the last column of Table 7.14 would maintain the fidelity of the program while keeping costs at a minimum, thereby maximizing return going forward.

The largest impact on reduced utilization expenditures came from the inpatient setting. We explored this further to determine how much of this reduction was from reduced length of stay (LOS) versus fewer encounters. Our analysis (not shown) revealed that the majority of the savings resulted from a reduction in the average number of inpatient encounters per patient, while LOS remained relatively constant. Whether future benefits of reduced LOS are possible remains to be seen, but it could be a potential opportunity to consider.

We should also address the fact that not all utilization expenditures are direct costs. That is, there exist expenditures related to utilities and facilities that are incurred whether a patient is treated or not. Previous examination of our internal account systems suggests that roughly 45% of costs are directly related to caring for patients. When we recalculate changes in utilization expenditures to reflect only 45% of the original values, while maintaining program costs as constant, we produce a net loss per patient: The calculated benefit in year two would be 45% of the year two value or $0.45 \times \$2990 = \$1346$. This is less than the per-patient costs of $2004 by more than $650 per patient.

Lastly, we should at least mention the intangible benefits associated with better patient outcomes (e.g., fewer hospitalizations) and reduced stress and anxiety of both patients and their families. While not quantified here, going forward we could attempt to quantify the impact by administering valid tools (e.g., PHQ-9) both before and after enrollment in the program and then by using published literature to equate improvements to economic benefits.

Because this analysis is retrospective and performed for a summary report instead of prospectively for a proposal, our sensitivity analysis looks a little different. Instead of examining the effect on return of variation in estimates or assumptions about what *will* happen, we seek to examine how variability in observed results *could have* affected the financial returns, to inform future decisions about continued viability. This may also inform future projects and proposals, and the complexity of this analysis is determined by the needs of the individual project.

Table 7.14 Yearly staffing costs, sensitivity analysis, 2019 US $, assuming 250 patients per year

Staff member	10% higher[a]		20% higher[a]		Redistribute staff time	
Staff	FTE	Cost	FTE	Cost	FTE	Cost
Physician	1.375	$341,000	1.5	$372,000	0.8	$198,400
RN	1.65	$99,000	1.8	$108,000	2.0	$120,000
Social worker	1.1	$82,500	1.2	$90,000	1.5	$112,500
Admin	1.65	$55,00	1.8	$60,000	1.5	$50,000
Total		$577,500		$630,000		$480,900
N patients	250		250		250	
Cost per patient		$2310		$2520		$1924

[a]Compared to year two of the program

7.3.1.5 Interpretation

The results of this analysis indicate that the level of monetary return of the collaborative care model depends on several definitions and assumptions. In the base case, we demonstrated that the ROI was negative in year one and positive in year two on a per-patient basis. Assuming that year two would be more representative of future years (since year one involved a learning curve and experienced less than optimal patient enrollment and participation), then there is evidence that future years can continue to produce net monetary benefits, plus nonmonetary gains associated with improved clinical outcomes and reduced burden for family caregivers. Additionally, it may be possible to improve return if the effort needed from physicians can be reduced and shifted to RNs and social workers.

However, this conclusion depends on several things. First, we are considering reduced utilization expenditures to be a benefit even though they may not reflect the true monetary benefit to our healthcare system; some or most of these expenditures are reimbursed to us by public or private payers, and some fixed costs would exist regardless of whether patients are cared for or not, meaning that they cannot truly be reduced. Using only utilization expenditures directly for patient care, a net monetary loss results; we would either need to reconsider how to more efficiently utilize staff or accept this loss (given that it is on a per-person and direct-cost basis, as opposed to the true bottom line) to have better patient care and quality of life.

Second, we are assuming that these benefits are solely attributable to the introduction of the collaborative care model and are positing that the use of the model will continue to provide a similar benefit in the years to come. We are also ignoring issues related to economies of scale (efficiencies that are related to the number of patients included) and assuming that the observed per-patient benefit will be similar even if the number or type of patients included varies.

In this example, what is truly concluded will probably depend on the situation and what the authors and their audience determine are the appropriate assumptions and definitions to use. For example, whether they consider the full reduction in utilization expenditures to reflect a benefit or whether they consider only the 45% directly associated with patient care will heavily influence what they decide about the financial strength of the program. Similarly, if the main objective was to improve patient and caregiver mental and emotional well-being, the costs would probably also be weighed against formal measures of any changes in those symptoms (which we did not explore in this example but only alluded to and suggested that we may measure them going forward).

Our goal in performing the analysis and creating the report is to clearly describe what was done, how costs and benefits were measured, and what variability exists and its effect on the measured return. The interpretation in this case is largely situation specific.

Additionally, this entire analysis would be different if alternative metrics were chosen. For example, in a collaborative care program that seeks to manage multiple chronic diseases like diabetes, hyperlipidemia, hypertension, etc., one could very easily use clinical metrics related to the control of glycemic, lipid, and blood-pressure indicators to determine success and then equate those changes to monetary benefits through published evidence of their association to costs. That is, there exists literature on how many adverse events can be avoided by keeping each of those metrics in control or by lowering them by a specific amount. We could have approached this as an exercise in estimating reasonable reductions in those metrics and then extrapolated to estimate the number of adverse events avoided and the associated cost avoidance. That type of analysis is more like what was done in the first example on nursing home falls.

In this analysis, the authors do not try to identify or even describe the antecedents to the reduction in care utilization. The reason, in part, is because their goal is not to estimate what might happen but instead to report on what did happen. A fruitful exercise in this type of situation would be to compare not only the realized costs and benefits to what was estimated prior to implementing the model but also to dig into the drivers of these costs and benefits (the frequency of each type of event of care, LOS for inpatient stays, common diagnoses and procedures, etc.) to see if one can more fully understand the causes of the observed results.

As is often the case with these examples, we could explore and pursue a litany of possibilities and avenues, but we need to be careful to place the analysis within the specific context and framework for which it is applicable.

7.4   Example 4: Investing in Facility Improvements

The Scenario: Hospital and clinic administrators are often faced with decisions regarding whether to invest in their facility to expand, renovate, or improve. These investments can be substantial, and there may be a variety of justifications for what is prudent. However, sometimes a business case can be made by examining how the investments may affect the quality of care delivery and exploring potential revenue gains or cost reductions enabled by the renovation.

Here, we will explore a scenario where a hospital has completed a renovation of their emergency department that not only updated the existing space, but also added capacity by creating additional examination rooms. Part of their justification for the renovation, we will see, is that the improvements may help reduce the percent of patients who leave the ED without being seen by a care provider, which is a common metric of ED crowding and quality of care. This example could be representative of several types of situations where investments are made to either the physical environment or the training or well-being of the staff that may result in improvements to care quality in addition to financial gain. The perspective of this retrospective analysis will be facility or hospital administrators and will represent a ROI analysis included in a summary report.

7.4.1   Sample ROI Analysis

7.4.1.1   Background

As a level one trauma center, the physicians and administrators at our hospital fully understand the crucial role our emergency department plays in providing timely and high-quality care for patients. We have known for some time that our ED was aging to the point where functionality was impaired and efficiency was affected. Additionally, our patient volume had grown to where patient wait times were rising. We suspected that this was contributing to a higher-than-desired rate of patients leaving without being seen (LWBS). During the proposal and planning stages of the ED renovation, we estimated how an updated facility and increased capacity (from three additional examination rooms) could reduce wait times and ultimately the LWBS rate.

The renovation was completed approximately 15 months ago, which has allowed us to collect data regarding LWBS for a full year to assess the extent of any improvements resulting from this renovation. This report summarizes those original estimates and compares them to what we have observed in the first 12 months of operation of the fully renovated ED.

7.4.1.2   Baseline Assessment and Assumptions

During the proposal stage, we attempted to estimate the potential financial return associated with reducing the LWBS rate. To do this, we used a combination of historical data and assumptions. Specifically, we had data to inform: the average monthly volume, patient acuity upon arrival, overall LWBS rates, and average revenue loss due to a patient leaving without being seen. We also made several assumptions when we lacked certain data. First, we assumed that the main reason for a patient leaving without being seen was due to wait times so that reductions in wait times due to increased efficiency and capacity allowed by the renovation would directly reduce LWBS rates. Additionally, we understand that multiple other factors influence the likelihood that a patient will leave, but we chose patient acuity as another main driver: Those with less urgent needs would be more likely to leave than those who were high acuity.

Specifically, we categorized patients into two acuity levels: "urgent" and "nonurgent" and assumed that nonurgent patients were three times more likely to leave than urgent patients.

Using historical data on the overall LWBS rates and the percent of presenting patients who could be categorized as either nonurgent (40%) or urgent (60%), we estimated the contribution to LWBS (and associated lost revenue) by acuity. We chose to approach the estimation this way because we expected that the renovations would have a significantly larger impact on reducing LWBS for nonurgent patients than for urgent patients. Table 7.15 summarizes the values either calculated or assumed for the baseline projections of financial impact of LWBS.

We used the following expressions and known quantities—along with our assumption about the relative rate of LWBS—to estimate the contribution of nonurgent patients to LWBS and therefore the potential opportunity for improvement.

Specifically, overall LWBS can be written as a function of the LWBS of each acuity group:

$$\text{LWBS}_{\text{all}} = [\text{LWBS}_{\text{nu}} \times P_{\text{nu}}] + [\text{LWBS}_{\text{u}} \times P_{\text{u}}] \qquad (7.2)$$

In this equation, P_{nu} and P_{u} are the proportions of all presenting patients who are nonurgent and urgent, respectively. Similarly, there are placeholders for each group's LWBS that we will solve for.

Table 7.15 Baseline estimates of ED efficiency

	Total	Nonurgent	Urgent
Ave monthly volume	3500	1400 (40%)	2100 (60%)
LWBS	8.44%	(unknown)[a]	(unknown)[a]
Cost per LWBS episode	$650		

[a]Estimated below by assuming that nonurgent patients' LWBS rate is three times that of urgent patients

Recognizing that the proportion of nonurgent patients is simply one minus the proportion of urgent patients, and that the LWBS rate for nonurgent patients is assumed to be three times that of urgent patients, we can rewrite Eq. 7.2 as follows:

$$LWBS_{all} = [3 \times LWBS_u \times (1 - P_u)] + [LWBS_u \times P_u] \qquad (7.3)$$

Collecting like terms and solving for the LWBS for urgent patients produces the following:

$$LWBS_u = (LWBS_{all})/[3 - 2P_u] \qquad (7.4)$$

When we plug in the values for the overall LWBS rate (8.44%) and proportion of urgent patients (60%) from historical data, we obtain an estimate of the LWBS rate for urgent patients of 4.69%. To obtain the estimate for the nonurgent patients' LWBS, we simply multiply that rate by three and get 14.07%.

Here, we assume that wait time is primarily a cause of LWBS for nonurgent patients (but not for urgent patients), and that the difference in LWBS rates between urgent and nonurgent patients is *because of* wait time. That is, if nonurgent patients' LWBS rate could be made to equal that of urgent patients (4.69%), the overall LWBS rate would drop from 8.44 to 4.69%. Therefore, we assume that the contribution made by nonurgent patients, through excessive wait time, to the overall LWBS rate is the difference between those values, and the total contribution to monthly revenue loss is calculated as:

$$(8.44\% - 4.69\%) \times 3500 \times \$650 = \$85,338 \qquad (7.5)$$

When multiplied by 12, this value equates to a total revenue loss of $1,024,053 annually. We determined that the impact of the renovation on wait times could be substantial enough to result in a relative reduction in the nonurgent LWBS rate of 50%, which would theoretically result in a return of (50% × $1,024,053) = $512,027 per year. Given that the renovation was projected to cost $1.38 million, a 50% reduction would recoup the cost in less than three years (2.7 years).

The value calculated in Eq. 7.5 is considered to be the *potential* monthly savings that could be realized if the LWBS rate for nonurgent patients could be reduced to that of urgent patients. Our stated assumption is that this difference is primarily driven by wait times, so in our proposal we intended to pursue this potential savings by reducing wait times. However, it does not really matter whether wait time is the only reason for the difference in LWBS rates between urgent and nonurgent patients—any reduction in the dollar amount in Eq. 7.5

represents a financial return in this scenario. The reason to approach it as we have here is to focus on the benefits we can attribute to our intervention. We have said that we do not believe that the LWBS rate of urgent patients is (as) affected by wait time, so we do not want to attribute any observed reductions in LWBS rates for that group to our intervention. We also do not want to let other variables, like the relative frequency of urgent versus nonurgent patients seen at our ED, to erroneously impact our calculated benefits.

The process outlined above from Eqs. 7.2 to 7.5 is not immediately intuitive for most people. If you struggle to follow the algebra without the intermediate steps presented, consider this simplified example: Assume half of the patients are urgent and half are nonurgent (so equal numbers of each). If the overall LWBS rate is 6% and nonurgent patients are three times more likely to leave, then the respective LWBS rates are 3 and 9%. Why? Because 9% is three times that of 3%, and their average is 6% (the overall rate). The example presented in this section simply includes more complicated calculations by using nonround numbers and assumes that each type of patient is not equally represented in the population. So, even though nonurgent patients are more likely to leave without being seen, there are fewer nonurgent patients, so they contribute less to the overall average. The 8.44% is a *weighted* average of the individual rates, where the weights reflect their relative frequency in the population.

Finally, the logic as presented applies to other situations where unequal contributions to an event or outcome occur based on some characteristic or variable. Examples might include less experienced providers being more likely to commit an error, patients without caregiver support being less likely to adhere to treatment or medication, or physicians exhibiting signs of burnout being more likely to turnover or retire. In each case, there could be a goal to address the deficiency in the specific aspect (experience level, the presence of caregiver support, or physician burnout) that *leads* to the undesirable result (errors, medication adherence, turnover).

Therefore, we cannot expect that by addressing the characteristic associated with the outcome or event of interest that we will completely eliminate the outcome or event from occurring, but instead we hope to make it as likely or unlikely as is the case for those without the characteristic. That is, there will always be some probability of an error, but hopefully you can train or educate the less experienced providers so that their error rate approaches that of their more experienced colleagues, for example.

7.4.1.3 Project Results

Over the first 12 months after the completion of the renovation, we collected data on patient acuity and LWBS rates *within* the two categories of acuity previously described: urgent and nonurgent. Table 7.16 shows the average monthly values (the observed results).

The LWBS rate within nonurgent patients of 9.66% represents a 31.3% reduction from our estimated rate prior to the renovation. While this reduction is less than our goal of a 50% reduction, it reflects significant improvement during the first year. Therefore, using the same calculations as described for the proposal, the total contribution to lost revenue from LWBS that can be attributed to nonurgent patients was $650,365 during the 12-month evaluation period. This represents a reduction from the baseline estimate ($1,024,053) of $373,689.

The true cost of renovation was slightly over budget, at $1,432,708. Therefore, the one-year ROI is −73.92%, calculated as:

$$(\$373,689 - \$1,432,708)/\$1,432,708 \times 100\%$$

The payback period is just over 46 months or slightly less than four years. This is approximately 1.3 years longer than anticipated.

7.4.1.4 Sensitivity Analysis

The original goal for reducing LWBS for nonurgent patients was not attained. Additionally, the renovations cost roughly $52,708 more than budgeted. Together, these contributed to a lower ROI and longer projected payback period than originally anticipated.

If during the second year we can achieve the goal of a 50% reduction in the nonurgent LWBS rate from the pre-renovation value (while maintaining the LWBS rate for urgent patients), we would increase the yearly savings from $373,689 to $687,633, thereby reducing the payback period to a total of 2.5 years (slightly less than the pre-renovation projection) or an additional 1.5 years. This would require a reduction in the LWBS of an additional 2.62 percentage points, from 9.66 to the goal of 7.04, which staff believes is possible.

Table 7.16 Observed results

Measure	Value
Average monthly volume	3642
Percent who were nonurgent	42.1%
Overall LWBS	6.51%
LWBS within urgent patients	4.22%
LWBS within nonurgent patients	9.66% (2.29 times that of urgent patients)

This is a relatively short sensitivity analysis section. It certainly could be longer as other aspects could be explored. For one, the relative improvement is highly dependent on the assumption of the pre-renovation ratio of the LWBS rates for urgent versus nonurgent patients. We assumed that nonurgent patients left at a rate three times that of urgent patients; in the observed results, their rate was 2.29 times higher. But, if the true rate was greater than three the observed improvement is *greater* than what we have estimated (and so would be the realized return), and if it is less than three the opposite is true.

So, one option would be to vary that assumption and repeat the calculations to obtain other potential return rates. Another option would be to notice that the observed LWBS rate for urgent patients was 4.22%, slightly lower than our pre-renovation estimate of 4.69%. However, it is close, and it might be reasonable to assume that the renovation could have a small impact on the LWBS of even urgent patients, giving support to the initial estimate.

We could also double down on our assumption that wait time does not affect urgent patients and claim that if the renovation truly had no impact on urgent patients, their true LWBS before the renovation was the same as afterward, or 4.22%, instead of 4.69%. In that case, we could go back to Eq. 9.2 and plug in 4.22% for the LWBS rate of urgent patients, leaving only $LWBS_{nu}$ as the one unknown. Solving for this variable would produce a value of 14.77%, which is only slightly higher than our original calculation of 14.07%, but would produce a slightly larger improvement given the post-renovation value of 9.66%.

At this point, recall the discussion earlier in the text that indicated the importance of being thorough and creative but not confusing. Given the only slight change this final exercise would have resulted in, it is perhaps not worth the risk of confusing the reader to include it in this case. However, it illustrates the kind of exploration that one may perform in this type of analysis.

7.4.1.5 Interpretation

The results of this analysis suggest that the renovation resulted in significant improvement in wait times and a reduction in the rate of LWBS for nonurgent patients. While we did not achieve our original goal of reducing this rate by 50% in the first year, we realized significant improvement and believe it is feasible to reach this goal by the end of year two. If we can accomplish that goal, we anticipate that the accumulated benefits will begin to exceed the cost of renovation slightly ahead of schedule or about halfway through year three.

Additional interpretation regarding potential reasons why the initial rate reduction was not achieved in year one, or lessons learned that may be applied to future renovation projects, would also be appropriate here but would be situation specific.

Without the assumption that wait times influence rates of LWBS, most of this analysis would not be possible. If this had been a prospective analysis as part of an attempt to secure funding, probably more significant evidence would have been required to assure the reader of that connection. But, given that this is an internal project and was given the go-ahead in part because of the benefits it was thought it would produce in reduced LWBS rates, it is safe to assume that this assumption was widely adopted within the organization.

Finally, one may ask whether it is necessary to insert the complication of trying to separate the LWBS rates for urgent and nonurgent patients when any instances of LWBS result in a revenue loss, regardless of whether the patient would be considered to have urgent needs. The answer is that it is not necessary, but it may help in a couple of ways.

First, those who are skeptical about the connection between wait time and LWBS may be more easily persuaded of such a connection in nonurgent patients (there is, in fact, published literature on this). Secondly, whether in this example or in examples of physician turnover or occurrences of errors, this exercise allows for a measure of how much improvement is possible. That is, where will probably always be some percent who leave the ED, or commit a medical error, or leave a practice to go somewhere else. Splitting the groups as we have produces a range for what is possible: We likely could not get the LWBS rate of nonurgent patients *below* that of urgent patients, but with the appropriate estimates we can establish a reasonable expectation of what is possible. Similarly, a 50% reduction in the LWBS for the nonurgent group is easier to achieve than a 50% reduction overall. Therefore, we are setting ourselves up for success by framing the issue in terms of only the patients we expect to be influenced by waiting time.

7.5   Comments About the Hypothetical Examples

The examples presented above are relatively brief and do not exhaust all possible scenarios. However, hopefully they provide a flavor of how the individual pieces of a ROI analysis fit together to produce a report. There is no one way to examine ROI and no right way to present the results. In each case presented, the goal was to be clear and transparent about what was done, why it was done, and what the implications were or would be for the projects and activities reflected in the calculations. In general, your goal should be to give the reader all the necessary information so that they may make a logical and informed decision about the financial return of the project. Additionally, you should structure the report to support the achievement of that goal.

Chapter 8
Tips and Templates

8.1 Tips

While much can be gained from reading about how to perform ROI analyses, you will always learn more from actually *doing* them. Therefore, I would encourage you to find opportunities to perform ROI analyses that will present you with situations where you will need to make assumptions, find estimates, and calculate results. In all likelihood, the situation you face when you endeavor to quantify the financial return of some quality improvement initiative or other investment will not look exactly like any of the examples presented throughout this text. Therefore, it will be up to you to determine how best to extend the concepts and techniques presented here so that they may be applicable to your unique needs. As with anything of this nature, as you perform more and more analyses, you will gain invaluable knowledge and may identify specific tips or tricks that will help you in future analyses.

In this chapter, I will present a few of my own discoveries that you may find to be helpful. I hope that you will steal these and use them as your own and that you will build on them and improve upon them to amass a mountain of resources and information that you can reliably pull from.

8.1.1 Accessing Relevant Information

8.1.1.1 Keep a Folder of Source Information

It can often seem like the only time you cannot find your car keys is when you are late and you need them more than ever. That is why many have a designated location for them by the door, such as a hook or a drawer. That way they will always know where their keys can be found.

Similarly, you will find that the only time you cannot locate the article that you vaguely remember but are sure is relevant to a specific ROI analysis is when you need

© Springer Nature Switzerland AG 2020

C. A. Solid, *Return on Investment for Healthcare Quality Improvement*,
https://doi.org/10.1007/978-3-030-46478-3_8

it the most. Therefore, you should begin to accumulate and index relevant information before you ever find a need for it. Specifically, I suggest designating a location (an electronic one, ideally on a cloud-based storage app like Dropbox, Box, or Google Drive) where you can store and search any and all information that may be relevant for future ROI analyses. These may include:

- Published studies (whether or not they include ROI analyses or just clinical or care quality information)
- Results of previous research projects or quality improvement interventions you know about or participated in
- Relevant books
- Websites, blogs, key reference pages (e.g., population estimates, discount rates, etc.)
- Notes from meetings, conferences, presentations, etc.
- Previous ROI analyses and resources.

The information included is where you will locate things like estimates of disease prevalence and incidence, previous experiences with the effectiveness of a certain type of intervention or quality improvement activity, costs, benefits, methods for establishing the monetary value of an intangible benefit, etc. I am speaking of anything and everything that may ever be of use. Table 8.1 has a list of several types of information that may be helpful to collect.

Depending on how much you accumulate, who will access it, and your personal preference for the level of organization, you may even create subfolders that will allow you to categorize the information for ease of retrieval. Personally, I find the most intuitive first level of classification is by topic or disease state. That is, individual folders may be named "hypertension," "diabetes," "stroke," or may describe an event or setting, such as "nursing home," or "falls," or "hospital-acquired condition," etc.

Below that, it may be helpful to include additional folders to classify information related to cost, benefits, monetary estimates, general assumptions, or other topics. Obviously, the exact structure is a matter of personal preference, but whether the information is reflected in the folder structure or not, it can be helpful to consider the different types of information that may be useful to accumulate. This includes information regarding:

- Incidence and prevalence
- Quality of life and satisfaction
- Efficiency and waste
- Trends and knowledge
- Interventions and effectiveness
- Costs and Benefits.

Once you are on the lookout for it, you may find that your real struggle is limiting the information to that which is truly useful. That is, this type of system can quickly become cluttered with information because there is no clear line between what is useful and what is not. In general, be ruthless: Read the information carefully to determine if there are numbers or values that could actually be used for a ROI

Table 8.1 Information to collect for use in ROI analyses

Information	Details and examples
Incidence and prevalence of disease or events	Previous examples or studies that present rates of disease, adverse events, or utilization can be used to estimate baseline or pre-intervention expected rates and counts of affected individuals
Quality of life and/or satisfaction	Reported measurements of quality of life decrements associated with specific conditions or events, tools or surveys used to assess patient and staff experiences and satisfaction, or impact of poor quality of life on related outcomes
Efficiency and waste reduction	Methods to assess or measure efficiency and/or waste reduction, areas potentially vulnerable to waste (e.g., ordering of laboratory tests, extra days in the hospital for certain conditions, excess staffing)
Trends and knowledge	National or regional trends in disease incidence and prevalence, mortality, or policy impacts; methods others have used to try to account for pre-existing trends when assessing the impact of a specific intervention or project
Interventions and effectiveness	Examples of previous interventions that may be relevant; can be helpful to estimate the expected improvement associated with particular activities, the amount of resources and time that will be required to achieve a certain level of improvement, or to incorporate learnings that can allow you to design and implement a more effective quality improvement strategy
Costs and benefits	Any information regarding the costs of treating a disease, types of treatments, adverse events, or associated subsequent outcomes (e.g., increased stroke likelihood due to uncontrolled hypertension); could include sources of costs and benefits, monetary values associated with different activities or outcomes, or methods to monetize specific costs or benefits

analysis and then, highlight them. Remember that percentages or lifetime risks are not as useful as rates per time at risk or actual counts and details regarding time period so that you can calculate the rate on your own.

8.1.1.2   Keep a Folder of Examples of ROI Analyses

I suggest filing examples of ROI analyses others have done in a catalog of useful ROI references or in a separate location. These examples may include ones that are likely to be relevant to your area or type of work, but you may also find benefit in ones that contain very little that is directly applicable to what you are likely to do. There is such variety in how these analyses are performed and presented that having several examples can not only provide you with some useful templates for how to present your own analysis but may also spark something in your own imagination that you would not have otherwise thought about.

As mentioned, the topic or clinical area of the examples you keep need not be directly relevant to your work. That is because part of their benefit is in their structure and the model they provide for the level of complexity that may be necessary for your own pursuits. They can serve as a template for what to present, how to present it, and in what order. Additionally, you can examine the language used and how the background and motivating information is presented, as well as how the interpretation is framed.

In cases where the ROI analyses do reflect topics or clinical areas that may be relevant to your own work, these examples can also serve as a way to "check your work" and make sure you have thought of every contingency. For example, it can sometimes be difficult to identify all of the potential costs or benefits associated with an intervention. If there is an example of a previous ROI on the same or similar topic, the information it contains can help ensure that you have not missed any potential source or have not incorrectly identified a benefit as unmeasurable or not monetizable when in fact, there may be a way to legitimately do both.

Finally, other ROI analyses can be excellent sources of relevant information. Often, through either the text or their list of references, they may provide specific sources that will be of assistance to you in your analysis. Take caution, however, since even though this can save you time in your own research, there may be additional resources or more recent publications that should be included in your search.

8.1.1.3   Take the Time to Create Templates

One of the biggest challenges that organizations encounter in performing ROI analyses is that they often require more time and resources than anticipated. The reasons for this are numerous, but individuals and groups often scramble to put something together in time to meet a pre-determined deadline. Unfortunately, often this means that little time or effort is spent on creating systems for future iterations of the analysis or to aid in similar endeavors that may be encountered. While understandable, the truth is that creating usable templates for you or your team can produce significant efficiencies down the road.

The initial basis for templates can be established from the examples housed in the folder of a previous ROI analysis, or from other sources like this text or other endeavors. Creating the template forces one to think more generally about the topic and the steps required to compile information and perform base case and sensitivity analyses. There may be a variety of useful templates, including those for:

- Overall format of presenting ROI results
- Abstracting information from published or online materials
- Combining inputs to create base case calculations
- Varying inputs to explore sensitivity analyses
- Tables for presenting specific inputs and their sources.

This list is certainly not exhaustive. Additionally, certain templates may be specific to a particular topic or kind of intervention. That is, interventions that generate value through cost avoidance by lower utilization or fewer adverse events often require different assumptions and estimates than those involving investments in equipment or technology and therefore would benefit from different templates. While templates can save time, they can also be valuable by reducing the likelihood of omitting key information or skipping steps that could jeopardize the fidelity of the analysis.

8.1.2 Presenting ROI Results in Oral Presentations

Given the volume of information, numbers, metrics, and alternative scenarios often considered in ROI analyses, presenting the key information to an audience can pose some challenges. If you were to simply present what appears in written form orally, the result would be a dizzying amount of material that would only serve to confuse or bore (or both) those in attendance. However, you can do a few things to improve the effectiveness of what is presented.

8.1.2.1 Do not Assume Your Audience Understands ROI

In most presentations to a wider audience, the presentation of ROI for quality improvement is unlikely to be the primary purpose. Instead, when ROI is presented it will likely be part of a larger presentation regarding the quality improvement pursuits, either prior to starting or after completing an intervention or investment in materials or equipment. Therefore, it is likely that at least some, if not all of those in attendance are only vaguely familiar with ROI and its related concepts.

Therefore, it is worthwhile to explain not only what it is, but why it is important and how it can be used in tandem with other information about the quality improvement activities to evaluate success and value. Describe what scope and perspective are and how they provide a framework for the analysis; go on to describe these attributes for the results being presented so that viewers are clear about what the results do and do not reflect. The definition of key metrics should include practical and relatable examples (e.g., the rate of return of a bank account or other investment to illustrate ROI values), along with a description of what value the metrics reflect and what other types of value are not included in the calculations.

Additionally, emphasize the difference between ROI and the broader concept of value. If new to the topic, it can be difficult to understand why certain types of costs or benefits are not included in the ROI for a particular perspective or a given scope. Ensuring that these concepts are understood will be crucial for the audience to fully grasp what was done and what the results indicate.

8.1.2.2 Present Summary Tables

In place of bullets or text describing the assumptions and estimates used, summary tables can be useful and more palatable for those receiving the information. Keep in mind that unlike someone reading a report, audience members will have a limited time to absorb the information and cannot "flip" back and forth as if in a report if something confuses them. Often, a table of assumptions and estimates is effective if only to illustrate the volume of uncertainty involved in the upcoming calculations. More details can easily be inserted on "appendix" slides, which many presenters prepare in anticipation of questions. If asked, they have them at the ready; if not, they are not shown.

When displaying multiple values that reflect base case and sensitivity results, shading or highlights can help the viewer quickly understand how the values are intended to be compared and considered. Remember that if you have to extensively explain your slides to the audience, they are likely too complicated. While it may not be realistic to create a presentation that could "stand on its own" without any description, aim to create visuals that require only a sentence or two of explanation.

Also consider that graphs or figures may be more effective than tables, even if the graphs display less information. Charts of the costs and benefits over time can be effective for demonstrating how the intervention will produce both and how they combine to produce relevant metrics like ROI, BCR, and payback period.

8.1.2.3 Reduce, Reduce, Reduce

When in doubt about information, equations, or values in an oral presentation, cut them. Recall that the ROI results are likely being presented as supporting material for a demonstration. Provide the audience with an interpretation that relates the results back to the clinical and practical implications of the quality improvement activities. Summarize information whenever possible and remind the audience of the aims as well as key assumptions, even while presenting results.

As stated previously, judicious use of appendix slides can help reduce material in the main presentation. Equations are good candidates for these types of slides because while a deep dive into the specific calculations can bring a presentation to a screeching halt, there may be those who want to understand the details of how the metrics were developed.

8.1.3 Responding to a Request for Proposals (RfP)

It is becoming more common for RfPs to include a request for a ROI analysis as part of the proposal. At first blush, this may seem like a reasonable response to the increasing awareness of the importance of the value of quality improvement. However, RfPs frequently fail to provide sufficient guidance for applicants; the level of detail for what is expected will vary by funding source and opportunity. It is prudent for organizations to develop a consistent strategy for how to respond in such situations.

When Little to No Guidance is Provided in the RfP
When the RfP simply states that a ROI analysis is required but offers no additional guidance, it can be difficult to know the appropriate level of detail one should provide. In this situation, you should first consider whether the lack of guidance may be due to limitations on space or whether it is for some other reason.

For example, if the proposal's length has a stated limit, the expectation may be that the ROI analysis will be brief and provide only a high-level overview. Sometimes those releasing the RfP simply want to prompt those who will be submitting proposals to consider the value of their proposed activities when they plan and design them. In this case, the ROI analysis may receive only cursory scrutiny.

Another possibility, however, is that the organization that released the RfP does not have a clear idea of what they want and have included the request for a ROI analysis because of internal or external pressures. That is, because of the increased prominence of value assessments within the current healthcare climate, the organization may feel obligated to request a ROI analysis. This can be a dangerous situation because the potential funding agency may not have any specific expectation for the resulting analysis, or worse, may not have an adequate level of understanding of ROI to appropriately evaluate the ROI analysis ultimately submitted. Regardless of the situation, there are multiple strategies to consider.

Asking for Clarification
If it is acceptable to ask those who released the RfP to provide more clarification regarding what is expected for the ROI analysis, a good strategy when you inquire about it is to provide some options of how you might proceed and ask for their preference. Asking open-ended questions such, "Can you provide more specifics for what you would like to see for the ROI analysis?" may not be effective. Frankly, they may not know what they want to see and asking them will either earn you no answer or an answer that requires an unreasonable amount of work (if they are unfamiliar with ROI analyses they may also be unfamiliar with how much work goes into one, and they may ask for more than is reasonable). Prompting them instead to indicate their preference between a few options that vary in complexity demonstrates that you are familiar with ROI analyses and have the capacity to pursue a number of different routes when it comes to the value assessment.

When offering alternatives, a narrative may be sufficient to describe the key aspects that differ. Explain in broad terms what you consider to be drivers of costs and benefits and provide examples of differing levels of detail for how estimates would be determined and how values would be calculated.

For example, in the hypothetical case study of reducing nursing home falls, you could provide some alternatives when asking about clarification as follows:

> We are writing to inquire about the level of complexity expected for the ROI analysis the RfP requests. We anticipate that the main cost drivers will be the time and resources required to train staff, as well as facility-related costs for IT upgrades and ongoing monitoring costs. Additionally, we know there will be costs related to data collection and analysis. We plan to use internal estimates of costs that are based on our previous experiences with area nursing homes in similar projects.
>
> Monetary benefits will manifest as reduced costs through avoiding fall-related injuries. We have considerable research available to us regarding the frequency of different types of injuries, the associated cost to treat each one, and the reduction in frequency we can anticipate from a fall-prevention intervention.
>
> To present the estimated ROI, we could provide only the resulting estimates and calculations of overall costs and benefits in order to demonstrate the expected return while conserving space for additional project considerations. Additional details would be available upon request. This is the level of detail we suspect is appropriate. Alternatively, we could present the details of the estimates and values in order to display the full picture of how ROI is calculated. This would require significantly more space within the application. Please let us know your preference.

In this way, we demonstrate that we know what we are talking about and suggest a level of detail but leave the door open if they decide they would like the more rigorous exploration. If nothing else, this provides foreshadowing for what the evaluators can expect. Even if they do not have any prior expectations, after reading this they will not be surprised by what level of detail is included in the submission, or why.

Instead of or in addition to a narrative, another strategy is to include one or more table shells. Here, the idea is to provide the potential reviewers with a specific image of what they can expect to receive as part of the ROI analysis. Whether they confirm that the proposed tables are sufficient or whether they suggest adjustments, the result is more specific guidance about what level of detail they expect, which was the original goal.

When It is Not Possible to Ask for Clarification
It may not be possible or appropriate to ask for clarification from those who released the RfP. Or, you may not receive a response to your inquiry. In either case, you are forced to produce an analysis without any guidance regarding how much detail (or which details) to include and present. Do not assume that the evaluators will understand ROI the same way you will. At a minimum, include a few sentences of rationale for what you will present and why. Citing examples from similar projects or from your previous experience provides support for the level of detail you decide to include in your results.

Additionally, state that more detail is available upon request so that those evaluating your proposal know that you did more than what is presented. For example, if space is limited, you may make only a brief mention of the results of your sensitivity analysis, especially if they are not appreciably different from your base case. Sometimes simply stating, "When key assumptions and estimates are varied the anticipated ROI remains positive" can be enough, as long as you have the more detailed results available upon request.

When the RfP Provides Specific Guidance or Instructions for ROI

Sometimes the RfP will give specifics about what is expected for the ROI analysis. In this case, carefully consider how those specifics match up to your understanding of what constitutes a reasonable and responsible ROI analysis. If the requested information is similar to what you would produce you are likely ahead simply altering your output to match to the requested format or type of information. If, however, you believe that you can produce a much more meaningful analysis than what is requested (e.g., sometimes there is a table shell that you are asked to fill out that does not fully encompass what you believe to be the main drivers of financial return), then you have a few options.

One possibility is to completely ignore what the RfP requests and instead submit what you believe to be more appropriate. This may be acceptable, especially if it looks as though those who wrote the RfP are not well-versed in ROI methods. However, it is never a bad idea to include a sentence or two about why you abandoned the suggested format or requested information in favor of your own set of results. Be clear, but not condescending, about why the information you are providing represents the most useful for evaluating the financial feasibility of the project. If possible, cite outside sources and authorities who support your decision of what to present.

Another option is to submit your own set of results, but to also attempt to provide the information by the RfP. Sometimes it can be effective to first present what you believe the RfP is requesting and briefly describe why you believe other or additional information is merited. Then, you can detail the additional results and demonstrate why they are more effective for those evaluating the proposal. Here, too, there is a fine line between thoroughness and condescension. You will not want to imply that the requested results are completely inadequate, just that you believe some additional information is helpful (or that you are not able to provide the information requested because of any one of several reasons).

Communication and Transparency

Regardless of the situation, when performing a ROI analysis at the behest of a RfP, clarity and transparency are key. Clearly describe your understanding of what is being requested and your intention to address that request in the most effective way possible. Provide enough information so that those evaluating the proposal will understand what you did, and offer to provide more detail upon request. As with any prospective analysis, you will want to avoid the perception that you are manipulating the data to create a favorable scenario. Instead, you want those reading the proposal to feel as though you are being objective, open-minded, and reasonable. If they feel that way, it likely will not matter what form your presentation takes.

8.1.4 Publishing and Disseminating Results

When a quality improvement intervention successfully improves the quality of care and patient outcomes, some or all of that information warrants dissemination through a peer-reviewed journal, a white paper, or a report to key stakeholders. A write up of the project allows others to understand what was done, assess why it was successful, and apply the learnings to their own setting when attempting to improve care quality.

Sometimes, the results of a ROI analysis are worth publishing either as part of a larger publication or as their own paper. Several aspects of a ROI analysis may be publication-worthy: the sources or data used to obtain relevant costs or benefits, the methods used to measure or monetize observed benefits, or the learnings gained from the process of assessing value alongside quality. Consider several tips when sharing the results of a ROI analysis.

First, the tips for good oral presentations apply to written summaries and publications as well. Do not assume the reader understands ROI, use summary tables, and avoid superfluous details whenever possible. Another key for developing an effective publication is to get clear about the message and the audience. When you do this, you provide focus and direction regarding the information presented. If the goal is to assure hospital administrators that a specific type of intervention is financially feasible, then the paper should focus on the sources and estimates of costs and benefits to demonstrate how they accrue and accumulate. If the goal is to provide guidance on how to estimate costs and benefits associated with a specific intervention, the paper may instead focus on lessons learned and advice for others hoping to perform a similar analysis.

A subset of the ROI analysis may also be worthy of publication or dissemination, even if the entire ROI analysis is not. For example, the successful development of methods or tools to effectively monetize benefits that were not previously monetizable may merit dissemination. These may include novel surveys or patient-reported outcome measures developed to capture an intervention's effect.

Currently, ample opportunity to publish ROI-based papers exists because there is a paucity currently available in the peer-reviewed space. Sharing your experiences, successes, and failures helps to further value-based examinations and assessments. Publishing these analyses is vital to promoting intentional and thoughtful evaluations in the future.

8.1.5 Develop a Process

In my experience, groups that endeavor to perform ROI analyses face two common stumbling blocks. The first is waiting until too late to begin the planning or execution of the analysis. Frequently, organizations spend weeks or even months planning an initiative. They carefully determine the appropriate quality measures; they meet several times to decide what data will be needed and how they will either secure existing datasets or collect necessary information; and they create a detailed analytic plan for how improvements in quality will be detected, risk-adjusted, and compared across relevant variables. Upon completion of that planning, the team will then turn to the task of how to estimate the potential ROI.

The problem with this method: Soon after exploring what will be needed for the ROI analysis, often those charged with planning the intervention will discover that their chosen quality measures are inadequate to capture value and the data are insufficient to estimate measurable benefits. At this point, they face either revisiting aspects of the original project plan or using measures, estimates, and resources that are less than ideal and that produces a ROI estimate that fails to fully encompass the true financial return. Unfortunately, organizations frequently opt for the latter, simply because they have already exhausted the available time and resources for project planning. This situation is gravely similar to another common situation: not exploring ROI until *after* the quality improvement project has been completed. Both situations consist of too little information suitable to create robust or even accurate evaluations of relevant costs or benefits.

The second most common stumbling block is not allocating sufficient time or resources for the analysis. Frequently, this compounds the issues experienced by waiting to begin ROI explorations until after quality initiative plans have been finalized, but sometimes it is completely separate. Those who take on the assignment of identifying and quantifying costs and benefits without full knowledge of what is involved often find themselves in over their heads. They discover that they lack the time or means to fully explore the necessary aspects and have to instead settle for more general calculations that fall woefully short of what they had originally intended.

In either case, the results often provide little guidance or evidence for the financial feasibility of the project. In contrast, those who recognize the need for ROI analyses to be performed in concert with quality intervention planning and who understand the level of time and effort required to do it well will typically formalize the procedure and incorporate it into their usual planning process.

A good strategy is to develop a process so that the time and effort required can be predicted. Define key roles and responsibilities and track the time it takes to perform the analysis. Then, include it as part of any quality improvement planning or summary process, even if it is not required.

8.1.5.1 An Example Process

Consider this example process for avoiding common stumbling blocks encountered when planning and performing ROI analyses. While general in nature, this could easily be expanded with the added detail of the specific situation and circumstances (Table 8.2).

The goal of this process is to think about the value assessment prior to starting the project so that you properly plan for the time and effort for the analysis.

Table 8.2 Example process for ROI development

Step	Description
1. Compile relevant information	Gather information from previous activities, published articles, and online materials related to what is known about the topic's quality and value to date. This will include measures previously used to assess quality and value, the level of success regarding improvement, and available data
2. Connect quality and value	Determine the overlap between quality and value. What aspects of measurable quality can also be used to assess value? Will we need additional data and/or measures to fully capture the desired value?
3. Make preliminary estimates	Using the information gathered to this point, estimate the value that would be realized for different levels of quality improvement. Use this to inform the necessary sample size, resources, and time frame to determine feasibility
4. Adjust and reassess	Make necessary adjustments to the broad strokes of the project or activity to balance the feasibility with the desired levels of quality and value achievement
5. Formally design intervention	Design the quality improvement initiative while keeping in mind the implications for achievable value. Select measures of quality and value and plan the analysis for quality and value (ROI) assessment
6. Test and estimate	Perform a preliminary ROI analysis to estimate the potential return

8.1.6 Increasing Influence

Whether your ROI analysis is part of a proposal to secure funding for a future project or a retrospective examination to establish the fiscal repercussions, often the ultimate goal of the analysis and the larger proposal or report within which it resides is to influence others. Prospectively, the goal is often to convince an individual, department, or organization that the project has merit and is financially feasible. Retrospectively, the goal is often to convince those same stakeholders that the project was worth it or that it could be scaled to a different setting or population with no worse a financial outcome. And yet, the ROI analysis will be only part of the larger endeavor to persuade, convince, and influence. In my experience, six primary factors are involved in being influential when it comes to quality improvement activities. They are:

1. **Clinical Knowledge**: This first one should be obvious; if trying to effect change for a particular condition or adverse patient event, your level of clinical knowledge about those patients and that condition go a long way toward your ability to influence anyone to change how treatment or care is provided.
2. **Practical Experience**: The natural complement to clinical knowledge is experience on the front lines of care, seeing patients, providing services, running a facility, and the like. Your level of practical experience in the field helps you

identify the roadblocks and envision how things could be better if certain aspects of care delivery were adjusted. The more practical experience you have, the more you can speak to the need for change and potential impact it could have in real-world practice.

3. **Understanding of Data and Measurement**: To prove a change has happened, you need to determine what to measure and how to measure it in a way that is valid and reliable. This involves identifying or collecting data with minimal or no bias, determining what constitutes a "meaningful" change, and analyzing the results in a way that addresses uncertainty and allows for accurate interpretation. The more representative your data, the more sound your methods, and the more robust your analysis, the more the intended audience will have confidence in the project's ability to detect and quantify improvement.

4. **Demonstration of Value**: Here is where ROI comes into play, but it is often not the whole story. Demonstrating the value of a project may take many forms, only one of which may be ROI. Frequently, it behooves those seeking funding or summarizing previous activities to include a discussion of any improvement in patient experiences, quality of life, or of reduced waste inefficiency.

5. **Credibility**: Certainly, clinical knowledge and practical experience go a long way toward establishing credibility. However, some things can augment credibility in the eyes of either a potential funder, a clinician, or a policy maker. Previous examples of successful interventions or explorations into the drivers of care quality within a particular population demonstrate a deep understanding of the particular situation or project being addressed. One of the most effective, and universally accepted, ways for augmenting credibility is through publishing peer-reviewed articles. Having a significant library of authored publications on a given subject signals to the intended audience that you are serious about this issue and have been studying it for some time.

6. **Storytelling**: Technical knowledge, lived experiences, and sound analytic methods are all necessary aspects of a good project and therefore the ability to influence those who can change how care is delivered and paid for. However, influence increases when we can paint a vivid picture for the audience of why the project is necessary, what the current landscape of care looks like, and what a vision for the future of care for this topic could look like. The more artfully and skillfully you can weave together the different components of a project's background, methodology, and results, the more impact it will have on those reviewing it. To motivate and inspire readers or listeners to change requires that it stirs something inside of them and encourages them to believe in your vision for what could be and that it is necessary.

You may ask why this matters and why it appears here. Frankly, because this is a text about how to perform ROI analyses, a discussion about the larger endeavor of influence within quality improvement and the healthcare environment is somewhat beyond the scope. However, it appears in the section on "tips" because I truly believe that considering the ROI analysis within the larger context of whatever proposal or report where it is housed will allow you to more effectively leverage the topics we have covered. Moreover, some of the decisions that performing ROI analyses require can be guided or at least informed by the overarching goals and vision of the larger document or presentation.

8.2   Templates

What follows are several examples of templates that may be helpful for different aspects of the work necessary to perform ROI analyses, either prospectively or retrospectively. Feel free to steal these, share them liberally, and tailor them to your own needs. Downloadable versions of these are available on my website, www. SolidResearchGroup.com/ROIforQI. When used in the form presented in this book (or close to it), please credit this text when it is appropriate.

8.2.1   Literature Abstraction Template

When pulling relevant estimates from published literature, it can be helpful to have a structured system for abstracting the information that allows for quick comparison and an easy summary across several articles. This is particularly the case in a prospective analysis when there are typically so many more estimates needed. The example in Fig. 8.1 was created in Excel and includes columns to collect the citation, the author(s), study type, setting, patient population, outcomes and time frame, the estimate of interest and its value, and any notes. Under each entry, there is a space to provide comments and summarize the study, including its relevance to a particular project or analysis.

Figure 8.2 includes an example of how it might look after a couple of articles had

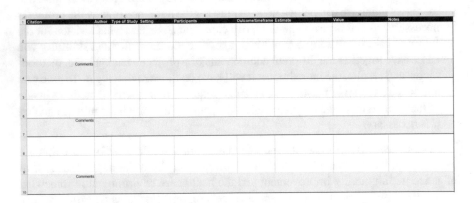

Fig. 8.1 Literature abstraction template (blank)

Citation	Author	Type of Study	Setting	Participants	Outcome/timeframe	Estimate	Value	Notes
Dong C, Della-Morte D, Rundek T, Wright CB, Elkind MS, Sacco RL. Evidence to Maintain the Systolic Blood Pressure Treatment Threshold at 140 mm Hg for Stroke Prevention: The Northern Manhattan Study. Hypertension. 2016 Mar;67(3):520-6. doi: 10.1161/HYPERTENSIONAHA.115.0685 7. Epub 2016 Feb 1.	Dong C	Prospective cohort study	Northern Manhattan study	Stroke-free patients from 1993 to 2001. 1,750 pts aged 60+ without DM or CKD; mean age = 72 / 8 yrs, 63% women, 48% Hispanic, 25% non-Hispanic white, 25% non-Hispanic black; 40% on antihypertensives, 43% had SBP < 140 mmHg, 20% 140-149, 37% > 149.	Stroke, median follow-up = 13 yrs	stroke incidence, all pts	9.1 / 1000 person years	Varied across race, gender, age
						stroke incidence, SBP < 140	6.2 / 1000	
						stroke incidence, SBP 140-149	12.3 / 1000	
						stroke incidence, SBP > 149	10.8 / 1000	
						stroke HR, SBP 140-149 vs <140	1.72 (1.15-2.57)	All pts
						stroke HR, SBP 140-149 vs <140	1.58 (1.01-2.47)	Excluded those with DBP >= 90 mmHg
						stroke HR, SBP 140-149 vs <140	ranged from 1.6 to 2.3 across race, sex, age groups	Excluded those with baseline antihypertensive use (See S1)
Comments: This study provides some estimates of stroke incidence for levels of SBP, but does not provide direct information for the effect of a reduction in 10/5 SBP/DBP HHmg. Authors also indicate that their cohort represents a lower SES group than we would expect in our project.								
Law MR, Morris JK, Wald NJ. Use of blood pressure lowering drugs in the prevention of cardiovascular disease: meta-analysis of 147 randomised trials in the context of expectations from prospective epidemiological studies. BMJ. 2009 May 19;338:b1665. doi: 10.1136/bmj.b1665.	Law MR	Meta-analysis	articles 1966-2007	Randomized trials of BP lowering drugs recording coronary heart disease (CHD) events and strokes	CHD and strokes	reduction in CHD for reduction of 10 mm Hg systolic or 5 mm Hg diastolic	22% (17% to 27%)	
						reduction in stroke for reduction of 10 mm Hg systolic or 5 mm Hg diastolic	41% (33% to 48%)	
					HF incidence	reduced HF incidence	19% to 24%	
Comments: Provides direct impact of lowering 10/5 points on reduced CHD and stroke. Information on HF is complex; may require examination of individual studies.								

Fig. 8.2 Literature abstraction template (filled out)

been abstracted. Note that additional rows are added as needed so that each estimate that may potentially be of use is given its own row.

Note that for each article, key information is documented and there is space to include notes that may be specific either to the particular study or how it applies to the intended project. While not fully displayed with only two entries, when there are several this format allows one to easily and quickly compare studies and even gather a range of estimates to use for base case and sensitivity analyses. The comments allow for space to summarize and indicate which ones may be more or less relevant to a particular situation or analysis.

This can be especially helpful when you return to an analysis after putting it away for a while. For example, once a proposal is submitted you often have to wait for some period of time to find out whether it will be funded. Having a summary like this makes it much easier to jump back into the analysis without fear of missing or forgetting some key piece of information. Additionally, after an intervention has been completed and you want to compare the observed results to what was proposed or estimated this tool allows you immediate access to what those estimates were. Finally, having a summary like this allows for more efficient sharing among colleagues. Instead of each team member studying dozens of individual papers and reports, they can get the key details from this file.

8.2.2 Outline and Checklist Templates

8.2.2.1 Outline

As mentioned previously, there is more than one way to present the results of a ROI analysis. Each individual situation will call for certain information to be presented in a certain way. Specifically, how you present the results will be shaped by several attributes of the analysis, including:

- Whether it is prospective or retrospective
- The type of quality improvement activity, such as

    - Improving patient outcomes
    - Increasing efficiency or reducing waste
    - Investing in equipment, the facility, or staff.

Different situations have different requirements for clearly expressing all of the relevant information. Further, the structure of the presentation of results will depend on aspects like:

- The clinical or functional topic
- The implications of improvement (e.g., reducing hypertension may lead to other outcomes like reducing cardiovascular events, but avoiding infections is its own benefit)
- The chosen scope and perspective
- The desired generalizability
- The targeted audience.

For all of these reasons, there is not a specific format one can point to as the accepted way to structure a written report or presentation of a ROI analysis. Let us look at a couple of examples of how different characteristics of the analysis may inform the general outline for presenting the results.

Example #1: A Prospective Analysis for an Intervention to Reduce Disease Prevalence

In this example, the key aspects that will inform how it is presented include the fact that it is a prospective analysis for an intervention intended to improve patient outcomes. Specifically, the goal is to reduce the prevalence of a disease, which should reduce the risk of adverse events that could affect patient quality of life, disease burden, and healthcare expenditures. A general outline might look like the following:

I. Background

    a. Describe the current prevalence rate in the target population.
    b. Explore the clinical implications and financial burden of the current disease burden.

c. Identify that there is an opportunity for improvement and describe it.
d. Define the scope and perspective.
e. Define key metrics (ROI, BCR, payback period).

II. Present estimates and assumptions used for analysis, including those for:

a. The affected population, including its size
b. The likely effectiveness of the intervention to reduce disease prevalence
c. The implications of reduced prevalence on clinical outcomes
d. The associated costs of treating adverse clinical outcomes of the disease
e. The likely costs of the intervention.

III. Base case and sensitivity analysis

a. Identify the values used for the base case and justify their use.
b. Calculate key metrics.
c. Identify the values used for the sensitivity analysis.
d. Calculate best- and worst-case scenarios, and any other relevant scenarios.

IV. Interpretation

a. Summarize the results to justify the proposed project.
b. Acknowledge the uncertainty and variability and offer alternatives if key assumptions turn out to be false.

The chosen perspective may not affect much of what comes after the background. In this case, whether the perspective is that of patients, providers, payers, or someone else, the motivation for reducing hypertension will often be the same: to reduce the occurrence of hypertension-related adverse events. The associated benefits will certainly vary depending on the perspective (as will the costs associated with the intervention), but that is really a function of what is presented, not how.

Example #2: A Retrospective Analysis on Improved Efficiency or an Investment in Equipment or the Facility

In a retrospective analysis, often the background section will be less detailed. While in a prospective analysis it is essential to demonstrate the existence of an opportunity and motivate the reader or audience as to its need, in a retrospective analysis it is often enough to simply point out that the activities were performed. Additionally, often there are fewer estimates or assumptions since there are presumably observed data for use in this type of report or presentation. What follows is an example of an outline that may serve to present the necessary information.

I. Background

a. Describe the pre-activity situation and perhaps the project's motivation.
b. Explain the opportunity for improvement and its potential impact.
c. Define the scope and perspective.

II.   Provide definitions and any estimates or assumptions

    a.   Anticipated costs, benefits, and timeline.
    b.   Supporting evidence for these expected values.

III. Base case

    a.   Present the observed results with actual data.
    b.   Calculate key metrics.

IV.   Sensitivity analysis

    a.   If prudent, identify what differed from expectations (cost, timeline, etc.).
    b.   Determine what impact those had on the results (i.e., drivers of ROI).
    c.   If prudent, explore nonmonetary benefits.
    d.   If relevant, extrapolate about future costs and benefits.

V.   Interpretation

    a.   Determine whether the activities produced an acceptable return.
    b.   Explore lessons learned.
    c.   Detail the next steps (if any).

As with the previous example, there are numerous places where alternative topics could be covered. Additionally, there may be situations where a different order of the specified topics would be beneficial. For example, it may be reasonable to present the base case (the observed results) before describing what had been anticipated—especially if there was uncertainty regarding the anticipated costs and benefits. In this way, these expectations, and their associated uncertainty, could naturally be folded into the sensitivity analysis. When presenting results retrospectively, a sensitivity analysis often contains sections that essentially convey "here's what would have happened if things had gone to plan." This can be very instructive for identifying and understanding drivers of the realized return.

A more general template is presented in Fig. 8.3. Obviously, there is room for alteration given that each unique situation may call for different sections to be added or removed.

As presented, this outline would be applicable to a prospective analysis. However, not much would need to change for it to apply to a retrospective one. In the section describing definitions, estimates, and assumptions, a retrospective analysis would present observed costs instead of anticipated costs and observed effectiveness instead of estimated effectiveness. Additionally, the amount and type of information presented in the sensitivity analysis would be different for a retrospective analysis, even if the headings of the outline sections would not change. Finally, the interpretation might change depending on the goal of the retrospective analysis and the specific project.

Each template provided is meant to be a guide. The specific circumstances of your project will dictate what will be presented. Having a template can help ensure the key aspects are not forgotten.

ROI Analysis Outline Template

I.   Background

    a. Describe the baseline or pre-intervention situation:

        i. Current rates of disease or events

        ii. Explain the overall motivation and demand for change

    b. Describe the desired change

    c. Define the scope and perspective

II.   Definitions, estimates, and assumptions

    a. Affected population

    b. Anticipated costs

    c. Estimated effectiveness of intervention

    d. Resulting impact on outcomes or costs

    e. Other assumed benefits

III.   Base case and sensitivity analysis

    a. Key values used for base case

    b. Definition of metrics (ROI, BCR, payback period)

    c. Calculation of base case metrics

    d. Values used for sensitivity analysis

    e. Calculation of sensitivity analysis metrics

IV.   Interpretation

    a. Determination of return and its implications

    b. Acknowledgement of uncertainty and key assumptions

    c. Generalizability or future steps

    d. Summary and conclusion

Fig. 8.3 Outline template

8.2.2.2 Checklist

While you may be able to use several reasonable structures when presenting ROI results, frequently there is key information that should be included somewhere in the report or presentation. This is where a checklist can be useful to ensure that nothing of substance is omitted. The checklist in Fig. 8.4 can be a starting point for you. Take it and alter it for your own purposes and needs, potentially including specific references for yourself or others for common language or tools (e.g., spreadsheets) that may be part of the process you develop.

In general, however, the checklist represents the bare essentials for the most common types of ROI analyses performed for quality improvement.

The order of items in this list is intentional but does not suggest that this is the only order possible. You have seen in examples throughout this book that certain information can be presented in several places throughout a report. Additionally, you may decide to add items regarding the inclusion of tables or figures. I discussed previously that including a table that summarizes key estimates can help with clarity. Often, figures are useful to illustrate main results such as payback period or overall ROI. The intent is to develop a system that will help you create consistently effective reports that include key information and communicate results.

8.2.3 Costs

How you choose to aggregate and classify costs will be unique to the setting and situation, and therefore, I have included multiple versions of the templates that may be useful and also may spark ideas for your own needs. Please feel free to use and alter them as needed. In addition to these, the examples throughout this book provide additional options that you may find useful.

In Table 8.3, time period columns could also be further split into pre-intervention stages (training, ramp-up), and in addition to ongoing costs, perhaps there will be costs associated with terminating or shutting down the intervention. It may be useful to create a table that uses these activity classifications (like Table 8.5), either instead of or in addition to a more common breakdown like those in Tables 8.3 and 8.4. If the intervention is likely to occur over multiple years, it may be reasonable to include a column for each year of the program, in part so that costs can be easily discounted to reflect a common currency year. Finally, the "personnel" and "facility" rows may merit more detail and be split into individual roles (clinician, data analyst, project manager, etc.) or categories (salaries, benefits, reduced efficiency during training, etc.).

Checklist: Presenting Results of Return on Investment Analysis for Quality Improvement

- ☐ **Define Metrics**
    - ☐ ROI
    - ☐ Benefit to cost ratio (BCR)
    - ☐ Other (payback period, etc.)
- ☐ **Describe aim of project, number affected, etc.**
- ☐ **Identify relevant assumptions and estimates**
    - ☐ Cite sources or justify assumptions and estimates through other means
- ☐ **Describe Impact of Interventions**
    - ☐ Pre-intervention incidence/prevalence/utilization/event rate
    - ☐ Impact of Intervention
    - ☐ Post-intervention incidence/prevalence/utilization/event rate
    - ☐ Summary statement regarding specific project (impact on number of patients, events, etc.)
- ☐ **Costs of Intervention**
    - ☐ Describe methods/sources for costs
    - ☐ Include both one-time costs and on-going costs
- ☐ **Benefits**
    - ☐ Cost avoidance per timeframe due to lower incidence/prevalence/utilization/event rates
    - ☐ Increases in revenues
    - ☐ Decreases in expenses
    - ☐ Indirect benefits if quantifiable
- ☐ **ROI and Related Metrics**
    - ☐ Base-case calculations (ROI, BCR, savings per patient, payback period, etc.)
    - ☐ Sensitivity analysis
    - ☐ Indirect benefits not quantifiable
- ☐ **Interpretation**
    - ☐ Context and/or threshold
    - ☐ Risks and alternatives
    - ☐ Generalizability
    - ☐ Limitations

Fig. 8.4 Checklist for presenting ROI results

Table 8.3 Cost-capture Example #1

Type	Description	Initial cost	Monthly cost (intervention)	Monthly cost (ongoing)
Personnel				
Facility				
Materials or equipment				
Travel				
IT				
Outreach				
Other				

Table 8.4 Cost-capture Example #2

Type	Initial cost	Year 1	Year 2	Year 3
Personnel				
Facility				
Materials or equipment				
Travel				
IT				
Outreach				
Other				

Table 8.5 Cost-capture Example #3

Type	Planning	Ramp-up	Implementation	Shutdown
Personnel				
Facility				
Materials or equipment				
Travel				
IT				
Outreach				
Other				

8.2.4 Benefits

When capturing benefits, you should clarify how you intend to capture the change attributable to the intervention (utilization, adverse events, efficiency). One method is to capture benefit sources both before and after the intervention (or between comparison groups). This could be done on a monthly, quarterly, or yearly basis, or aggregated into more descriptive periods like "Initial Benefit" and "Ongoing Benefit" (Table 8.6). Another method is to capture the change itself by summarizing benefits before and after the intervention, which is then equated to financial gains.

To capture and display the change, the columns of Table 8.6 might include headings like "Before Intervention," "After Intervention," and "Difference." This assumes that the time frame is clear and that it is reasonable to aggregate the time periods before and after the intervention. The most common example of this situation would be if the evaluation time frame allows for equal periods before and after the intervention. That is, your intent is to compare the six months prior to the intervention with the six months after the change is implemented. As with any data presentation, you will need to determine the most appropriate way to display your results. Alternatives to these examples or the use of multiple tables may be warranted.

Table 8.6 Examples of how to display benefits

Type	Description	Initial benefit	Monthly benefit (intervention)	Monthly benefit (ongoing)
Health encounters				
Hospitalization				
Rehospitalization				
Length of stay				
ICU use				
Laboratories				
Complications				
Infections				
Outpatient visits				
ED visits				
Other				
Facility				
Personnel				
Equipment				
Other				
Efficiency/waste				
Wait time				
Medication errors				
Turnover				
Patient outcomes				
Mortality				
Morbidity				
Satisfaction				
Quality of life				

											Savings	Payback	
					Post-	Post-					per	period	Cost of
		follow-up	Baseline	Baseline	Risk	intervention	intervention	Absolute	Cost per	Estimated	patient	(years)	program
Scenario	Patients	in years	Risk	events	Reduction	risk	events	reduction	event	savings			
Base-case	500	3	0.1	150	0.2	0.08	120	30	$15,000	$450,000	$900	4.44	$2,000,000

Fig. 8.5 Sensitivity analysis

8.2.5 Calculations of Base Case and Sensitivity Analyses

To arrive at the values contained in the tables just presented, it is usually necessary to make some calculations based on the number of individuals affected, incidence or event rates, changes, and the associated dollar value of differences. Setting these types of calculations up in a spreadsheet can not only ensure consistency but will also allow for easier explorations of variability during sensitivity analyses.

A common calculation is shown in Fig. 8.5. Here, cells in orange represent values input by the user, with the rest of the values calculated from those values. So, in the base case estimate, the user predicts a population of 500 patients that will experience a 20% reduction in the event rate (from 10 to 8%) over the three-year period. This reduces the number of events by 30, each which cost $15,000 to treat, resulting in an overall net benefit of $450,000. Additional metrics can be added, as demonstrated by the calculations for savings per patient and payback period.

The real power of this type of template, however, is during the sensitivity analysis. By varying inputs either individually or in combinations, you can quickly see how variable the results are and which assumptions look to be drivers of the realized value. Figure 8.6 includes some examples.

In this example, a 10% lower reduction (50 fewer patients) results in a corresponding 10% reduction ($45,000) in net benefits. A less effective intervention, one that reduces risk by 15% versus 20%, results in more than a $100,000 reduction in net benefits, and so on. Using a spreadsheet, additional rows can be copied as needed and different scenarios can be explored and interpreted. This demonstrates not only how robust the program may be to variations in assumptions, but also highlights for those creating the proposal whether there are critical milestones they need to ensure are met (e.g., level of recruitment, effectiveness of the intervention, etc.).

This type of template can also be used to look at benefits over time periods, which allow for different assumptions and estimates to be applied differently over time (e.g., perhaps it is reasonable to assume that recruitment will increase or the

						Post-	Post-				Savings per	Payback period	Cost of
Scenario	Patients	follow-up in years	Baseline Risk	Baseline events	Risk Reduction	intervention risk	intervention events	Absolute reduction	Cost per event	Estimated savings	patient	(years)	program
Base-case	500	3	0.1	150	0.2	0.08	120	30	$15,000	$450,000	$900	4.44	$2,000,000
1 Lower recruitment	450	3	0.1	135	0.2	0.08	108	27	$15,000	$405,000	$900	4.94	$2,000,000
2 Less event reduction	500	3	0.1	150	0.15	0.085	127.5	22.5	$15,000	$337,500	$675	5.93	$2,000,000
3 Lower baseline rate	500	3	0.08	120	0.2	0.064	96	24	$15,000	$360,000	$720	5.56	$2,000,000
Combinations:													
1 & 2	450	3	0.1	135	0.15	0.085	114.75	20.25	$15,000	$303,750	$675	6.58	$2,000,000
1 & 3	450	3	0.08	108	0.2	0.064	86.4	21.6	$15,000	$324,000	$720	6.17	$2,000,000

Fig. 8.6 Sensitivity analysis, Part 2

Scenario	Patients	Year	Baseline Risk	Baseline events	Risk Reduction	Post-intervention risk	Post-intervention events	Absolute reduction	Cost per event	Estimated savings	Present Value*	Savings per patient	Payback period (years)	Cost of program
Base-case Year 1	500	1	0.1	50	0.2	0.08	40	10	$15,000	$150,000	$150,000	$300		
Base-case Year 2	500	2	0.1	50	0.2	0.08	40	10	$15,000	$150,000	$145,631	$291		
Base-case Year 3	500	3	0.1	50	0.2	0.08	40	10	$15,000	$150,000	$141,389	$283		
Base-case Total	1500			150			120	30		$450,000	$437,020	$291	4.58	$2,000,000

*Discount Rate: 0.03

Fig. 8.7 Sensitivity analysis, Part 3

effectiveness of the intervention will decrease over time). The template can also be used to discount values if projecting over a longer time period. In Fig. 8.7, we see that when discounted at a 3% rate, the total monetary benefit of $450,000 equates to approximately $437,000 in present value.

8.3 Summary

A variety of tips and tricks may save you considerable time and effort to perform a thorough and rigorous ROI analysis. These include keeping files of relevant information and sources, whether the information relates to a particular clinical area, costs and benefits, or ROI analyses in general. These can cut down on the time needed to search for information and may also serve as examples of what to present. Leveraging templates can also help you reduce time and effort, whether they are for abstracting information from published studies, creating an outline, displaying costs or benefits, performing base case and sensitivity analysis calculations, or presenting results.

8.4 Key Concepts

- Tips to reduce the time and effort to perform ROI analyses include keeping files of relevant information and examples.
- When presenting ROI results in oral presentations, remember that individuals can become overwhelmed by large amounts of numbers and equations; if possible, keep the presentation visual and have additional slides you can access if there are specific questions.
- Developing a process for performing ROI analyses can help keep efforts consistent and ensure that no steps are missed or skipped; ideally, this process would be embedded with processes to define and plan for quality measurement.
- Several factors can affect one's ability to influence potential funders or healthcare practitioners, one of which is the ability to tell a compelling story.

- Several useful templates may help increase the efficiency of performing a ROI analysis; lengthy activities or those that involve a lot of information (e.g., abstracting information from published literature, exploring scenarios in a sensitivity analysis) are excellent candidates for the use of templates.
- Checklists may also be helpful; there is no one correct way to present results, but there are typically key aspects that should be included in any ROI presentation.

Chapter 9
Expanded Topics in ROI

9.1 ROI in a Value-Based Environment

The current healthcare environment is one of change and adjustment. In terms of Medicare reimbursement, the increase in value-based payments (the Merit-based Incentive Payment System, Hospital and Physician Compare, etc.) combined with a) the growing understanding of the importance of the continuity of care across settings and b) the impact of community-based programs does the following: it reflects a desire to shift focus away from "services" or "treatment" toward a more holistic approach to population health. The implications of this shift are far-reaching, and providers and facilities face challenges related to the associated administrative burden and striking a balance between care quality and cost. One could argue that these new takes on healthcare delivery make ROI an even more crucial tool to evaluate the value (however you chose to define it) of quality improvement interventions. However, the new rules of the game also make certain aspects of ROI more challenging.

9.1.1 Reducing Encounters Versus More Efficient Encounters

At the most basic level, shifting from fee-for-service (FFS) reimbursement to value-based reimbursement has implications for how to measure fiscal benefits and costs for ROI calculations. Under an FFS model, the costs of hospitalization could be tallied by summing the individual services provided during the stay, and each would represent a cost to both the hospital and ultimately to the payer. Therefore, when a payer like CMS funds a quality improvement initiative, they receive benefits in the (common) form of lower utilization that results from the improved quality and efficiency of care that is provided, as in Fig. 9.1. That is, in addition to improvements in patient outcomes, we see that reductions in waste, increases in efficiency, and other improvements typically funnel back to the payer because all activities in an

C. A. Solid, *Return on Investment for Healthcare Quality Improvement*,
https://doi.org/10.1007/978-3-030-46478-3_9

Fig. 9.1 ROI in a
fee-for-service environment

FFS model are billed for and reimbursed at some level. As a consequence, comparing the realized benefits to the original investment is somewhat straightforward because almost any measurable and monetizable improvement in quality will result in a benefit that ultimately produces some return for the payer in addition to any benefits it may produce for providers, patients, or others.

However, in a value-based environment when payments for services are bundled or are reimbursed based on quality measure performance, some of those services provided to patients will represent a cost to the hospital but not to the payer. There may be circumstances, for example, where payers will agree to reimburse a fixed amount for the encounter (assuming it's not an extended stay or complex diagnosis), regardless of what services the hospital administers. Therefore, reducing unnecessary services (i.e., waste) or improving efficiency may produce benefits for the hospital that may not funnel back to the payer, at least not monetarily (Fig. 9.2). Put more broadly, the highest ROI for payers will involve reducing the number of encounters,

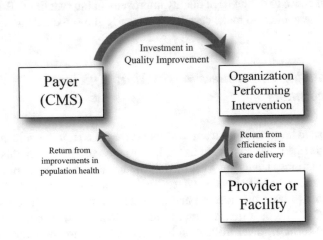

Fig. 9.2 ROI in a value-based environment

while the highest ROI for facilities and hospitals will involve reducing services within an encounter (i.e., making an encounter more "efficient").

Further classified, the improvements in efficiency and effectiveness of an individual encounter that ultimately provides benefit to the provider reflect improvements to *care delivery*, while reductions in the quantity and frequency of encounters that benefit a payer equate to improvements in *population health* since a healthier population requires fewer visits to the doctor or the hospital.

This is a shift that has the potential to put the interest of payers and providers slightly at odds with each other. Or, at a minimum, there may be activities that providers and facilities can engage in that will produce significant benefit in the process of care delivery but which cannot be included as part of the financial return to a payer. There is a danger, then, that providers and organizations seeking to solicit funds from payers (like CMS) will have an incentive to focus on improvements in population health and patient outcomes (which produce financial benefits for payers) instead of focusing on improvements in efficiency and process where the benefit is retained by those receiving funding.

There may be no direct solution to this conundrum, but at a minimum, it is a concept that should be addressed by those funding projects and those designing them. If anything, this highlights the need to interpret results within a larger context of the overall care landscape and to discuss benefits and value in a larger sense and to more than just those who put up the money for the initiative. At the end of the day, a ROI analysis is a tool to help demonstrate the merit of a quality improvement intervention; this new paradigm does not diminish the effectiveness of this tool but underscores that ROI represents a portion of the overall evaluation of the importance, necessity, and value of quality improvement activities.

9.1.2 Benefits Across Care Settings

Along those lines, the initial reaction to the example just discussed might be that in a value-based world it will be more difficult to demonstrate a significant ROI to payers (e.g., CMS) because changes in processes or services at the local level may not translate into a change in costs or benefits to the payer. However, as healthcare systems continue to improve the coordination of care across settings, improvements in care quality and the health of patients will facilitate lower health expenditures overall, which does impact payers.

Therefore, while improving the discharge process for hospitalized patients, for example, may not result in a monetary benefit for payers for the index hospitalization, studies have shown that good discharge planning results in better patient outcomes going forward and a lower risk of a subsequent encounter (across settings), which likely will result in a monetary benefit for payers. What this means for those applying for funding from a payer is that they will need to be diligent in identifying and monetizing benefits from more than just an index health encounter or a single care setting. While this does not necessarily imply larger or more complex interventions (although it may), it does imply that more thought and research may be needed to understand the impact across the entire spectrum of care and the community so that the appropriate benefit is reflected in the ROI analysis. When relevant, this notion may encourage more system-wide or even community-wide interventions, which will require providers to communicate and collaborate with a variety of services and programs.

This may increase the costs of interventions in order to accurately track and assess care over multiple settings. Investments in staff time, resources, technology, and data collection could all be affected by expanding interventions to more fully encompass the entire spectrum of care. However, given what is now understood about the importance of care continuity and the support of family and informal caregivers, it is also likely that these types of interventions would demonstrate more benefit. Some of the increased benefit may simply come from the additional information available from multiple settings, but the hope is that it would also improve overall care, outcomes, and patient experiences, thereby raising the overall level of benefits beyond which could be realized in a single setting.

In the coming years, the extent to which interventions are expanded to include multiple care settings will be directly proportional to the amount of additional funding that is provided for such endeavors. As an industry, it will be important to remember that these types of interventions not only carry with them additional cost but likely additional benefit that would otherwise not be captured and ultimately should be evaluated based on their return, not simply their cost.

9.1.3 Benefits Associated with Quality Monitoring Programs

In the past, hospitals and facilities might have received monetary payouts from risk pools or local programs related to the quality of care they provide, and these (usually nominal) benefits could be considered when calculating an internal ROI for a quality improvement intervention, but they likely would not have significantly moved the needle. However, with the explosion of national quality monitoring programs and the ever-increasing percentage of reimbursement tied to performance, the benefits and penalties realized from these programs will continue to have larger and larger fiscal implications for facilities and physicians. The good news for providers: This may motivate initiatives that previously were not financially viable because the gains in efficiency or reductions in waste would not have translated into a large enough monetary benefit to cover the costs of the intervention. However, going forward, if the added benefit of the increased quality-performance-based payout combined with the financial benefits of increased efficiency now results in a large enough monetary gain for the facility or providers, they may be incentivized to pursue those endeavors.

Providers will have to continue to balance quality improvement efforts with the need to remain "high performing" in other areas. That is, shifting resources away from an area where a provider has previously performed very well could potentially result in lower performance and subsequently a reduction in reimbursement; the complexity of resource allocation for quality improvement will need to become an increasingly precise science.

However, among the major challenges involved in many quality monitoring programs is the ability of the individual measures to validly and reliably reflect the quality and the overall measurement methodology to correctly incentivize behavior and rewards the appropriate activities. With the expansion in the number of programs, instances have emerged where providers are evaluated for the same basic aspect of quality by two or more programs, often using different measures or evaluation methodologies. This may be a concern not only because of the additional burden it may impose on providers and facilities but also because any inconsistencies in methodologies may serve to deteriorate the credibility of the measurements they employ. Throughout the industry, we have a duty to continually examine the validity and reliability of how quality and value are measured, assessed, and either rewarded or penalized through reimbursement programs.

9.1.4 The Impact of Social Media

Like it or not, social media is seeping into the healthcare environment. Beyond the measures of patient experience already contained in quality measures like HCAHPS, social media postings by patients are having a growing impact on how hospitals and providers approach patient care. Several published studies have already appeared regarding the association between certain social media trends and hospital ratings or quality measure performance, and facilities are realizing that "customer service" is an important aspect of their financial viability.

It is likely that gathering data related to the patient experience will become more prevalent in quality improvement interventions across the board, and the benefits associated with improving those experiences will become more tangible and measurable, even outside the currently employed formal measures. As the tools to measure and quantify the impact of patient experiences on the bottom line become more precise and accurate, this may encourage and accelerate the acceptance of monetary estimates of quantities that may have previously been considered neither measurable nor monetizable.

If possible, the opportunities provided by social media or more direct data collection regarding the patient experience of care may allow for the realization of more types of benefits, which would improve the ROI of patient-facing interventions. Therefore, we should consider what may be possible using social media or other nontraditional data sources whenever we are attempting to assess either the financial return or the larger value that quality improvement activities may produce.

9.1.5 Putting It All Together

Developing and conducting examinations of ROI in the ever-changing environment of health care will require vigilance to stay ahead of the challenges and be at the forefront of the positive changes brought about by value-based payment policies. Understanding the implications and taking a larger view of population health management will allow providers, administrators, and organizations to effectively estimate or calculate ROI and leverage those results to motivate quality improvement. In short, interventions with the highest ROI will likely be those that embrace the more holistic approach to population health and incorporate information, if not interventions, across multiple settings and that are specific to the local environment and community.

9.2 Life Years and Quality-Adjusted Life Years (Cost-Effective and Cost-Utility Analysis)

Some of the most common questions regarding the evaluation of value in health care fall under the umbrella of cost-effectiveness or cost-utility analyses. Most of the time, these questions involve the concept of quality-adjusted life years, or QALYs, a utility-based metric that tries to combine the length of life with the quality of life. While cost-effectiveness and cost-utility analyses are separate tools that deserve, and have, their own volumes dedicated to how they are conducted and interpreted, they also deserve a mention in the current text because of their relationship to ROI through the common goal of assessing value.

9.2.1 Background

In the most general terms, a cost-effective analysis considers two potential courses of action and compares the difference in their cost relative to the difference in their outcomes. In the healthcare space, this type of analysis could involve any number of outcomes, such as the number of lives saved, improvements in patients' laboratory values or vital signs, or some other outcome of value. Although the terms "cost effectiveness" and "cost utility" are often used interchangeably, the latter is actually a special case of the former.

In a cost-utility analysis, the outcome of interest is QALYs. A life year (LY) is simply a unit of time: one year lived. In a study of 10 patients over two years where one died at six months, another at nine months, and a third at 15 months (with the remainder surviving the full two years), the total number of LYs would be:

$$0.5 \text{ Years} + 0.75 \text{ Years} + 1.25 \text{ Years} + (7 \times 2 \text{ Years}) = 16.5 \text{ LYs}$$

This calculation is similar to how time at risk is calculated: It is a combination of the number of individuals and the time associated with each of them. It is often used to demonstrate benefit or improvement of a treatment or intervention intended to reduce mortality or extend life. The quantity of LYs is a more complete representation of the benefit than would be the binary outcome of life or death because it allows for comparisons about the differences in lifetime added. That is, reducing the number of deaths is important but so is delaying deaths in many cases.

If, for example, those 10 patients represented a control group or "usual care" comparison and a treatment or intervention that cost $20,000 resulted in a different 10 patients living a total of 19 LYs, then that $20,000 investment theoretically resulted in an additional 2.5 LYs, which equates to $8,000 per LY gained. That may or may not reflect fewer deaths. It may simply be a function of a longer life or delayed mortality. Whether that cost is acceptable depends on the situation and a whole host of other factors.

A QALY is simply an LY that is adjusted to reflect the level of quality of that life year. QALYs can range from 0 (dead) to 1 (one year lived in "perfect" health), with values less than 1 but higher than 0 reflecting some measure of health burden.[1] Therefore, if a treatment extends the life of a patient by two extra years at a quality of life that is estimated to be at 60% of that which they would experience in perfect health, then it results in an additional $2 \times 60\% = 1.2$ QALYs to the individual.

The motivation for using QALYs instead of LYs is the notion that not all LYs are equal and that extending life may not be a benefit in and of itself if the quality of that extended life is poor. Said another way, all LYs should not be considered equal in terms of the benefit they infer. For example, patients with complete renal failure require either regular dialysis or a kidney transplant to survive. Studies have shown that someone living a year getting thrice-weekly in-center hemodialysis for multiple hours at a time enjoys a lower quality of life than someone living a year with a fully functioning transplanted kidney. Both have their life extended through renal replacement therapy, but one experiences a higher quality of life, which provides a greater benefit. Similarly, if someone with a terminal disease is offered a treatment designed to extend their life, they likely will consider not only the length of the potential extension but also the quality of life they may experience as a result. Some may choose a shorter, higher-quality timeline as opposed to a longer, lower-quality one.

The formal method for applying QALYs in cost-utility analysis is to compare the difference in cost to the difference in QALYs for two activities. In the previous example of LYs, if everyone involved lived for the entire time in perfect health, the result would be the same: $8,000 per QALY. If instead the treatment or intervention not only extended life but improved the quality of life for all involved, the associated benefits would increase, causing the cost per unit of benefit (QALY) to go down. Specifically, assume that without the treatment or intervention, patients were living with a condition that decreased their quality of life to roughly 60% of that experienced

---

[1] Some publications use the term "disability-adjusted life year" (DALY), where the disability is a decrement from perfect health, to arrive at essentially the same quantity as a QALY.

in perfect health, while those who received the treatment or intervention saw their quality of life increase to 75% of that experienced in perfect health, then the difference in QALYs would be calculated as follows:

$$(19.0 \times 75\%) - (16.5 \times 60\%) = (14.25 - 9.9) = 4.35 \text{ QALYs}$$

Note that in neither group do participants contribute full health LYs to the calculation: the 19 LYs experienced by those who received the treatment or intervention only experienced 14.25 QALYs, while those without the intervention experienced 9.9 QALYs, even though they experienced a total of 16.5 LYs. Also note that the improvement in QALYs (4.35) is greater than the improvement in LYs (2.5), due to a combination of longer life *and* higher quality of life associated with the treatment or intervention.[2] In this example, while the cost per LY is $8,000, the cost per QALY is approximately $4,600, or significantly cheaper.

The formal metric for the comparison we just made is the incremental cost-effectiveness ratio, or ICER:

$$(\text{Cost}_1 - \text{Cost}_0)/(\text{QALY}_1 - \text{QALY}_0) \tag{9.1}$$

In Eq. 9.1, Cost_1 and QALY_1 reflect the cost and benefit of the treatment and their counterparts reflect the cost and benefit of the control or "usual care" group. This type of analysis is often used to make decisions about whether changes should be made or implemented, so that the comparison group often represents the current situation, usual care, or the status quo. If the ICER in Eq. 9.1 is over a certain threshold, the proposed treatment or change in care is considered to be too expensive to make it "worth it," and the proposed change is rejected. How to set an appropriate threshold is an entirely separate topic; national health policy may loosely use values around $50,000 or $60,000 or some multiple of the average taxable income or some other metric of what an individual life is "worth."

It is not hard to imagine that these types of analyses carry with them a whole host of additional challenges, and they are not without their detractors. Setting a threshold invariably means assigning a value to a human life, which poses an intractable debate on what is fair and reasonable. And, as with any contrived model, it cannot account for every situation or circumstance. For example, those in declining health have loved ones and caregivers whose life quality and care burden are not encompassed in the patient's QALY. Reducing caregiver burden has benefit but is not reflected in the QALY or the ICER.

---

[2]In a situation where extending life requires invasive treatment or results in poorer quality of life, the difference in QALYs may be smaller than the difference in LYs: Even though life was extended, quality of life diminished. This is often the argument against aggressive treatment at the end of life: Any minimal extension in life lived may be accompanied by worse quality than if the individual was allowed to live out their remaining life at home or a preferred setting.

9.2.2 Relationship to ROI

All types of cost-effective analyses, including cost-utility analysis, attempt to assess "value," but in a very specific way. Some contend that these analyses could be used in conjunction with ROI analyses to explore both the financial viability and the ratio of the incremental cost to the incremental patient benefit.

It should be noted, however, that cost-utility analyses often involve simulations where patients are assumed to travel between "states" of health, each with associated utility levels based on underlying probabilities of moving between states (e.g., 10% chance of moving from state of "hospitalized" to "death," etc.). Each state has a utility associated with it so that when the simulation is run each patient accumulates and contributes QALYs as they travel between states. The simulation is run many times (at least 1,000 times, typically), and the results provide some measure of precision because they produce a range of results that reflect the underlying variability assigned through the state probabilities.

Certainly, in some situations it is reasonable to explore costs and benefits from multiple perspectives to demonstrate net benefits to both those burdened with the costs of an intervention (payers, providers, funding agencies) and those who are the target for the improved care (patients, families, informal caregivers). When and if it is prudent to include a cost-effectiveness or cost-utility analysis in tandem, or even instead of, a ROI analysis is for those conducting the analysis to determine.

9.3 Deterministic and Probabilistic Sensitivity Analysis

In prior chapters, there has been no attempt to classify or categorize sensitivity analyses, and no suggestion that they should conform to any specific type or method. However, because in published literature the terms "deterministic sensitivity analysis" and "probabilistic sensitivity analysis" are used, defining and comparing these methods here is warranted.

Frequently, these terms are relevant for model-based or distribution-based ROI analyses, where specific inputs are considered "parameters" that have an assumed underlying distribution, and the value used in the base case represents the assumed mean and therefore most "likely" value to occur. Therefore, sensitivity analyses involve explorations into how variations in these parameters according to their distributions would affect the resulting ROI.

In deterministic sensitivity analysis, individual parameter values are manually varied to lower and higher values within their assumed distribution. This is similar to the type of sensitivity analysis described in the previous chapters, except with the additional constraint of the distributional assumption for the specific estimate. Deterministic sensitivity analysis often involves varying only one value at a time to determine its specific effect on the results.

By contrast, a probabilistic sensitivity analysis randomly draws values for all parameters simultaneously from their individual distributions and then calculates the result. This is repeated many times (usually thousands) to provide a range of possible results that are intended to encompass the majority of possibilities assuming the individual distributions are accurate.

In many cases, the added complexity associated with having to assign probability distributions to each input and performing the additional calculations or simulations outweighs any added benefits of the method. That is, while this method can produce more specific estimates of the likelihood of different outcomes, the insights it provides may not be significantly greater than what would have been gleaned from a deterministic analysis. For most ROI analyses, thoughtful examination of best- and worst-case scenarios provides a full picture of likely outcomes and therefore is usually sufficient.

9.4   Contingent Valuation

This topic was covered briefly in Chap. 4 as a potential tool for measuring or monetizing non-MMA benefits. However, it is worth another look to more fully develop the pros and cons of this method and its usefulness for ROI. Whenever quality improvement occurs, it is likely that some value will be difficult to quantify or translate into monetary terms. In these situations, sometimes attempts are made to employ tools and techniques to accomplish the monetization of benefits so that they can be included in ROI analyses.

Methods that attempt to establish the willingness to pay (WTP) or a willingness to accept [compensation] (WTA) are such tools. These fall under the larger umbrella of contingent valuation, which has its roots in economic theory, and have been used in the healthcare setting to evaluate public health initiatives as well as individual initiatives.

The process involves presenting hypothetical scenarios to individuals either in interview or survey form and asking them how much they would be willing to pay or willing to accept compensation for the different scenarios. An example might be a question posed to individuals with Type II diabetes about treatment mechanisms:

> Imagine you were able to control your blood glucose with a daily oral medication instead of injections, but that this medication was more expensive. How much more would you be willing to pay for it?

Once several answers are obtained, the idea is that if there was some other type of intervention that could remove the need for regular insulin injections, it would be worth at least as much money as those individuals were willing to pay out of pocket for it.

The difficulty with contingent valuation is that it is more complicated to apply in practice than it is to understand conceptually. Detractors of these methods cite several functional and intellectual challenges associated with developing and administering these types of questions. An excellent summary of these issues is offered by Haveman and Weimer [1]:

> One source of concern is the cognitive demands that it places on respondents in terms of understanding the policy being valued. Unless respondents understand what is being valued, and believe their answers to be consequential in influencing the policy choice, they cannot be expected to give meaningful answers to serve as the basis for an inference about the willingness to pay of the entire population. Considerable research, mainly by environmental economists, is contributing to the craft of designing effective questionnaires for contingent valuation. Another source of concern is the fear that respondents will answer strategically in the sense of giving false answers that they believe will lead to a better outcome for themselves than would result from truthful answers. Both theory and evidence suggest that giving respondents referendum-type questions about public goods minimizes the dangers of strategic responses. That is, rather than directly asking a respondent to state her willingness to pay, she is given a random dollar amount and asked if she would vote for the policy if it would cost her that amount in higher taxes or increased costs for other goods.

In essence, respondents know that the situation is hypothetical and therefore their responses are either inauthentic or reflective of desires and intentions more than their true behavior or preferences. As described by these authors, there are methods that attempt to make responses more "truthful" through the use of framing and other techniques, but the take-home message is that these types of sources for monetary benefit should be used with caution and under the consultation of an expert in their development and application.

9.5   The Changing Landscape of Quality Improvement

9.5.1   The Evolution of Care Delivery

As the nature of care delivery continues to change, so too will the methods and processes of effective quality improvement. The explosion of available data, federal monitoring programs, and quality measures has been well documented. These aspects alone have significant implications for how healthcare professionals measure, detect, and monitor changes in quality and efficiency. There is an increasing opportunity to assess care value, but with that comes a heightened responsibility to prudently and skillfully apply the tools and techniques of value determination. Further, health policy is regularly adjusted to incentivize certain activities and encourage providers to seek certain outcomes. Bundled payments, performance-based bonuses and penalties, and risk-sharing arrangements (e.g., accountable care organizations) raise the stakes for those who seek to juggle efforts to improve quality and maintain financial solvency.

Our previous understanding of healthcare delivery systems as segmented or siloed fragments functioning independently from other settings or locations is insufficient and inaccurate. As an industry, we are becoming fully aware of the importance of certain facets of care that occur outside of the walls of a hospital or clinic, such as social determinants of care as well as access to care and health insurance. We also understand the importance of care continuity across settings, as well as the crucial roles of peer-groups, social support networks, and family caregivers. Together with the digital progression of smartphone apps, activity tracking devices, and in-home digital assistants, the assessment of care quality and value needs to evolve and adapt as well. Where targeted methodologies like Plan-Do-Study-Act (PDSA) or Lean may have sufficed in the past, a more holistic approach will likely be necessary going forward, which has major implications for how quality and value will be assessed.

9.5.2   Implementation Science and Emerging Methodologies

An emerging field in quality improvement is implementation science. This field seeks to understand why an intervention may or may not be successfully implemented and sustained by understanding the nature of healthcare delivery systems and the individuals who make up those systems. The National Institutes of Health define implementation science as: "...the study of methods to promote the adoption and integration of evidence-based practices, interventions and policies into routine health care and public health settings" [2].

While it might seem like a relatively academic pursuit, many are beginning to believe that insights provided by implementation science can greatly impact the likelihood of success and therefore the value and financial return of a given intervention.

According to Bauer et al. [3]:

> The business case for implementation science is clear: as healthcare systems work under increasingly dynamic and resource-constrained conditions, evidence-based strategies are essential in order to ensure that research investments maximize healthcare value and improve public health.

While this quote refers to research, the same could be said about quality improvement efforts, which are what frequently leverage evidence-based strategies to improve care.

The field is vast and touches on numerous disciplines and areas of study. Those who seek to understand how healthcare delivery systems function and adapt to change leverage theories and frameworks that acknowledge the complex interplay between individual choices and the social and professional networks that live within these systems. By better understanding and modeling these complex networks of individuals, one can begin to explore how to encourage certain behaviors and decisions in order to effect real and sustainable change.

Any healthcare delivery system—hospitals, clinics, nursing homes, etc—is made up of a physical space and individual members (i.e., doctors, nurses, techs, support staff, administrators, etc.). The system functions as a result of interactions between the members within that space. Therefore, the organizational structure, the social culture, the politics, as well as internal and external forces related to budgets, regulations, guidelines, and the like all influence what happens and how it happens. A host of variables influence whether an intervention will be successful and sustainable (Fig. 9.3).

Some implementation scientists believe that the appropriate model for any health-care delivery system is that of a "complex network." The fields of network theory and complexity science are used to describe all sorts of natural phenomena, such as biologic processes, ecologic systems, and social systems like cities, companies, and organizations. Networks are defined by the structure and nature of how individuals are "linked" to one another: they may be highly spread out, randomly distributed, or more locally clustered with "hubs" (select individuals with lots of connections).

Depending on the structure, the network will display certain characteristics, such as how closely "connected" any two members are (i.e., the "six degrees of separation" idea) and how adaptable or resilient the network is when faced with a change. A particular kind of complex network that many feel is applicable to health care is that of a complex adaptive system. It is "complex" because of the large number of members and the variety and depth of the type of connections between the members; it is "adaptive" because it is dynamic in that its members can learn from previous experiences. As an aside, there is a wealth of information about these systems and their practical applications that, frankly, is fascinating. For now, however, it is enough to define a complex adaptive system as a dynamic network of individuals who are both semiautonomous and interdependent. That is, they each can make their own decisions and have a "job to do," but they also rely heavily on many other members of the system, both those in their immediate vicinity as well as those they may only be connected with through others.

The behavior of the network is not defined by the individual members, but by the interactions between the members within the system as well as with external forces;

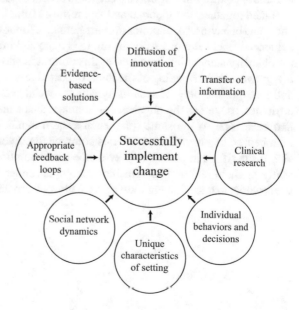

Fig. 9.3 Many factors influence whether a change will be successful and sustainable

the ability of the system to adapt depends on the members to grow and learn from their experiences. What this all implies for implementation is that evoking a desired change does not so much require a change to the "system" but to the decisions and interactions of the individuals who make up the system.

To understand how and why individuals behave a certain way and make decisions, implementation scientists often turn to the ideas developed within behavioral economics. As explored by countless authors in many other settings, studies dating back to the 1970s have revealed cognitive biases that are inherent in all humans and that shape and color the decisions we make based on the information available to us. For example, we're susceptible to how information is presented ("framing"), what is offered as a comparison ("anchoring"), and how readily we can conjure up a recent or similar situation or event ("availability" and "representativeness"). As a result, behavioral economists have uncovered ways to leverage these biases to "nudge" individuals to perform certain behaviors. For example, if we want school children to choose more fruits and veggies at lunch, placing them sooner in the lunch line and at eye level will make them more likely to select than if they appeared later and lower. Marketers, too, have learned these biases to sell more products.

When an entire system is built to encourage certain behaviors and decisions it is called a "choice architecture," and if constructed correctly it can make it much easier to induce change in behaviors and processes involved in care delivery. For example, if trying to reduce infections by incorporating an infection prevention bundle, aspects of a choice architecture may include the following: posters reminding staff of the frequency of infections and how they can occur, stated intentions regarding adherence to the bundle, reminders that most staff members are complying with the bundle, equipment placed in plain sight to remind staff to use them, and electronic reminders to remove central lines or urinary catheters after a number of days to prompt action.

Taken together, the theories and frameworks from complexity and network sciences and behavioral economics provide guidance for how to structure and implement evidence-based solutions when trying to change and improve care quality. From an introductory standpoint, however, at this point it is enough to understand that there is a growing understanding of the interconnectedness of healthcare delivery systems and that the interplay of system dynamics, social pressures, individual skills and attributes, as well as the physical environment shape and promote certain decisions and behaviors. At the same time, each system is unique in its characteristics and members so that how these attributes combine to influence outcomes can vary from site to site. If we hope to apply evidence-based solutions in ways that will consistently produce real and sustainable change, an understanding of the theories and frameworks that implementation science draws from will be crucial.

9.5.3   *Where Does ROI Fit in?*

Under the umbrella of the changing landscape of quality improvement, assessments of value including ROI will continue to be important, and if anything they will continue to gain favor as a tool to determine whether an intervention should be pursued. As care delivery evolves, and technology and data collection evolve with it, there will certainly be additional opportunities to evaluate financial return and other measures of value throughout the care process. With more attention paid to the implementation methodology and understanding the overall care system as a complex network, these opportunities may include assessments of the implementation methodologies themselves, as opposed to the individual care practices or policies. A solid foundation of how to measure and assess value will improve our ability to adjust to these changes and apply critical thinking about value in new ways. A better understanding of implementation science and some of the prevailing theories of how to bring about effective and sustainable change will enhance our ability to design and evaluate quality improvement initiatives.

9.6   ROI in Statistical Process Control

The methods of statistical process control (SPC) include run charts and control charts, which have gained favor over the last few years as a way to track and monitor the performance of quality improvement activities. In these instances, it is a natural extension to try to use these tools to assess the financial return or overall value of any improvements in quality that are observed.

Details of how to construct run charts and control charts and when to use the different types are left to other sources. Here, however, we will explore some options for how to leverage the information already available in these charts to estimate financial return.

At the most basic level, run and control charts attempt to quantify the amount of "common cause" variability within a process and provide rules for when a "special cause" of variation has occurred. Within quality improvement, we are not as interested in individual outliers that may have resulted from some shock to the system or explainable source, but instead we are interested when the entire process has shifted as a way to demonstrate improvement in quality or outcomes. Take the example presented in Fig. 9.4, where the percent compliance, presumably with the use of a treatment bundle or process, shows a noticeable increase.

While this is a simple example, we can see that the control chart can provide credible values for what should be used as "before" and "after" values if one were to try to describe the true change and the associated value. That is, even though there is natural variability in compliance, the median values charted on the graph can serve as excellent reference points for the amount of change.

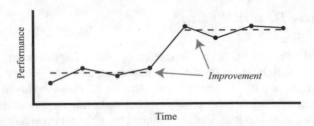

Fig. 9.4 Using a run chart to demonstrate improvement to assess value

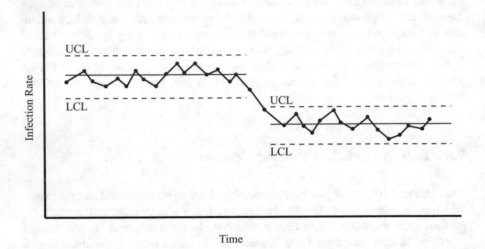

Fig. 9.5 Changes in quality demonstrated by control chart

When charts include more detail, including control limits for changing processes, as in Fig. 9.5, these limits may provide reasonable values to use in sensitivity analyses.

Because the control limits are based on the underlying variability seen in the process, they inherently include a level of uncertainty that may be relevant for those attempting to conduct analyses that provide a full picture of not only the level of quality improvement but also of the realized value.

In general, the methods of SPC leverage basic statistical tenants and therefore offer a sound basis to estimate value. For those who understand these methods, it will be relatively straightforward to extend the insights SPC provides for quality to those for value.

9.7 Summary

Several concepts of interest are beyond the scope of this text, either because they are tangential to ROI or because they are computationally advanced. A common question for those performing ROI analyses is how to incorporate patient-centered metrics such as life years or quality-adjusted life years into a discussion of financial return. These tools are used most often to identify preferred treatments and inform policy decisions. Techniques included in deterministic and probabilistic sensitivity analyses provide a more systematic way to explore uncertainty and variability and may be fruitful in some situations.

When attempting to ascertain the value to patients, sometimes methods that estimate the willingness to pay are utilized; however, several caveats are involved in using these methods and they may have limited application in traditional ROI. The emerging field of implementation science offers insights into how best to implement quality improvement interventions, and in the future may be a key component of establishing the financial return of an intervention. Finally, the use of statistical process control in ROI is not without precedent; it can often demonstrate changes in quality while accounting for variability and lead to reasonable and credible estimates of value.

9.8 Key Concepts

- As care models continue to change from FFS to value based, assessing value and calculating ROI will likely require more nuanced explorations; in a value-based setting, benefits previously realized by payers from improvement activities may be redirected to providers and facilities.
- This requires careful consideration of how value and ROI will be measured, presented, and evaluated.
- Cost-effective and cost-utility analyses share some attributes with ROI analyses but are typically used for a different reason; however, some of the lessons learned regarding how to assess the value of a life year may be useful in ROI.
- Deterministic and probabilistic sensitivity analyses involve more formal processes for exploring the variability and uncertainty in the examination of ROI; the added complexity needed to conduct them often outweighs the advantages they offer.
- Techniques to establish the willingness to pay, or to accept compensation, associated with changes in care quality or processes may be used to estimate the associated value; however, several caveats and cautions should be considered before using them.
- The future of quality improvement is likely to leverage information developed by implementation scientists, and the concepts and frameworks embedded in this

discipline can help identify and define appropriate measures and representations of value.

- Statistical process control methods can be useful when performing ROI because they can identify changes and consider variability of the observed data.

References

1. Haveman RH, Weimer DL (2001) Cost-benefit analysis. In: International encyclopedia of the social & behavioral sciences, pp 2845–2851
2. National Institutes of Health Fogarty International Center (2019) Implementation science news, resources and funding for global health researchers. NIH. https://www.fic.nih.gov/ResearchTopics/Pages/ImplementationScience.aspx. Accessed 3 Jan 2020
3. Bauer MS, Damschroder L, Hagedorn H, Smith J, Kilbourne AM (2015) An introduction to implementation science for the non-specialist. BMC Psychology 3:32. https://doi.org/10.1186/s40359-015-0089-9

Glossary of Terms

ACA Affordable Care Act of 2010

APM Alternative Payment Model: one of the payment model options available for those who treat Medicare patients

Base case The most likely or observed circumstances that is used to construct an initial estimate of ROI

BCR Benefit-to-Cost Ratio: an alternative or supplement to ROI, and is calculated as the benefits divided by the costs, can be interpreted as "the benefits per dollar spent"

Benchmark A value by which to compare and evaluate results or outcomes

Break-even point The point in time where benefits have accumulated to the point where they exactly equal the costs spent

CAUTI Catheter-associated urinary tract infections: a common quality measure is one that tracks the rate of this infection in healthcare settings

CEA Cost-effectiveness analysis: an economic method to establish the financial justification for a particular activity

CLABSI Central line-associated bloodstream infections: a common quality measure is one that tracks the rate of this infection in healthcare settings

CMS The Centers for Medicare and Medicaid Services

Complex adaptive systems A type of system that is made up of independent but semi-autonomous individuals who interact with each other in multiple ways

CUA Cost-utility analysis: an economic method to establish the cost per quality-adjusted life years that a change in policy or activities would yield

Discount rate The annual percentage rate used to calculate the present value of future costs or benefits

ED Emergency department

FFS Fee-for-service: a health reimbursement policy by which providers and facilities are paid based on the services that they provide, regardless of patient outcomes

Future Value (FV) The amount that a current monetary value would equal in a future time period

© Springer Nature Switzerland AG 2020
C. A. Solid, *Return on Investment for Healthcare Quality Improvement*,
https://doi.org/10.1007/978-3-030-46478-3

Hazard rate The instantaneous rate of change, or the likelihood of an event (death, disease, hospitalization, etc.) in the next short time period given that it has not occurred

ICER Incremental Cost-effectiveness Ratio: a ratio of the difference in cost to the difference in QALYs in a cost-effectiveness or cost-utility analysis

ICU Intensive Care Unit

Implementation science A field that endeavors to understand how innovations or changes are best implemented and sustained in healthcare delivery systems

Lean A quality improvement strategy for implementing changes

MACRA The Medicare Access and CHIP Reauthorization Act of 2015, which mandated the creation of an incentive program for providers where reimbursement was in part based on performance on quality measures

MIPS The Merit-based Incentive Payment System: a program to reimburse physicians based in part on their performance on quality measures

Moral hazard The tendency to either engage in more risky behavior or consume more healthcare services because of the presence of health insurance

Net benefits Benefits less costs

Payback period The period of time until costs are covered by accumulating benefits

PDSA Plan-Do-Study-Act: a quality improvement strategy for implementing changes

Perspective The selected point of view for a given ROI analysis

Present Value (PV) The current value of a cost or benefit that occurs in the future

QALY Quality-adjusted life years: a calculation of the total survival time adjusted to reflect the quality of life during that time

QI Quality improvement

QPP Quality Payment Program; the federal program under which MIPS and APM operate

Relative risk A ratio of the probability or likelihood of an event or disease incidence

Reliability An indication of how well a quality measure can detect differences in quality between entities

ROI Return on Investment

Savings per patient Net benefits per patient affected

Scope The selected time frame and affected population for a ROI analysis

Sensitivity analysis The process by which various values in a ROI calculation are altered to examine how different scenarios may affect the resulting financial return

Validity An indication of how well a quality measure reflects the concept it is attempting to measure

Index